D1557582

HENRY STUBBE,
radical Protestantism
and the early
Enlightenment

HENRY STUBBE, radical Protestantism and the early Enlightenment

JAMES R. JACOB

*Professor of History, John Jay College of
Criminal Justice and the Graduate School
of the City University of New York*

CAMBRIDGE UNIVERSITY PRESS

Cambridge

London   New York   New Rochelle
Melbourne   Sydney

Published by the Press Syndicate of the University of Cambridge
The Pitt Building, Trumpington Street, Cambridge CB2 1RP
32 East 57th Street, New York, NY 10022, USA
296 Beaconsfield Parade, Middle Park, Melbourne 3206, Australia

First published 1983

Printed in Great Britain at
the University Press, Cambridge

Library of Congress catalogue card number: 82–12919

British Library Cataloguing in Publication Data

Jacob, James R.
Henry Stubbe, radical Protestantism and the
early Enlightenment.
1. Stubbe, Henry   2. Radicalism – Great
Britain – Biography
I. Title
322.4'2'0924   HN400.R3

ISBN 0 521 24876 0

Contents

To PEG

Preface

In an earlier book I explored the ideological foundations of the natural philosophy of Robert Boyle and his followers in the early Royal Society. In this book I complete the task begun there of uncovering and examining an alternative understanding of the relations between knowledge and society, science and power, that challenged the outlook and aims of the Royal Society during the Restoration. This alternative understanding, spawned during the mid-century crisis, survived well into the eighteenth century and continued to threaten that version of the scientific Enlightenment which upheld established Christianity, by offering its own radical version of enlightenment which did not. This study provides a way we did not have before of understanding the connection between the radical Protestantism of the Interregnum and the radical Whiggery of the early eighteenth century.

The central figure in this story is Henry Stubbe (1632–76). I do not claim that he was a major thinker, but he was certainly a very exceptional one, who until now has been both misunderstood and depreciated. His career, once revealed, lends new meaning to Restoration science and connects it more closely with the central issue of the period, the question of church settlement. At once vivid and elusive, Stubbe as eccentric thinker and actor has made the writing of this book a virtually undiluted pleasure – full of concealed turnings, drama and chiaroscuro. I hope some of this also manages to get through.

My debts are numerous and run deep. Conversations and correspondence with fellow scholars have proved immensely stimulating and reassuring. For these I should especially like to thank Randolph Trumbach, David Edge, Corinne Weston, Lois Schwoerer, Ernst Wangermann, Steven Zwicker, Mark Goldie, Elizabeth Eisenstein, Steven Shapin, Clarissa Campbell-Orr, Joyce Appleby, the late Andrew Appleby, Richard Schlatter, Hugh Ormsby-Lennon, David Erdman, Michael Hunter, Israel Rosenfield, and the members of the Intellectual History Seminar of the Institute for Research in History who read and criticized, in their inimitably deft and friendly way, preliminary drafts of two parts of this book. To John Jay College of Criminal Justice of the City University of New York I owe my sabbatical year during which much of this book was worked out, and I would like to thank Gerald Lynch, Theodore Gill and William Preston, Jr, for understanding the needs of a humanist in the context of a college which represents an interesting, if sometimes testing, social experiment. My friends have been so loyal and devoted, and so ready to provide needed diversion, that I must thank them too: 'Tina Stiefel, Randy Trumbach, Joe Friedman, Jerry Szeglin, Jim and Gertie Roche, Ernst and María Wangermann, Jeremy Maule, Diana Boernstein, Pat Cunningham and John Cunningham.

Several repositories have contributed their riches of books and manu-scripts to this effort: the British Library, the Bodleian Library, Christ Church Library, Oxford, the Public Record Office, Pepys's Library (Magdalene College, Cambridge), the Library of the Royal Society of London, London University Library, the New York Public Library, the Bobst Library, New York University, and the Widener Library (especially the Houghton). The local record offices of Somerset and Bristol have also to be thanked; brief visits to each proved immensely valuable. The University Library, Cambridge, served as my working library during summers and a sabbatical, and I cannot praise its staff enough for their unfailing courtesy and efficiency.

Thanks are due to the Trustees of the Will of the late J. H. C. Evelyn for permission to quote from the Evelyn Papers, and to the editors of the following publications for permission to reprint portions of what originally appeared in their pages: *Social Studies of Science* for my 'Boyle's Atomism and the Restoration Assault on Pagan Naturalism,' 8 (1978), pp. 211–33; *Notes and Queries* for my 'The Authorship of *An Account of the Rise and Progress of Mahometanism*,' n.s., 26 (1979), pp. 10–11; and *Science, Pseudoscience and Society*, ed. Marsha P. Hanen, Margaret J. Osler and Robert G. Weyant (Waterloo, Ontario, 1980), for my 'Aristotle and the New Philosophy: Stubbe Versus the Royal Society,' pp. 217–36.

To four scholars my debts are exceptional. Christopher Hill and Quentin Skinner have provided encouragement and assistance of the most vital sort for several years. I am also very grateful to John Pocock for a searching critique of the manuscript of this book. We do not always agree, but his suggestions have led, I hope, to substantial improvements in my argument. These three scholars have been among my best teachers for two decades, though I was never their pupil: such is the power of books. Finally, Margaret Jacob has been my intimate friend and fellow artisan for many years. With her I learned my craft, with her I still practice it, and to her this sample is gratefully dedicated.

Spelling and punctuation have been altered where the original would prevent or seriously impede comprehension. Dates conform to modern usage as to year.

Introduction: the historiographical problem

This book is a piece of detective work in more than the usual sense. Not only is it the first book-length treatment devoted to its principal subject, the career and influence of Henry Stubbe; it is also an attempt to solve a puzzle, and this is where the real detective work comes in. Henry Stubbe has received a bad historical press. His career has been divided into two parts by those scholars who have studied him. In the first part, up to 1660, he is quite rightly seen as a republican Independent, a late Interregnum apologist for the 'good old cause' and a spokesman for Sir Henry Vane the Younger.[1] In the second part after the Restoration, however, he has been cast, quite wrongly as it turns out, in the role of a turncoat who rejected the Revolution and became a conservative defender of the established church, the monarchy and Scholastic learning against innovation and particularly against the innovations represented by the new philosophy of the Royal Society and its principal advocates Thomas Sprat and Joseph Glanvill.[2] It is his published attacks on them that have commanded the most scholarly attention, and quite rightly too because they probably constitute the most sustained and vociferous polemical challenge that the Society has ever faced. Stubbe's attacks, moreover, are especially important because they occur at the very moment when the new philosophy and the modern idea of science and its applications were being formulated and institutionalized.[3] This does not mean, however, that, for all the scholarly energy devoted to examining Stubbe's attacks, the issues posed by them have been seen in the proper light because they have not.

Those attacks have been consistently misread partly because Stubbe's career has been divided into two parts, and it is equally true to say that his career has been kept divided by scholars partly because those have been misread. Historians of radical political thought have been interested in Stubbe as a late Interregnum republican theorist and have not ventured beyond 1660 because his explicit republicanism ceases at the Restoration. Historians of science have concentrated on Stubbe's career after 1660, and particularly between 1669 and 1672, because during those four years he mounted his attack on the Royal Society. No one, until now, has explored Stubbe's career with any seriousness after he levelled that attack. True, he

1

lived only four more years, but his activities during those last years prove crucial, as we shall see, for properly interpreting and integrating his life and thought.

In this study I have considered Stubbe's polemical career from first to last and so have bridged the division between the pre-Restoration radical Stubbe studied by historians of political thought and the post-1660 conservative detractor of all things modern and progressive, especially the Royal Society, the straw man conjured up by historians of science. What emerges is no longer the fractured, bifurcated Stubbe of earlier historiography, but something quite different. The first two chapters treat Stubbe's pre-Restoration thought in greater detail than ever before and expose the close links between his early religious and political views – also something not before attempted, yet extremely important for understanding the continuity between his thinking before and after 1660. During the late Interregnum Stubbe, borrowing principally from John Selden, Thomas Hobbes and James Harrington, developed and advocated a civil religion which would survive the Restoration, undergoing several mutations in the course of the 1660s and 1670s. Stubbe, from the late 1650s to his death in 1676, was committed to a radical civil religion, based upon a vitalistic and materialistic metaphysics, which would have reduced Christian doctrine to a deistical minimum, common to the Jews, the Muslims and the primitive Christians, and undermined the claims of the clergy to separate moral and legal authority, if not in fact eliminating them altogether. This civil religion also entailed a policy of toleration for Protestant Dissenters, regularized poor relief and moderate levelling, and a commitment to a secularizing society in which men would pursue national unity, peace and prosperity for all and turn their backs on conservative and clerical Protestantism.

Stubbe's vision of a new society, bound together by civil religion, derived not only from a vitalistic materialism, but also from a profoundly secular conception of history, particularly Christian history. Man's past, according to Stubbe, is not the product of God's supernatural interventions. This providentialist view of history is just another clerical invention foisted upon men by priests and designed to enhance their authority. History, on the contrary, is the result of its own internal processes. There is nothing beyond history making it turn out as it does. All history is secular history.[4] Thus Stubbe's secular historicism is entirely consistent with his vitalistic metaphysics. There is no spiritual order governed by supernatural forces operating in either nature or history. There are only nature and history, and the spiritual and divine are conflated with the natural and historical. Chapters 3 and 4 of the following account are devoted to showing how Stubbe's view of history and nature survived the Restoration and continued to permeate his thinking.

After 1660 Stubbe was no longer free openly to espouse his radical political and religious views, his civil religion, given the comparatively strict censorship and the extreme reaction, both in church and parliament, among gentry and clergy alike, to the Interregnum.[5] Thus, during the 1660s and 1670s Stubbe's works, with one bold exception which landed him in jail, were marked by subterfuge and replete with double meanings – another reason that previous readers of Stubbe have been so misled. Stubbe was by no means alone during the Restoration in this resort to deception in order to avoid the censor.[6] Indeed Steven Zwicker has claimed that Restoration polemical literature is generally characterized by 'the language of disguise.'[7] The task has been, therefore, to probe beneath the surface and ferret out Stubbe's Restoration radicalism. The rewards have been well worth the effort. What emerges is the fact that Stubbe remained committed to one version or another of his former, pre-Restoration civil religion. He continued to put forward (albeit by stealth) many of his earlier views – his vitalistic naturalism and his commitment to a primitive, natural religion which provided a historical foundation for his critique of clerical claims to separate spiritual authority, his Erastian tolerationism and his belief in universal charity to the poor and moderate economic levelling. He was no longer explicitly republican but some of his statements are crypto-republican, and were understood by others to be so. Although he embraced the monarchical Restoration, if not the ecclesiastical one, his adherence to monarchy was highly provisional and departed radically from Restoration orthodoxy. He rejected justifications for monarchy resting upon arguments from divine right and even suggested that subjects have the right to resist their king in certain circumstances. He would also deploy his civil religion for the reform of monarchy by calling for toleration, a reduction of clerical power and a dedication to the secular goals of increasing England's wealth and power to the exclusion of the goals of the clerical Reformation. There is evidence to suggest that he subscribed to the notion of mixed monarchy which was officially proscribed after 1660.

Having shown that Stubbe's radicalism survived the Restoration (albeit in new forms), it is possible in chapter 5 to reinterpret his attacks on the Royal Society and to show that far from representing a conservative reaction to the new philosophy, as the standard interpretation would have it, those attacks represent yet another deployment of his civil religion, this time against the alliance being forged during the early Restoration between the Royal Society and latitudinarian Anglican Christianity. The latitudinarian churchmen in the Royal Society constructed a natural philosophy that demonstrated the existence and providence of a supernatural God and the immortality of the human soul. To latitudinarian Fellows of the Royal Society like Robert Boyle, John Wilkins, Sprat, Glanvill and others these doctrines, proved by science and inculcated by the clergy, would establish the church on proper foundations and preserve it from its enemies. Science was thus seen by the latitudinarians to be crucial to the survival of the church. Nor did they envisage a bare survival. Rather they argued that scientific inquiry was a principal key to increasing trade and profit, domestic peace and imperial expansion, all of which would advance the church's interests and help bring in the Reformation.[8] Stubbe was the first to point out the character of this alliance between latitudinarian churchmen and the Royal Society, or at least its leading publicists – and with good reason. The alliance flew in the face of the objectives of his civil religion which was meant to tear down a clerically dominated society and clerically dominated learning and replace them with something much more secular and pagan. Thus the debate between Stubbe and the polemicists for the Royal Society was not a confrontation between a reactionary Scholastic holdout and the forward-looking Royal Society, that is between error and the advancement of learning, as it has always been claimed to be. It comes down instead to a conflict between two views of how to achieve progress and reform. The Royal Society would attach science to the Restoration settlement in church and state and achieve progress through a steady increase in knowledge of the natural world.[9] Stubbe, on the other hand, would link scientific inquiry and the accumulation of knowledge to the progressive secularization and de-Christianization of society. His was a program for the radical reform of knowledge *and* society; theirs, for the reform of knowledge alone. His vision was one which distressed leading natural philosophers in the Royal Society and which they set out specifically to answer. Nor did the confrontation die with Stubbe. It was the dialogue that would last well into the eighteenth century because views very like Stubbe's were taken up by John Toland after the Revolution of 1688–9 and much later by Joseph Priestley.[10]

The artificial division of Stubbe's career at 1660 which gives the earlier part to historians of republican theory and the later to historians of science is clearly responsible for the consistent misreading of the message underlying his attack on the Royal Society. But there were other reasons for this misreading, reasons from which scholarship has only recently recovered. The study of the history of thought in the seventeenth century was until quite recently bedevilled by an admiration for the achievements of the great natural philosophers of the age. It blinded historians both to the larger social and cultural forces that nurtured natural philosophy and, what is more important in terms of this study, to other forms of intellectual novelty as impressive in their own way as those of mathematical physics. Thus what was opposed to the new philosophy was seen to be backward and all that was in line with it, progressive. Because Stubbe couched his criticism of the Royal Society in terms of an assertion of the values of Aristotelianism, that convenient bugbear of science and progress, it was easy to slip into interpreting his debate with the Society as a clear case of a conflict between darkness and light, stubborn ignorance and the search for truth.

What was lacking in this quick assessment was any careful evaluation of the terms of the debate, the rhetoric of the argument and the Restoration context in which it took place. When these factors are taken into account, two things become readily apparent. First as to rhetoric, Stubbe, in vaunting the claims of Aristotle and the ancients over the moderns represented by the Royal Society, was appealing to the past not because he was a conservative, but because the past to which he appealed constituted a source of primitive purity and prudence against which to set, measure and reform the corruptions of the present. We have learned from the works of Christopher Hill, John Pocock and others that this appeal to the past was not necessarily conservative and could in fact be a device whose consequences were sometimes extraordinarily radical. In this regard, as we shall see, Stubbe's appeal to ancient authority in his attacks on the Royal Society was the equivalent of the contemporary appeal to the ancient constitution as a corrective to 'the Norman yoke.'[11] More specifically, as we shall also see, Stubbe's championing of Aristotle over Epicurus and the corpuscular philosophy of the Royal Society was close, once his message is decoded, to the contrast set up by his contemporary Harrington between ancient and modern prudence.[12] Indeed it will be argued in chapter 6 that at times Stubbe's views represent a cryptic Restoration revival of Harringtonian vocabulary, distanced though they are from Harrington's meaning.[13]

Second, when the context of the debate between Stubbe, Glanvill and Sprat is taken account of, it becomes clear that the issues were a great deal more complex than a simple confrontation between outmoded Scholasticism and progressive science. This context will be explored in detail in chapter 5.

This complete reversal of our understanding of Stubbe's career after 1660 and his attacks on the Royal Society in particular is confirmed by the findings presented in chapters 6 and 7, which deal with Stubbe's activities from 1672 to his death four years later. As court propagandist in 1672, he rings yet another change on his perennial civil religion, and in the course of defending the third Anglo-Dutch War adopts a position which makes use of Harrington's vocabulary but which departs drastically from his meaning. Stubbe's position again calls fundamental Christian doctrines into question and points towards an at least partial return to the civil religion of early Christianity. The year 1673 is a particularly revealing one in Stubbe's career, and the tracing of his politics during that year constitutes the main subject of chapter 7. Stubbe leaves the court, joins the opposition and becomes a spokesman for some of the more extreme elements, probably including the first Earl of Shaftesbury, in the country party which was just then emerging. The standard interpretation which sees Stubbe as a turncoat upholder of the status quo would have no way of taking Stubbe's politics during 1673 into account, and in fact has uniformly and totally ignored this stage in his career. It could hardly be claimed that Stubbe was simply doing the expedient thing, as it is claimed he had done in 1660, by joining the opposition in 1673. Seen in the context of his continued commitment to radical ideals throughout the Restoration, however, his migration from court to country with Shaftesbury that year becomes another step by which he hopes to achieve the goals of his civil religion and a reformed monarchy.

Stubbe died in 1676 but his ideas lived on, and the tracing of this posthumous influence is the subject of chapter 8. What emerges is not only that there is a continuity between Stubbe's thinking before and after the Restoration, but that there is a longer continuity linking Stubbe's Interregnum and Restoration radicalism with that of the radical free-thinkers Charles Blount and John Toland before and after the Revolution of 1688–9, a linkage continuing well into at least the second decade of the eighteenth century and probably beyond. Stubbe can now be added to the list of those men like Milton, Andrew Marvell, Henry Neville, John Wildman and Algernon Sidney who nurtured the radical ideals growing out of the 1640s and 1650s and continued, often by resort to subterfuge, to preach a message subversive of Restoration orthodoxy, men whose ideas were later taken up by the early Enlightenment in England. In fact Stubbe's career and later influence provide the best example up to now of precisely how that Interregnum radicalism survived the repression of the Restoration from one year and decade to the next, to be reborn briefly during the Exclusion crisis and more permanently during the 1690s and first two decades of the next century. Other scholars have addressed this question of the survival and mutation of radical ideas after 1660, and what follows is much indebted to this valuable body of work.[14] If this study contributes something to answering the same question, it is because the evidence for Stubbe's career, read in the proper light, tells in the clearest, most concrete way so far the story of this survival and adaptation in the hard and rocky soil of the Restoration. It is this historical specificity that seems so precious and important.

This study also contributes to the story of the continuity of seventeenth-century radicalism in another important way. In the last decade or so it has been shown that the natural philosophy of the Royal Society, as it evolved from Boyle to Newton, was shaped in part in the crucible of the English Revolution, understood as a social and political transformation stretching from the 1640s to the early eighteenth century.[15] This latitudinarian natural philosophy was designed in particular to preserve and enhance Anglicanism by answering the various radical political and religious threats to Anglican hegemony thrown up by the Revolution. The process by which latitudinarian natural philosophy developed in response to more radical conceptions of nature and society has been clearly worked out for the 1640s and 1650s and for the two or three decades after the Revolution of 1688–9.[16] What this study does is again to provide a clear, connecting link between the Interregnum and the early eighteenth century. Henry Stubbe's vitalistic naturalism and paganizing civil religion posed a threat to latitudinarian Anglicanism similar to that posed by sectaries, republicans and Diggers during the Interregnum, and by the likes of John Toland during the early Enlightenment. The dialogue between latitudinarian natural philosophers and their social and political enemies wielding subversive views of the relations among God, man and nature was continuous from Boyle and the founders of the Royal Society to Newton and the early Newtonians: on the radical side Henry Stubbe provides the principal missing link, establishing that continuity. During the early Restoration, when most radical natural philosophers had been reduced to silence, he kept up the attack and indeed renewed it in his remarkable series of tracts challenging the Royal Society. He may be said to have brought that challenge to a new level by exposing for the first time the character of the active and deliberate alliance growing up between the Royal Society and a certain kind of Anglican orthodoxy, namely, latitudinarianism or liberal Anglicanism. This is his original and profound contribution to the radical tradition, no less important for being completely overlooked by historians of the Royal Society. Before this contribution can be properly understood, however, the undergrowth of misunderstanding must be cleared away. Hence the purpose of this book. The result will be another new insight into the dynamics of intellectual change during the later seventeenth century in England and another new strand to be introduced and woven into the rich tapestry of 'the century of genius,' which as I shall show in the last chapter, helps to revise our understanding of the origins of the Enlightenment.

1

Hobbesian Independent

Hobbes had an enormous impact on late seventeenth-century England, and nowhere more than on religion. From the 1650s on through the century Christian apologists took up their pens to answer the Hobbesist threat. If the anti-Hobbesist literature offers any measure of Hobbes's impact, one might be led to conclude that his influence was pervasive, that Hobbesism in religion had spread or was at least in danger of spreading throughout the land. What is remarkable, however, given the degree of anti-Hobbesism, is the fact that so little explicit Hobbesism in religion gets into print or even enters public discourse during the Restoration. Censorship of course would work to keep it out of print, and, since Hobbesian views were so heretical, people who held them were probably reticent to express them in public. If anyone had any doubts on this score, the example of Daniel Scargill would serve to remind him of what lay in store for the avowed Hobbesist. Scargill was a young Cambridge don who in 1668 was brought before University authorities and forced publicly to recant his Hobbesian views. He was never heard from again on any issue.[1]

Seen in this light, Stubbe's case is particularly interesting. Others have noted his association with Hobbes during the 1650s, but no one has shown the character of Hobbes's influence upon him both before and after the Restoration. In this chapter I shall examine Hobbes's impact upon Stubbe before 1660 as a prelude to charting Stubbe's Hobbesism and analyzing its significance throughout his career. What I shall show in this chapter, and later, is that although Hobbes was a major influence on Stubbe, Stubbe's views sometimes diverged sharply from Hobbes's own. Stubbe, in other words, was not a consistent follower of Hobbes; he was not a strict Hobbesist. Thus in Stubbe's career we see Hobbes's ideas being taken up and exploited in ways that were not true to Hobbes's own position. This study then should throw new light upon the old question of Hobbes's impact, the question of Hobbesism during the Restoration. If Stubbe's career is any example, Hobbes's influence could take some peculiar forms. Stubbe's career in turn suggests that what its detractors called Hobbesism might be something other than Hobbes's own views. A great thinker's ideas made popular, accessible and polemical, as Hobbes's were in Stubbe's hands, become rather different from what they were to start with. The historian must, therefore, cast a wider net if he is to receive the lost world of Restoration Hobbesism.

Little is known of Stubbe's life before 1656, and what we know comes mainly from Stubbe's earliest biographer Anthony Wood whose admirable account in *Athenae Oxonienses* drew its inspiration from Wood's obvious fascination with his subject. According to Wood, Stubbe was 'the most noted person of his age that these late times have produced.'[2] One may well wonder precisely what Wood meant, but he may have been referring to the fact that in his youth Stubbe was something of a hothouse plant, forced, that is, into early, almost premature, bloom because he possessed the skills of the pen and the pugnacity to deploy them in the service of causes to which he and his patrons were committed.

He was born in Lincolnshire in February 1632. Sometime thereafter his family moved to Ireland, and when the rebellion broke out there in 1641 his mother brought him to London where she is supposed to have supported them 'by her needle.'[3] She earned enough to send him to Westminster School where his exceptional abilities were taken notice of by Richard Busby, the headmaster, and the younger Sir Henry Vane, himself a former pupil at the school. Vane became Stubbe's earliest patron providing for him at the school and sending him in 1649 to Christ Church, Oxford, where during the next few years he gained a reputation for impudence and proficiency in Greek and was for the former 'whipt . . . in the public refectory.'[4] His career as a satirical wit, for which he was later to become notorious, may already have begun.

With Vane for his patron he could not help but serve the parliamentary cause. In 1651 parliament drew up the engagement oath and to Stubbe was delegated the task of bearing it to the University. As Wood quotes him, ''Twas I that brought the engagement down to Oxon (though I took it not, being then an undergraduate) and having got Dr. S. F. [Samuel Fell as it should seem] and Dr. R. [Reynolds] to be turned out, I saved the remains of the cavaliers of Ch. Ch. and Queen's coll. and gave them opportunities to live securely and educate others in their principles.'[5] Wood does not provide a citation for this quotation but if it is to be credited, Stubbe was already playing an important role in the political life of the University and displaying that devotion to liberty of conscience, in this case as extended to 'cavaliers' or royalists, which was to be a hallmark of his thought. The quotation also suggests that as bearer of the Engagement, he was a wholehearted supporter of the new government and had no difficulty accepting the de facto character of its authority. This commitment also throws light on Stubbe's Hobbesism, since Hobbes's *Leviathan* was among other things an elegant justification of de facto authority.[6]

In 1653 he took his BA degree and then did a two-year stint of military service on the parliamentary side in Scotland, about which, alas, there is no more to say. In 1655 or 1656 he returned to Oxford and a Studentship at Christ Church; and in 1656 took his MA degree. From this year we can begin to trace the development of his ideas.

Two of the most vital new intellectual forces of the 1650s were the theological ideas growing out of the religious movement known as Independency and the philosophy and religion of Thomas Hobbes. Oxford was one of the places where these two new forces were felt most strongly, and Stubbe was one of the principal innovators there on both fronts, engaged as he was in promoting Hobbes's philosophy and in championing the cause of extreme Independency in defiance of the Presbyterians. Stubbe was in fact a Hobbesist and a radical Independent. On the surface nothing could appear more contradictory. Hobbes after all is supposed to have been devoted to the idea of an absolute sovereign who would enforce strict obedience to all his commands civil *and* religious. The Independents, on the other hand, stood for religious toleration, the freedom of the individual Christian to associate with a congregation separate from and independent of any higher ecclesiastical authority.[7] Despite the obvious tensions between these two religious views, Hobbes's and the Independents', Stubbe, and for that matter Hobbes himself, managed a kind of reconciliation between them, and the resulting theological position remained fundamental to Stubbe's thinking to the end. In fact one of the major purposes of this book is to explain and explore that curious mixture of Hobbesism and political and religious radicalism that Stubbe represents, and to show that it is important for understanding not only Stubbe himself but also the world of subversive religion in which he moved and to which he contributed after the Restoration. The remainder of this chapter is thus devoted to an examination of the marriage between Hobbes and radical Independency that Stubbe worked out. An ancillary purpose is to answer, insofar as the evidence allows, the question what was the nature and extent of Hobbes's connection with Stubbe and Independency?

By April 1656 Stubbe and Hobbes had become friends – and one may well ask how a young radical Independent and the theorist of absolute sovereignty could strike up a close relationship and even, as it turns out, an intellectual collaboration, for Stubbe had begun, with Hobbes's approval, if not at his instigation, to translate *Leviathan* into Latin.[8] Nor was this the only occasion for collaboration. Since 1655 Hobbes had been engaged in a pamphlet feud with Dr John Wallis, the Presbyterian divine and Savilian Professor of Geometry at Oxford. It was a quarrel partly about geometry, partly about religion and politics. But it often devolved into attempts on both sides to poke holes in the other's arguments or his way of handling the argument. Since it was conducted for the most part in Latin, Wallis and Hobbes accused each other of committing grammatical errors or of an inadequate command of classical sources. This is where Stubbe came in on Hobbes's side. He relied on the young precocious classical scholar with access to the libraries of Oxford to check and correct his Latin and supply him with grammatical arguments and the classical sources to back them up. On one occasion Hobbes even incorporated Stubbe's critique of Wallis's classical allusions and Latin grammar into his own attack on Wallis's mathematics and religion.[9] Stubbe's reproof of Wallis's Latinity was introduced into Hobbes's tract in the form of an anonymous letter, the work of a friend of a friend who had sent it on to Hobbes with instructions to publish it.[10] The collaboration between Hobbes and Stubbe in the first instance then was the product of their mutual animus against Wallis, and there was one object in particular of their hostility, namely, Wallis's Presbyterianism.

For Wallis, as for many other conservative Christians, Presbyterians and Anglicans alike, the true church was divinely ordained. Its authority, that is, came from God, not man. The form of its government was also based on a divine model revealed in the New Testament and set up by the earliest Christians in Apostolic times, and for Wallis of course this meant a Presbyterian model. According to him, the Presbyterian clergy, the one true ministry of God, was also invested with divine authority. An ordinary layman became a clergyman only when he was ordained by the clerical authorities in a ceremony that consisted literally of an imposition of hands. In this way each minister could be claimed to have received his authority from Christ through an Apostolic succession stretching down to the present.[11] One important result was, moreover, that the clergy could claim an authority derived from God, a spiritual power, separate and independent of that of the state, and it was over this issue that battle was joined between Wallis on one side and Hobbes and Stubbe on the other.

Wallis was perhaps the leading spokesman for the Presbyterians in the University. Nor was his religion only a recent phenomenon. His strong commitment stretched back over a decade to the time when he had served as a Secretary to the Westminster Assembly. Now in Oxford in the 1650s he championed the Presbyterian cause by preaching and publishing against Hobbes and the Independents alike. The focus of his position, and the points at which he drew fire from his opponents, concerned the nature of the church, the power of the clergy and the relationship between church and state.

Hobbes made his religious position clear in the last two parts of *Leviathan* at the beginning of the decade. The Christian church and all church officials should be subject to the civil sovereign, preferably (but not necessarily) a king.[12] Hobbes, like the Presbyterians, rested his case too on the Scriptures. They reveal, he argued, that the kingdom of God, theocracy on earth, belongs to the past (Moses and his successors down to the election of Saul) and to the future (the post-apocalyptic Millennium, when Christ will return to earth and rule his saints forever).[13] Christ himself had made it clear that his kingdom was, until the Millennium, 'not of this world.'[14] It would be realized on earth only with the end of time. In the meantime men, Hobbes taught, must obey their lawful civil sovereigns – and them alone – in all matters 'as well ecclesiastical as civil.'[15] Clergy there should be. But they should be appointed by and subordinate to the civil sovereign. Because Christ's kingdom lay in the future, moreover, their role should be only to teach Christianity and persuade men to accept it and live by it: they should have no power to command.[16]

It is a commonplace: Hobbes was an extreme Erastian. Thus he objected to any creed that insisted that Christ's kingdom was here and now as well as hereafter, that in this world it was embodied in the true church and its clergy ordained and instituted by him as a part of his commission from God during his incarnation. This doctrine, Hobbes maintained, would set up a clerical power independent of and rival to the civil authority and so undermine the civil sovereignty which it was Hobbes's chief purpose to see established. He was quite specific about who the principal enemies were in this regard: 'The authors . . . of this darkness in religion, are the Roman, and the presbyterian clergy.'[17]

Hobbes acknowledged that the Presbyterians had rejected many Roman tenets.[18] But this was not so important to him as the fact that they still shared with the Catholics 'the greatest, and main abuse of Scripture' – 'the wresting of it, to prove that the Kingdom of God . . . is the present Church.'[19] This one error provided both Romanists and Presbyterians with the theological basis for setting up an independent clerical authority – the pope for the Catholics and 'Assemblies of Pastors' in the case of the Presbyterians – thereby subverting the only true Scriptural authority in church and state, the civil sovereign.[20] Or as he said of the Roman and Presbyterian false assertion of clerical power, 'it . . . causeth so great a darkness in men's understanding, that they see not who it is to whom they have engaged their obedience.'[21] The effects could be serious: Hobbes blamed the Presbyterians, and in particular their doctrine of clerical authority, for leading England down the path to civil war.[22]

Related to the threat to civil authority posed by Presbyterians and Romanists alike was a shared metaphysic based, Hobbes argued, upon the false notion, derived from the ancient Greeks and especially Aristotle, of the existence of incorporeal spirits. Hobbes did not deny the existence of spirits, but his materialism compelled him to explain them as corporeal objects, refined bodies, matter in motion, attenuated but nonetheless material. An incorporeal spirit, then, according to Hobbes, was a contradiction in terms.[23] It was a key tenet of what he called 'vain philosophy, derived to the Universities, and thence into the Church, partly from Aristotle, partly from blindness of understanding.'[24] *Leviathan* attacked all universities, contemporary Oxford and Cambridge included, for perpetuating this metaphysics, and his opponents within the universities did not fail to notice and defend themselves against the charge.[25] Hobbes wished to rectify this 'blindness of understanding' by substituting his own philosophy for 'school divinity' in the university curriculum.[26] In place of Aristotle and his commentators he would have put his physics, mathematics, ethics and politics.[27]

Clerical power, according to Hobbes, hinged in large part on the doctrine of incorporeal spirits 'built on the vain philosophy of Aristotle'[28] and the schools. This philosophy allowed the clergy to maintain their power and independence by inculcating superstition and instilling fear in ordinary people and hence gaining their obedience, which should go instead to the civil authority. Hobbes provided examples of how 'vain philosophy,' the doctrine of incorporeal spirits in particular, worked to this effect.

For it is upon this ground, that when a man is dead and buried, they say his soul . . . can walk separated from his body, and is seen by night amongst the graves. Upon the same ground they say that the figure, & colour, and taste of a piece of bread, has a being, there, where they say there is no bread: And upon the same ground they say, that faith, and wisdom, & other vertues are sometimes poured into a man, sometimes blown into him from heaven; . . . and a great many other things that serve to lessen the dependence of subjects on the sovereign power of their country. For who will endeavour to obey the laws, if he expect obedience to be poured or blown into him?[29]

The connections between knowledge and power were clear to Hobbes. The universities purveyed a kind of knowledge that upheld clerical authority in defiance of civil sovereignty. Were Hobbes to have his way, his philosophy would be introduced into the universities and by dispelling fear and superstition undermine clerical authority in favor of the civil sovereign and civil peace. Thus Hobbes's attack was not upon Wallis's Presbyterianism alone; it was also directed against the curriculum that supported false theological doctrine.

Wallis understood the nature of Hobbes's challenge and addressed himself to it. As a professor of mathematics, Wallis's strategy was to point out the errors in Hobbes's geometry not as an end in itself but as a way of destroying the force of his whole argument. If, as Hobbes insisted, the introduction of his mathematics into the university curriculum would represent the beginning of effective educational reform and a major step towards undermining clerical independence to the advantage of the civil sovereignty, and if those mathematics could be shown to be riddled with error, his whole philosophy would be called into question and the threat he posed to Christian orthodoxy checked if not eliminated. In a letter to Christian Huygens in 1659, Wallis made these purposes clear:

Our Leviathan is furiously attacking and destroying our Universities (and not only ours but all) and especially ministers and the clergy and all religion, as though the Christian world had not sound knowledge . . . and as though men could not understand religion if they did not understand mathematics. Hence it seemed necessary that some mathematician should show him . . . how little he understands the mathematics from which he takes his courage.[30]

With respect to Hobbes, Boyle pursued purposes similar to those Wallis expressed here; in fact after the Restoration the two men collaborated in their attacks on Hobbes.[31]

During the last two years or so of the Protectorate, James Harrington, the author of *Oceana* (1656), about whom much more will be said in the next chapter, found himself engaged in controversy with 'the university wits,' as he called them, principally Matthew Wren and John Wilkins, who belonged to the circle of mathematicians and experimentalists (Wallis, Seth Ward and Boyle), who were attacking Hobbes and who after the Restoration were to be among the principal founders of the Royal Society.[32] The question then is: was there a connection between the two attacks, the one on Harrington, the other on Hobbes, besides the fact that they came from the same Oxford circle? The answer, I think, is that there was an ideological affinity as well. Wallis and Boyle attacked Hobbes's mathematics and physics because he argued that the introduction of his natural philosophy into the university curriculum would represent a major step towards undermining clerical power. His science and mathematics, Hobbes said, would expose 'the vain philosophy' for the fraud that it was and hence invalidate the claims of the clergy based upon it to independent spiritual authority. Indeed Hobbes's philosophy would have a further effect: to the extent that it took hold, it would bring the very idea of an incorporeal spirit into question and with it the fundamental Christian doctrines of the providence of God and the immateriality and immortality of the rational soul. For what was man's soul if it was not an incorporeal spirit that survived the death of the body to be rewarded or punished in the afterlife according to its deserts, and how could a supernatural God govern his creation providentially if not through incorporeal spiritual agencies like angels and demons? It was questions like these that Boyle and Wallis hoped to stifle by taking aim against Hobbes's mathematics and physics.

But what is the ideological affinity between this attack on Hobbes and the attack on Harrington coming from the same circle? On the face of it, the connection does not appear to exist. Hobbes was being attacked for his materialism, and Harrington was certainly not a materialist. Moreover, Matthew Wren, the member of the circle who led the attack on Harrington, argued against him by claiming that the basis of government lay not, as Harrington said, in the discovery of rational principles embedded in human nature but rather in the commands of the sovereign power. As Wren saw it, the fact that there were no timeless principles of government rendered otiose Harrington's argument for a perpetual republic or 'equal commonwealth.' Wren's view that government rested on command stood much closer to Hobbes's de facto theory than to Harrington's search for original principles on which to build 'immortal' commonwealths.[33]

None of this provides promising ground for establishing an ideological affinity between the attacks on Harrington and Hobbes delivered at exactly the same time by the same Oxford group – quite the contrary. Yet there is just such a connection, and it concerns religion and natural philosophy more than politics. Wren's political ideas may have resonated with Hobbes's and clashed with Harrington's, but in matters of natural philosophy, in particular the relation of God to nature, Wren would find Hobbes and Harrington equally unacceptable and the implications of their theories equally subversive of existing authority, especially clerical authority. Wren, though not a cleric, wrote his principal attack on Harrington, *Considerations upon Mr. Harrington's Commonwealth of Oceana*, at the request of a leading cleric, John Wilkins, Warden of Wadham College, Oxford, and dedicated it to him. Though it was published anonymously, Harrington in his reply took it to be the work of a cleric, so sympathetic was it to the clergy.[34]

What, first of all, was the difference between Wren's view of nature and Harrington's? How, secondly, does this difference establish the ideological connection between their controversy and the contemporary controversy between Wallis and Hobbes?

Wren shared the views of the Oxford natural philosophers – Wilkins, Boyle and Wallis – with whom he was connected. This group was developing at the time a natural philosophy that was at once mechanical and providential. It was mechanical because the universe was conceived of as consisting of atomic particles of matter in motion. It was equally providential because these particles did not move themselves: they had been originally set in motion by God at the outset of creation, and they were kept in motion according to his providential design by the intervention of supernatural spiritual agencies at work in nature. The fact that motion came from God Christianized the universe; that is to say, it preserved what was otherwise a mechanistic conception of nature from the materialism and atheism associated with ancient Epicureanism and latter-day Hobbesism, both of which were thoroughly mechanistic views which denied God's spiritual intervention in the universe. In Wren's view, and that of the Oxford philosophers, there was room in the cosmos for incorporeal spirits, supernatural agencies doing God's will; according to Hobbes, on the other hand, such spirits did not and could not exist.[35]

Just as Wren's natural philosophy was not Hobbes's, Harrington's departed from both. Where Hobbes denied even the possibility of spiritual intervention and Wren made provision for its existence, Harrington postulated a created order which worked according to spiritual principles and nothing else. For Harrington it was not a question (as for Wren) of God intervening through spiritual agencies to keep an essentially mechanical universe on track. For Harrington spiritual principles coming from God were built into and perpetually ordered the world. God and the world were not one and the same: Harrington was not a pantheist. But God was much closer to Harrington's world than to Wren's. He did not merely intervene in it; his principles were embedded and actualized in it.[36] Nature for Harrington *constantly* 'operates through spirits.'[37] God, moreover, gave men the reason by which to discover this spiritual order and apply it to the building of the polity.[38] Here then was the political pay-off: all men have the capacity to understand God's order, to bring themselves into line with it and hence to manifest the virtue that will make a republic, the immortal commonwealth, work. Not only is God's order built into the cosmos; it is accessible through human reason to the project of building a viable republic. For Wren and the Oxford philosophers there could be no such political pay-load. God's providence was too inscrutable and politics too contingent; the spiritual 'mechanics of nature' that Harrington postulated simply did not exist, and the capacities of human reason were not great enough.[39] Harrington's reply to Wren in this connection was to accuse him of being a 'mathematician' who was applying the mechanical philosophy to politics where it did not belong: 'Let me tell him that in the politics there is nothing mechanic, or like it. This is but an idiotism of some mathematician . . . The mathematician must not take God to be such an one as he is.'[40]

Now that we have explained the difference between Harrington on the one hand and Wren and the Oxford philosophers on the other, we are ready to answer our last question: what is the ideological connection between the controversy involving Wren and Harrington and the one involving Wallis and Hobbes? Why in other words did the Oxford philosophers argue against both Harrington and Hobbes, particularly in view of the fact that Wren's political argument against Harrington was itself strongly Hobbesian? The answer, as we have indicated, hinges upon the religious implications of the respective natural philosophies – Harrington's, Hobbes's and that of the Oxford philosophers. From the perspective of these latter, Hobbes and Harrington both threatened Christianity and especially the role of the clergy. Hobbes denied the existence of spiritual agencies and thus deprived the clergy of their traditional role as the interpreters of God's providence. If there were no incorporeal spirits, how could there be any divine providence and what then would be left for the clergy to explain? Harrington for his part went to the other extreme. The world was full of spiritual forces, and, what is more, all men by virtue of human reason could read them and be instructed by them in the lessons of republicanism. In the eyes of the Oxford philosophers Harrington was being unrealistic in making God's order too accessible to men, particularly when the order thus revealed prescribed an 'equal commonwealth.' Moreover, if men could read nature, a nature that embodied God's order and taught his political lessons, where again did this leave the clergy, those who specialized in interpreting God's will to everyone else? Here then is the source of the ideological affinity linking the attacks on Harrington and Hobbes mounted by the Oxford philosophers. From their perspective Harrington's estimate of human reason was too generous. Equally, the role which Hobbes would have assigned the clergy – there being no spiritual kingdom for them to interpret, he would have reduced them to serving as mere mouthpieces of the civil sovereign – was too mean. To paraphrase a point Margaret Jacob and I have made elsewhere: while Hobbes sucked too much spirit out of the world, Harrington pumped too much back in![41]

The battle between Wallis and Hobbes was joined in 1655, when the former produced his first tract attacking the latter's mathematics, *Elenchus Geometria Hobbianae*. Hobbes answered the next year with *Six Lessons, Directed to the Professors of Mathematicks*, an attack on Seth Ward, another Oxford mathematician, who had written that year against Hobbes in alliance with Wallis, as well as on the latter's tract of the year before.[42] And so the controversy went, a published attack from the one calling for and receiving an answer from the other, well into the Restoration.[43] Ward and Wallis were among the leading founders of the Royal Society after the Restoration, and in view of their ideological differences with Hobbes, differences that were reflected in the general outlook of the new Society,[44] as Hobbes himself indicated in 1674,[45] it is not surprising that he was never invited to membership of the Society.[46] Our chief interest for the moment, however, is in the controversy between Hobbes and Wallis before the Restoration. Wallis, as we have seen, drew support from Ward within the University. Hobbes also was not without his defenders in Oxford, Wallis's backyard, despite the fact that Hobbes lived in London at the time.

The fact of such support for the heretical Hobbes at Oxford is not so important as its source. Hobbes's Oxonian partisans in the battle against Wallis lay chiefly, it seems, among the radical Independents. Certainly his most enthusiastic champion was the young, outspoken extreme Independent and Vanian Student of Christ Church Henry Stubbe. In him the philosophical radicalism of Hobbes linked up with his own political and religious radicalism. Nor was he alone in this enthusiasm. He indicated that it was shared by other like-minded spirits in the University.[47] He, alas, is the richest source of evidence we have for the connection between Hobbes and radical Independency at Interregnum Oxford. But what evidence he provides is enough to indicate the reasons for the connection and to reveal another contemporary context for understanding Hobbes's thought. Just as Quentin Skinner has illuminated his political thought by examining its context, so Stubbe allows us to begin to do the same for Hobbes's religious thought.[48] The other purpose here of course is to discover the ways in which Stubbe adapted Hobbes's ideas, the nature and extent of his intellectual debt and devotion to the master.

We know about Hobbes and Stubbe because of Stubbe's letters to Hobbes among the Additional Manuscripts in the British Library.[49] By the time of the first letter, 1 April 1656, Stubbe already knows Hobbes and has been at work for some unspecified time on a Latin translation of *Leviathan*; he has reached chapter 8. By this time, too, Stubbe has become a leading spokesman for the Independents in the University. In this regard he is patronized by John Owen, Dean of Christ Church and Vice-Chancellor of the University, who is himself engaged in debate, within and without the University, with the Presbyterians.[50] There is still no final national religious settlement, and this is what is at stake in the controversy between Independents and Presbyterians throughout the land. In Oxford the atmosphere of the debate, as one would expect, is highly charged. In this situation Stubbe reads and reflects on *Leviathan*, meets Hobbes at least once in London, and sees his religious views as giving support to the Independent cause. Hobbes and Stubbe proceed to collaborate against Wallis, their mutual enemy. What we do not know, Hobbes's side of the correspondence not being extant, is how far Hobbes agreed with Stubbe. Hobbes of course had argued in *Leviathan* itself mildly in favor of Independency, writing of England at the time (1651): 'and so we are reduced to the independency of the primitive Christians, to follow Paul, or Cephas, or Apollos, every man as he liketh best.'[51] Does this mean that by the spring of 1656 and for the duration of the correspondence (the last letter is dated 9 October 1659),[52] Hobbes had come to accept some form of radical Independency as the best possible solution to the religious crisis, the one most compatible with the dictates of *Leviathan* in the circumstances? Perhaps it does.

What evidence does the collaboration between Stubbe and Hobbes reveal of a shared commitment in face of Presbyterianism and Wallis in particular? By 1656, when Stubbe writes the bulk of the surviving letters, he is engaged in translating *Leviathan* and promoting both Hobbes's philosophy and the Independent cause at Oxford.[53] Stubbe sends his draft translations to Hobbes as he does them,[54] In his letter of 7 October 1656, he says, 'I have here sent you the residue of the eighth and ninth chapter.'[55] He proceeds this way in order that Hobbes may have the opportunity to offer suggestions before Stubbe embarks upon revisions.[56] In this letter he announces that Owen, his patron, has asked him to write an answer to Wallis, who in 1656 'hath put out some theses against a branch of independency.'[57] In connection with his reply to Wallis, he says, 'I have received orders [presumably from Owen] to study church-government, & a toleration, & so to oppose Presbytery.'[58] So the translation must take second place for the time being. By way of excuse to Hobbes for this distraction he says of his dependence upon the patronage of Owen and the Independents, 'being obnoxious to others (for else the Presbyterians had outed me long ago) I must continue their favor, that so I may be capable to serve you.'[59] This should be read as a compliment to Hobbes rather than as evidence that Stubbe's Independency was merely expedient to his Hobbesism. The record is clear: he was both an Independent and a follower of Hobbes.

In the next letter, 25 October 1656, Stubbe asks Hobbes to contribute an anonymous 'letter' to the book he is writing for Owen against Wallis's theses: 'it would do much to disgrace ye Dr.'[60] To this end he has sent Hobbes a copy of the book by Wallis he is attacking.[61] Hobbes does not take Stubbe's suggestion, perhaps wishing not to be so closely identified with the Independent cause. On the same day Stubbe writes a second letter to Hobbes in which he modifies his request and merely says, having sent Wallis's anti-Independent tract to Hobbes, '& what hints you shall give me I shall endeavour to improve them.'[62] In this second letter he says that he has completed a draft of his attack on Wallis and shown it to Owen, who 'is well pleased, & hereupon hath given me the under-library keeper's place, which has made all the Kyrks madde.'[63] Stubbe's answer, at least in one form, was published in 1657,[64] and already late in 1656, he was rewarded for his efforts by being made second in charge of the Bodleian under the Keeper Thomas Barlow.[65] Stubbe's appointment is a clear case of the connection between politics and preferment in Interregnum Oxford.

Hobbes declined to write a letter to be included in Stubbe's tract, but he did furnish Stubbe his thoughts on the subject, as Stubbe had also requested.[66] Of these Stubbe writes to Hobbes: 'I observed . . . a great correspondence between my thoughts and yours, so that if Dr Owen who hath mine in his hands now at London, should but compare my notes with your remarks, he would conclude them to be but the transcript of yours.'[67] Hobbes undertook, furthermore, to address himself to Wallis's anti-Independent doctrines in his own attack on Wallis, entitled *Markes of the Absurd Geometry, Rural Language, Scottish Church-Politicks and Barbarismes of John Wallis*, delivered in 1657, as one volley in the succession of blasts and counterblasts that Hobbes and Wallis hurled at each other before and after the Restoration.[68] If his comments, supplied to Stubbe in November 1656, which, alas, are lost, square with his own published attack on Wallis in *Markes* in 1657, and there is no reason to doubt that they do not, then here is the strongest evidence we have that Hobbes and Stubbe had arrived at a common position as regards the religious question, that both were Hobbesist Independents. Of course we cannot be certain of this. Although it is true that Hobbes and Stubbe used the same arguments in their attack upon Wallis and the Presbyterians, whether or not Hobbes would have been willing to go further and identify himself with the cause of radical Independency itself of the sort Stubbe represented remains an open question. It is one thing for Hobbes to agree with Stubbe in the negative business of the assault on Wallis; it would be quite another for Hobbes to be counted positively in favor of Stubbe's Independency – and, as we shall see, there is some evidence to suggest that he was not. What is established, however, is that Stubbe saw no conflict between his dual attachment to Hobbes and to the Independents, that for him at least Hobbes's philosophy gave powerful support to the cause of radical Independency. It is also clear that Hobbes, for whatever reason, did nothing to disabuse his young admirer of this association and seems to have done a great deal to encourage it.

What then was the position that Hobbes and Stubbe shared, as revealed by their joint attacks on Wallis and Presbyterian 'church-politicks'? Hobbes's arguments amounted to restatements of those put forward in *Leviathan*. The authority of ministers comes from the civil sovereign and thus they do not have, as Wallis claimed they did, any independent spiritual authority. The clergy does not possess any extraordinary supernatural sanction conveyed by Apostolic succession and the imposition of hands. There is no divine right of ministers. Hence any layman might assume the office of a minister and even administer the sacraments should the civil sovereign appoint him to do so.[69] In these matters Stubbe was in complete agreement with Hobbes, as the correspondence makes clear.[70] Indeed to the tract in which Hobbes set out his opposition to Wallis's ecclesiology, Stubbe contributed an anonymous attack on Wallis's knowledge of classical sources and grammar.[71] Finally, when Wallis next answered Hobbes, the former identified Stubbe as the author of this anonymous attack and repeatedly referred to him as Hobbes's 'journey man.'[72]

Stubbe went to some lengths to maintain his anonymity in his collaboration with Hobbes in order to protect himself from attack or, as he put it, 'that my zeal to serve you be not my ruin & undoing.'[73] Owen confronted him twice with the rumor that he was engaged in translating *Leviathan* and made it clear that he disapproved.[74] The first time Stubbe equivocated, saying that he had indeed made a stab at it but gave up. He said on this occasion that the attempt was at Hobbes's request 'to whom I was obliged for that esteem, I had found at London,' suggesting that he moved in Hobbes's circle in the capital.[75] The second time Owen raised the issue Stubbe 'denied I was about any such thing, and offered the search of my study.'[76] In a third denial – this time in March 1657 to the Presbyterian Daniel Cawdrey, who was at the time engaged in a controversy with Owen and who in this connection accused Stubbe of being Hobbes's advocate – Stubbe went so far as to say of Cawdrey in his own defense: 'Had he written against Mr Hobbes so as befitted the unversity & his quality, I should have rejoiced in the confutation.'[77] Finally, in his own attack on Wallis published in 1657, he claimed to have visited Hobbes once but denied any knowledge of his doctrines, 'having never had leisure to examine his books.'[78] Such were the fears of an ambitious but vulnerable young don who, having made enemies of the Presbyterians, needed Owen's protection all the more.

It was not that he was oblivious of the heresies contained in Hobbes's works. After all he read *Leviathan* primarily for its extreme Erastianism, which was certainly heretical enough. But he also studied Hobbes's physics and as a result engaged in some alarming speculations. He wrote to Hobbes: 'You have been pleased in your physics to say that [the] first mover is moved: which I confess to be true, yet I am at a loss in eternity, & scarce see how he is first mover being moved: for in a circulation of causes, there is no first, but such as is arbitrarily designed.'[79] Here we may see one of the sources of that naturalism of which Stubbe was to be accused after the Restoration.[80] Like Hobbes, he is not denying God's existence. But, unlike Hobbes, he is finding it difficult to keep God and nature separate and distinct,[81] and his heretical, naturalistic interpretation of God's relation to the universe – Stubbe's vitalistic materialism, if you like, is based here upon his reading (or misreading) of Hobbes's physics. (As we shall see in chapter 3, there was another important source for Stubbe's naturalism.) It cannot therefore be claimed that Stubbe was innocent of Hobbes's meanings or potential meanings. If anything, he seems to have gone some way to spin heresies out of Hobbes, as we shall see in subsequent chapters.

At the same time that Stubbe took pains to conceal his part in the collaboration with Hobbes, he also discreetly worked on Hobbes's behalf within the University as well as outside. He was not so fearful as to be rendered completely secretive, and this may have been due to the fact that he was by no means the only don sympathetic to Hobbes at Oxford. In the course of Stubbe's correspondence with Hobbes he said repeatedly that Hobbes's works were widely read and appreciated in the University,[82] and this judgment is born out by other evidence.[83] Stubbe also did not hide the fact in friendly quarters that he was translating *Leviathan* – at least not until Owen's initial warning against it in early December 1656.[84] Nor was this all Stubbe did. He went to some effort to reconcile Hobbes and the University – to undo the damage caused by the entirely negative things Hobbes had said in *Leviathan* about the ancient universities. This attempt at reconciliation constitutes another aspect of the collaboration between the two men. Hobbes seems to have encouraged Stubbe's efforts in this regard, if indeed he did not instigate them. In any case the strategy for this attempted reconciliation was worked out between them, and Hobbes must have been glad that Stubbe was willing to act as a go-between. This facet of their relationship also throws more light on the connection between Hobbes and Oxford Independents.

Hobbes and Stubbe proceeded along two lines with respect to the

University. First Hobbes restated his position on the matter of the universities and so backed off from the extremely negative view he took in *Leviathan*. He now made a distinction between the universities and 'any doctrine tending to the diminishing of the civil power . . . taught there.'[85] The universities themselves, he said, 'I ever held . . . for the greatest and noblest means of advancing learning of all kinds, . . . as being furnished with large endowments . . . and frequented with abundance of young gentlemen of good families and good breeding from their childhood.'[86] But these noble institutions have been used to teach religious doctrines subversive of civil sovereignty both before the Reformation and more recently by Presbyterian divines who in so doing 'have contributed to our late troubles,' the civil wars. The solution then is to preserve the institutions but reform their teaching. Hobbes imagined that the recent university visitation had achieved precisely this reform. But he discovered that he was wrong when Wallis published his opinions. He would now like to see the University of Oxford 'by public act' disavow those opinions.[87] Hobbes told Stubbe of this argument before he published it, and Stubbe replied, 'In your praising, or rather speaking favourable of the University what you shall say, as if you heard it were now beginning to flourish after the visitation, will redound to Dr. Owen's honor.'[88] And after Hobbes published his revised view of the universities, Stubbe let it be known at Oxford that Hobbes's 'reconcilement to the university' was due to the influence upon him of certain recent books by the leading university Independents Owen and Lewis du Moulin.[89] He said this in a letter to Hobbes. This episode suggests two things – that Stubbe was attempting to build bridges between Hobbes and the Oxford Independents and that Hobbes was willing to let him do so. Here then is more evidence for a connection between Hobbes and Independency during the Interregnum, a linkage that was being forged, tentatively, from both ends. Certainly Herbert Thorndike, a contemporary enemy of both Hobbes and the Independents, saw an intellectual, if not historical, affinity between them.[90]

The second way Hobbes and Stubbe proceeded was by approaching Thomas Barlow, Stubbe's superior at the Bodleian. Barlow seems to have mentioned Hobbes's work favorably to Stubbe, and Stubbe passed the remark along to Hobbes who seized the initiative and through Stubbe sent Barlow a letter and a copy of his attack on Wallis, in which he comes round to a kinder view of the universities.[91] Barlow – again through Stubbe – replied cautiously, obviously sharing Hobbes's anti-Presbyterian Erastianism but equally chary of the heretical implications of Hobbes's views.[92] A month later Barlow spoke to Stubbe about possibly paying Hobbes a visit in London, and Stubbe also said, 'Mr. Barlow told me he should be glad to see you here, and I doubt not but you will believe the same of me,' whether for a visit or longer was left unclear.[93] Two weeks later

Stubbe wrote, 'I could be very glad to see you here, but it is hardly seasonable yet, & ye Presbyterians have so filled men's ears against you, that none would dare to exhibit that respect which they have for you, lest they might suffer in their preferment.'[94] Behind this delicate footwork may have been Hobbes's desire to gain a hearing or perhaps even a place within the University. The attack on the Presbyterians gave him an opening, and Stubbe was on hand to act as his agent.

In this connection the liaison between Hobbes and Barlow, tenuous as it was, is instructive. Barlow was no radical Independent, but, like Hobbes, he felt closer in ecclesiological matters to the Independents than to the Presbyterians. As Stubbe says to Hobbes: 'There is no man more against the *jus divinum* of the clergy than he [Barlow].'[95] During 1656–7, the period of the bulk of the correspondence between Hobbes and Stubbe, a party made up of diverse elements – radical Independents like Stubbe and Anglicans like Barlow – had begun to form, and Hobbes's Erastian philosophy furnished them with an intellectual meeting ground. Their differences, which were considerable, were not at this moment so important as their opposition to a common enemy, the Presbyterians, an opposition rooted in a shared commitment to the notion of an undivided civil sovereignty supreme in all cases 'as well ecclesiastical, as civil.' Hobbes's *Leviathan* was the most trenchant and penetrating exposition of that ideal – and of the threat to it posed by 'the Roman, and the presbyterian clergy,' especially the latter at Oxford in 1657. Hence the appeal of Hobbes to his erstwhile academic followers.

And what of the appeal Oxford held out to him? He must have thought that there was some chance, with people like Stubbe and Barlow in the University, that his views would gain a foothold there, not to say a permanent place in the curriculum. Whether his commitment to Stubbe and radical Independency was more than expedient to this goal is unclear, although evidence in Stubbe's letters indicates that it may well have been. After all, the details of church government were not so important to Hobbes as the supremacy of the civil sovereign in church affairs. He even maintained in *Leviathan* that Independency was 'perhaps the best' form of church structure because it was right that 'there . . . be no power over the consciences of men, but of the Word itself, working faith in every one . . . according to the purpose . . . of God himself.'[96] Hobbes's Independency, however, would have been an exceedingly quietistic one in which, once independent clerical power had been destroyed, the civil sovereign would regulate public worship, and the individual believer would be left free to conduct his devotions in private. For those who were personally devout there might be very few occasions on which public and private behavior would coincide, very little traffic between them. For the rest of the population there would only be the public ceremony. There would be in short a vacuum between the private and the public, an absolute embargo on the public expression of private religious sentiment. Though Hobbes may have adopted an attitude favorable to Independency in 1656–7, on this issue of the relation between public and private devotions Stubbe and Hobbes parted company. As we shall next see, Stubbe's Independency strayed far afield of Hobbes's sober, quietistic prescriptions.

The essential question raised by Hobbes's and Stubbe's Erastian Independency was how to reconcile the absolute authority of the civil sovereign with the dictates of private conscience. Hobbes's solution was to separate the two altogether and to relegate conscience to the social limbo of the private closet. The civil sovereign was thus left with a monopoly on religion considered as a public activity. In this very special sense Hobbes's philosophy called for a political or civil religion. Faith was ultimately bound up with politics: the civil sovereign was also the supreme ecclesiastical governor, and clerics were civil servants, nothing more. State and church were one. Hobbes in fact confined religion within the compass of a political straitjacket by giving the sovereign comprehensive public authority on the one hand and by leaving the individual believer to find his salvation in lonely isolation on the other. The political character of the religion was reduced to the barest minimum set by the civil authority in which the people or individual persons, insofar as they played a public religious role at all, were entirely passive. These strictures of course fitted with Hobbes's horror of popular enthusiasm motivated by religion.[97]

Stubbe's view was remarkably different. He was a Hobbesist insofar as he was a complete Erastian. He was also a Hobbesist insofar as he accepted Hobbes's materialistic metaphysic, and we shall have more to say about this. But his radical Independency led him to depart from Hobbes on the question of the character and content of civil religion. Hobbes's straitjacket could not supply the model. For Stubbe the public and the private in religion could not be kept apart. The stirrings and imperatives of private conscience were bound to invade the public arena. The people or individual believers and groups of believers acted as well as being acted upon. There was of course the problem of how to control these popular impulses, but the answer did not lie in the Hobbesian dichotomy between private and public worship.

Before we take up the question of the character of Stubbe's civil religion, we must first consider Stubbe in his role as a republican theorist. We shall then be in a position to understand his departures from Hobbes in matters of religion, as well as the degree of his intellectual dependence upon him.

2

Republican Independent

Stubbe had been committed to the new republic proclaimed in 1649 from at least 1651, when he was charged with bringing the Engagement to the University of Oxford. The patronage which he enjoyed from Owen and Vane, both staunch commonwealthmen, sealed his political loyalty. What his precise political views were before 1659, however, is not known. That year he took up his pen on behalf of 'the good old cause.' The evidence does not tell us who sponsored him in that enterprise, although his ideas reflect the views of Vane and anti-Harringtonian Army radicals before and after the dissolution of the Rump in October. The fact that Stubbe's republican tracts were published in late 1659 indicates that he wrote in the cause, if not the pay, of the Vanians.[1]

The central question Stubbe confronted in these papers was how to stop the drift towards the restoration of monarchy and put the republic upon a solid foundation, and his chief adversary, curiously enough, was a fellow republican, James Harrington, who produced the most sophisticated republican theory to come out of the mid-century revolution. Only the context can explain their disagreement. Stubbe was an admirer of Harrington's theory but argued that it could not be trusted without serious modifications to solve the crisis of 1659. It is these modifications that Stubbe set forth in his work.

Harrington's republican theory rested upon his reading of western history, and fundamental to his historical interpretation was the question of land distribution. In the ancient world republics had lasted for centuries, and he gives as examples the republics of the Hebrews, the Greeks and the Romans. The mechanism of their common survival was a particular relationship between the Few and the Many based upon a distribution of land in which the Many, the citizens, possessed enough real property to be released from economic dependence upon the Few, the aristocracy, and hence to play an independent role in the affairs of the state. This balance, at once economic and political, was what Harrington called 'ancient prudence,' in contrast to the system that displaced it, beginning with the decline of Rome and running up to his own day, the system of 'modern prudence.' Under this latter dispensation, roughly equivalent to feudalism, the balance between the Many and the Few had been broken in favor of the Few, as aristocrats had grabbed more and more land and reduced citizens to dependence upon them.[2] But the time was now at hand when conditions in England were favorable to restoring 'ancient prudence.' In the sixteenth century, Harrington explained, land had been transferred into the hands of yeomen and gentry through Henry VII's policy of seizing and redistributing the lands of the magnates and through Henry VIII's dissolution of the monasteries and sale of their lands.[3] As a result, the balance of power had shifted in the long run in favor of the Many at the expense of the Few (king and aristocracy). The parliamentary victory in the civil wars was proof of this transformation: the Many possessed more wealth than the Few and thus threw more resources on the battlefield to win the war. Here was the precious moment, then, in which 'ancient prudence' might be renewed and a republic created, and Harrington set out to prescribe how this should be done.

First, an agrarian law would impose a ceiling upon the amount of land any man might own, thus preventing the concentration of wealth (Harrington measured wealth for *political* purposes in terms of land and regarded other sources as politically negligible) and preserving the proper balance between the Few and the Many.[4] Harrington's republicanism was not anti-aristocratic; he did not seek to level the Few down to the Many. To quite the contrary, he wished to preserve the distinction. At the same time, however, he wished to guarantee that it was a *proper* distinction. A situation in which the Few engrossed the land of the Many would result in the return of 'modern prudence': hence the agrarian law. On the other hand, he thought it advisable that certain men possess sufficient land to afford the leisure to superintend the polity. Second, then, he would construct a bicameral legislature in which the upper house would represent the wealthy, particularly the larger landowners (one would have to have an annual income of at least £100 to sit there), and the lower house would represent everyone (any citizen would be eligible to sit). Representatives to both houses would be elected by all citizens and citizenship extended to all self-supporting males, thus excluding servants (of whom of course there were a considerable number in the seventeenth century) and wage laborers. The Few represented in the upper house would 'debate and propose' (make policy) and the Many represented in the lower house would 'resolve' (decide between the narrow range of choices presented to them by their superiors in the upper house). This functional division, Harrington thought, would preserve the aristocratic element in government and at the same time guarantee that the distinction between the Few and the Many would be the proper one.[5] Finally, Harrington stressed the principle of rotation in office as providing a means whereby all citizens would not only vote but stand a chance of serving in government from time to time.[6]

Stubbe delivered his replies to Harrington in a series of tracts published in late 1659 and early 1660. By then loyalties to the commonwealth had splintered, and there was a strong drift towards the restoration of monarchy. Stubbe's purpose in publishing his tracts was to offer a republican form of government which, if applied, would reunite those still loyal to the commonwealth and so counter and defeat the growing monarchical challenge. It is in this sense that he took on Harrington. Stubbe thought that his theory would provide a viable republican alternative to monarchy where Harrington's would not, where Harrington's in fact would even contribute to the destruction of the commonwealth and the advent of monarchy. How did Stubbe set about revising Harrington?

Stubbe answered the question in his *Essay in Defence of the Good Old Cause* (September 1659).[7] 'I cannot but declare my judgment for the promoting of Mr, Harrington's model . . . yet as limited to the good people which have adhered to the good old cause.'[8] Harrington's model with its agrarian law, complicated voting procedures, rotation in office and two-house legislature would serve Stubbe's purposes. But he would use it, in the first instance at least, to construct a system of dual citizenship that represented a fundamental departure from Harrington. He insisted that the people as a whole take part in government as voters, magistrates and representatives. This was what he meant by an 'equal commonwealth,' and for him this principle of equality was a *sine qua non* in the life of a republic. Equality of political participation was what would make it work and last.[9] Anything less would produce imbalance, instability and reversion to oligarchy or monarchy.

For Stubbe, however, it was this notion of equality that would prove the undoing of the republic. He argued that, given the conditions of 1659, for everyone to be admitted on an equal footing into the political life of the republic would be to give the advantage to its enemies, in particular royalist Presbyterians and Episcopalians who sought to destroy civil and spiritual liberty, the essence of the good old cause, for which the revolution had originally been fought. Those who opposed the commonwealth were more numerous than its champions. They also owned more land and could build a strong party out of their dependents: modern prudence was not dead. Finally, Presbyterians and Episcopalians were willing to sink their differences in order to defeat their common adversary, the supporters of the good old cause. They, moreover, possessed considerable support. Together they controlled ministers 'scattered over the land.' Their control also extended, Stubbe maintains, to the universities 'from whence they are masters of all the education of the youth in the nation: so that their party is strengthened with a succession of persons resolute & knowing in their way, & in esteem with the people, with whom to have been at the university and to be a scholar, wise man, & c. it is all one.'[10] Not only did the universities produce a disloyal ministry to overawe the people on behalf of the enemy. Oxford and Cambridge also spread disloyalty directly among the students who attended: 'they are there (the tutors being universally disaffected, or such as will not concern themselves on any side . . .) . . . either principled to overthrow the good old cause, or rendered indifferent towards it. This is such a truth as those faithful ones who have sent their children to *Oxon* have experienced to their sorrow.'[11]

What then was the solution, if not Harrington's equal commonwealth *tout court?* Stubbe used Harrington's model but redefined 'the people' to include those loyal to the good old cause and to exclude the rest. In *A Letter to an Officer of the Army* (26 October 1659)[12] Stubbe made a crucial distinction between 'the people' and 'the nation.' The people would be known as 'Liberators of their country' and would include those who opposed Sir George Booth's rebellion in Cheshire. Booth was a royalist who in August 1659 staged an uprising at Chester against parliament.[13] Stubbe seized on this incident, 'the last division which God providentially hath made in this nation,' as a means of separating the wheat from the chaff: all those who supported the rebellion would be excluded for the time being from what would otherwise be a Harringtonian commonwealth. This would effectively silence the enemies of the republic, Presbyterians and Episcopalians, and give political preponderance to sectaries who would then be free to put the republic on solid foundations.[14]

Stubbe allowed for the possibility that in future the distinction between 'people' and 'nation' might be lifted and a commonwealth in which all men, excluding servants, might participate equally, brought into being. This would happen should those now disloyal to the Commonwealth give up their opposition and come round to an acceptance of a republic and religious toleration.[15] Stubbe took a gradualist's view of building the republic. Harrington's equal commonwealth was the ideal 'whereunto we . . . may prudentially grow, but which we cannot at once fabrick, without running an extraordinary hazard of being again enslaved.'[16] For the first time Stubbe revealed an important element that runs through his political thought and is crucial to understanding his ambiguous position after the Restoration, namely, his emphasis upon contingency as a key factor in politics, that circumstances dictate principles of government and that as circumstances change new principles can be applied. For the moment the accomplishments of the revolution must be protected and England divided into patriots and non-patriots: in Harringtonian terms an unequal commonwealth must obtain.

Stubbe was also at pains to oppose two other views that might, but need not necessarily, be associated with Harrington, that were in fact a part of accepted political wisdom. First, he said, 'To be a part of the people it is not necessary that one actually have land in such or such a country [county]?.'[17] Here Stubbe referred to a crucial difference, perhaps the crucial one, dividing radicals and conservatives within the parliamentary and revolutionary camp. The *locus classicus* signalizing the split was the famous exchange between the conservative Commissary-General Henry Ireton and the Leveller Colonel Thomas Rainborough during the Putney Debates in October 1647.[18] Stubbe took the radical stand that citizenship did not hang on the ownership or possession of landed property, and his cryptic remark, uttered as a political dictum not subject to discussion, suggests that he might have been taking exception to the strong linkage in Harringtonian thought between citizenship and landownership. Second, he challenged the notion that soldiers 'in the pay of the state' be deprived for that reason of their citizenship.[19] This was a more specifically Harringtonian view. For him – and not only him – a standing army of mercenary soldiers constituted a gross imbalance that would lead to a reversion to some form of 'modern prudence': in contemporary terms the New Model posed such a threat.[20] Harrington's model, on the other hand, prescribed that the self-sufficient landowners should constitute the army. This would be an unpaid militia, the only form of military service compatible with citizenship and a stable republic, and not a paid army.[21] Stubbe would have none of this. For him the New Model was not so much a threat as a guarantor of the republic. Nothing else so strongly suggests where his political loyalties lay in late 1659; he was on this score a spokesman for Army radicals. Far from being excluded from citizenship, the soldiers in the New Model would constitute the core of citizenry in Stubbe's unequal commonwealth: such is one measure of the distance between him and Harrington, albeit both republicans.

Even so, in Stubbe's unequal commonwealth, as in Harrington's 'equal' one, the citizens – or, as Stubbe has it, 'the Liberators of their country' – would be soldiers and perform the obligations of citizenship in their military capacity. They would organize in militias across the country; frequent musters would build 'firm amity' and thus consolidate the good old cause. Each militia would elect deputies at their musters who in turn would ballot to elect 'the Select Senate or Conservators of the liberties of England.'[22] This Senate represented a sharp departure from the Harrington model. Its members were to be elected for life, and they were to be drawn, in an unspecified manner, from 'the several parties in the nation leagued in the establishment of a commonwealth, viz. Independents, Anabaptists, Fifth Monarchy Men, and Quakers.'[23] The senate was charged with preserving the good old cause, a task which lay 'in the management of the militia, universities and ministry: therefore the inspection and care of all those . . . must be vested entirely in them.'[24] In addition to the select senate Stubbe also suggested that a parliament be provided which would 'be chosen by the whole nation, and not the people only,' but of course its authority would be subject to the Senate in the crucial matters of 'militia, universities and ministry.'[25]

Harrington maintained that such a division between 'the people' and 'the nation', senate and parliament, would introduce instability by setting one segment of the population against another and so destroy the chances for building a lasting republic.[26] But to refute this contention Stubbe reached back to antiquity and plucked out an example of an unequal commonwealth that lasted for seven centuries: 'Lacedaemon and the country of Laconia inhabited by the helots made one commonwealth, a part only managing the government as to magistratical and military commands and performances, the other [the helots] being excluded all acts of government . . . , yet this commonwealth, so unequal, subsisted 700 years.'[27] Stubbe developed this point in a separate tract published in early 1660, *The Commonwealth of Oceana Put in the Balance, and Found Too Light, Or an Account of the Republic of Sparta, with Occasional Animadversions upon Mr. James Harrington and the Oceanistical Model.*[28] Harrington in turn answered later the same year by publishing *A Letter unto Mr Stubbe,* in which he argued that the example of Sparta could not be used to support Stubbe's case because the comparison went only so far and did not ultimately hold. In Sparta the people found themselves denied an effective voice in government by the senate. 'The nation' in Stubbe's commonwealth would also be denied just such a voice as a result of the division set up between them and 'the people.' But whereas in Sparta the people fought back and won, in Stubbe's scheme 'the nation' would not be permitted to do so; they would be permanently excluded.[29] Stubbe would establish an oligarchy that would prevent a republic from ever coming into being. Stubbe, on the other hand, saw Harrington's model as providing insufficient protection for the good old cause against its enemies.

One of the major themes of Stubbe's political pamphlets is the question of how to obtain a religious settlement that would nurture the spiritual and civil liberty that constituted the good old cause. For Stubbe such a settlement must rest on two foundations, toleration and extreme (Hobbesian) Erastianism: the civil authority must enforce a toleration.

Of the connection between these two principles and a viable republican polity, he says: 'The basis upon which the . . . people can erect any lasting government, must be such a toleration as each may be secured of the continuation thereof without molestation from, yea under the protection of, the magistrate.'[30] Again the context reveals Stubbe's meaning. In 1659 the principle of toleration was under attack from social and religious conservatives for whom the only workable formula for stability lay in the establishment of a national church in which, in one way or another, ministers and magistrates would have power to uphold orthodoxy by imposing rules for religious observance and behavior and punishing offenders. Those who stood to lose most from such a settlement were the sectaries, the very ones who would constitute the backbone of Stubbe's republic. Nor was Stubbe oblivious of the challenge thus presented.

In 1659 Stubbe wrote an attack on this conservative position and in particular on one of its chief exponents, Richard Baxter, whom Stubbe accused of being set to work by the advisers of Richard Cromwell 'to revile . . . the abettors of a commonwealth.'[31] Baxter had worked since the middle of the decade to persuade the government to build a more authoritarian state church.[32] He hoped that the Protectorate under Richard would adopt a religious settlement that would allow magistrate and minister at the parish level to work hand in glove at rooting out heretics and radical sectaries.[33] The work of Baxter's that Stubbe had in mind is *A Key for Catholicks* (1658), which he dedicated to the Protector in the hope that he, as Stubbe put it, 'would frustrate the subtility of the democratical politicians that are busy about the change of government, and would bring all into confusion under the pretence of the people's liberty or power, and would have the major part of the subjects to be the sovereign of the rest, that is the worst, that are still the most.'[34] This was a clear reference to Baxter's opposition to schemes like Stubbe's and the Vanian Army radicals' for dual citizenship and a select senate. Stubbe answered Baxter in *Malice Rebuked, or a Character of Mr. Richard Baxter's Abilities and a Vindication of the Honourable Sir Henry Vane from His Aspersions in His Key for Catholicks*. Stubbe finished this tract on 20 April 1659, and it appeared in September of that year bound together with his *Essay in Defence of the Good Old Cause*. The two works addressed the same problem, the challenge presented to the radical cause, and so it was natural that they should be published together.

As the title of *Malice Rebuked* indicates, Stubbe defended his sometime patron Vane against Baxter's attacks. Stubbe maintained that his had been an age of happy 'miracles,' by which he meant the destruction of king, church and nobility in favor of the good old cause, as he understood it.[35] But the achievement was now threatened by the likes of Baxter and their malice against patriots, especially Vane, the best and noblest of them all.[36] Contrary to Baxter, Stubbe shared Vane's view, stated in his *Retired Man's Meditations* (1656) that 'the mystery of iniquity . . . is the magistrate's intermeddling with Christ's power over the judgments of men.' Such 'intermeddling' compromises the true basis of religion, which is 'the evidence and demonstration of the spirit' at work in men.[37] To Baxter's prescriptions which would limit toleration Stubbe opposed his own radical Independency which insisted that religious truth was discovered by the holy spirit operating in individual believers: religion was thus removed from the scope of the law, and everyone was left to believe what he wished.

Stubbe, as we know, derived much of the intellectual thrust of his politico-religious position from Hobbes's *Leviathan*, and his arguments on this score in 1659 remained clearly Hobbesian.[38] But with the Hobbesism Stubbe now mixed for the first time in print another element deriving from the Hebrew scholarship of John Selden (1584–1654), an element that would bulk even larger in his thinking after the Restoration and indeed to the very end of his life. Selden had been at the head of the Erastian faction in the Long Parliament and the Westminster Assembly, and supported his religious position, close in spirit to Hobbes's own, with his Biblical and rabbinical studies. The Scottish Presbyterians in the Westminster Assembly were fond of arguing that their form of church government rested on divine right and pointed for evidence to support their case to the example of the Jewish Sanhedrin. But Selden shot back 'that the Jewish State and Church was all one, and that so in England it must be, that the Parliament is the Church.'[39]

There was much else in Selden's thought to delight Stubbe the Hobbesian Independent. Selden's rational views led him to deny the existence of 'spiritual jurisdictions' and the notion of heresy.[40] His remarks in the Westminster Assembly were recorded by his secretary Richard Milward and eventually published in *Table Talk* (1662).[41] There he revealed himself as a believer, but one who accepted a natural religion based upon God's commands as set down in Scripture.[42] The content of this religion he spelled out with great care in his major works of Hebrew scholarship *De Synedriis* (Amsterdam, 1679) and *De Jure Naturali & Gentium Juxta Disciplinam Ebraeorum, Libri Septem* (London, 1640), and it was on this latter work that Stubbe chiefly relied. In September 1659, the very month in which Stubbe published his Seldenian views in *An Essay in Defence of the Good Old Cause*, Selden's bequest of some 8,000 volumes was moved into the Bodleian, where Stubbe was Barlow's assistant, and shelved in 'the Selden end' by Barlow, Anthony Wood 'and others,' among them very probably Henry Stubbe.[43]

Selden claimed that the ancient Hebrews had practiced toleration and that it was their example in this regard that should be followed. Stubbe repeated his argument. The framework for ancient Hebrew practice lay in the distinction they made between

the sons of Noah and themselves: to themselves they say the law promulgated in the books of Moses was given; to the residue of mankind whom they call the sons of Noah, they say that they are not obliged to the law of Moses, but to seven precepts given to Noah . . . : hereby they are said to have been commanded to have abstained from idolatry; from blasphemy, or cursing the holy name [of God], from murder, from adultery and incest, from theft, and that they should erect a polity or magistracy for the keeping inviolably these precepts. The last . . . that they should not eat the members of any creature which had been cut off from it whilst it was yet living.[44]

Whether these were God's commands or innate ideas 'imprinted in the souls of all men at their original' was open to question.[45] Whichever it was, however, the rabbinical authorities were clear that these precepts 'were given to all mankind, . . . to the observance whereof they were so obliged . . . , that they could not without sin violate them.'[46] Stubbe, following Selden, suggested that here was the first universal, natural religion that might serve as the remote and primitive archetype or model for a civic, natural religion in England. It would, if you like, be the minimal, pared-down creed upon which believers might agree, the lowest common denominator, which in no way would be meant to cut individuals off from the promptings of the holy spirit. To reinforce this last point Stubbe specified that anything which one or another man would assert over and above this minimum would be subject to a mutual toleration. He then produced his radical Independent's objection to restrictions upon spiritual freedom: the transactions of the holy spirit within the human soul should not be regulated by men and men's laws.[47] He wound up his argument on a Hobbesian note, probably taken straight from *Leviathan*: 'Nay ought he [man] to venture his soul and eternity upon the uncertain and fallible experiences of another.'[48] When treating the seven precepts Stubbe went even further: ancient practice among the Hebrews was to refrain from punishing violations of even these simple precepts common to all. Hebrew toleration extended so far, and should be an example to England.[49]

Hebrew practice was an early example of toleration to be copied nonetheless for that. But elsewhere in his *Essay* Stubbe shed more exact light upon the relevance of the precepts of Noah to the English revolution and the good old cause – he brought the religion of Noah up to date. Men are social animals. They gather into communities, form governments and subject themselves to a sovereign, not only out of Hobbesian fear, but to uphold and extend this sociability.[50] This is man's animal nature. But he is also a spiritual creature, and with this realm government has, or should have, nothing to do. This is an area in which each believer is left alone to negotiate his own course without external intervention from either church or state. So far so good. But now Stubbe suggested in Hobbesian terms that man, considered even as a social animal quite apart from his spiritual nature, has a natural instinct for religion: that just as his sociable instincts cause him to place himself under a civil authority, so they also lead him 'to the acknowledgment of one God, that he is, and that he is a rewarder of such as diligently seek him.'[51] It is this religious instinct that among other things draws men 'into churches to maintain a spiritual communion.'[52] Man's animal sociability, in other words, is compatible with, and even to some extent conducive to, the cultivation of his spirituality. Though Stubbe did not here spell this out, he clearly associated this instinct for religion embedded in man's animal nature with the natural religion epitomized by the ancient Hebrews in the seven precepts of Noah. Both constituted natural religions, both were instinctive and universal and both approximated to the same thing, a simple creed acknowledging God's existence and man's obligation to follow him, though the religion of Noah was far more carefully delineated than Stubbe chose to be when he adumbrated the religious character of man's animal nature.

Stubbe's treatment of man's animal instinct for religion is clearly suggestive of Hobbesian religion, as worked out particularly in chapter 31 of *Leviathan*, 'Of the kingdom of God by nature.' Here Hobbes said that man's 'natural reason only' tells him that God exists and teaches us to honor him with prayers and thanksgiving. This is very close to what Stubbe said in his *Essay*, and the hypothesis of Hobbesian influence is strengthened by the fact that the very part of the *Essay* where Stubbe treated the natural origins of religion betrays a marked reliance upon *Leviathan*, particularly when it comes to elucidating one of Stubbe's other main points, the necessity of separating the realm of spiritual conduct from all human supervision, whether by church or state.[53]

But Hobbes was scarcely Stubbe's only mentor on this score. There was John Selden of course, and as we have seen Selden's scholarship was chiefly responsible for supplying Stubbe with his model for natural religion, the precepts of Noah, which Stubbe was willing to adopt as a basis of religious belief and practice in revolutionary England. Stubbe also probably knew of the religious views of a fellow student of Selden, James Harrington,[54] who preached a civil religion in which the citizen's devotion to the equal commonwealth would amount to a universal form of religious worship, another kind of natural religion, in which controversy and turmoil would disappear in favor of service to the republic.[55] In this regard it is worth noting that Hobbes and Harrington were in agreement against those Anglicans and Presbyterians who sought the restoration in one form or another of clerical authority.[56] Beyond this point, however, Hobbes and Harrington parted company. For Hobbes there would be no divine presence in the world of men and nature until the onset of the Millennium, when Christ would return to rule the world; hence, in the meantime, the clergy could legitimately claim to be no more than teachers appointed and supervised by the civil sovereign.[57] For Harrington the republic, founded on natural principles established by God and taken up by men, was sacred; hence there was no need for a separate clergy at all because the people, in their capacity as citizens motivated by ancient prudence, were their own priests. As we saw in the last chapter, for Hobbes spiritual intervention in the created world is impossible, and men must therefore be bound by their sovereign and by him alone rather than by a clergy pretending to spiritual authority; for Harrington spiritual principles were immanent in nature and made it possible for men to build a republic, and, therefore, all people in such a republic were spiritually illuminated by their own natural reason, and the claims of a separate clergy to a monopoly of spiritual authority were obviated.[58]

Where then does Stubbe stand in relation to Hobbes and Harrington, given the difference between them and the fact that he was influenced by both? With both Harrington and Hobbes, Stubbe attacked the claims of those clergy who argue that they possess a separate spiritual authority. But, unlike Hobbes, Stubbe did not deny the possibility of spiritual operations in nature: he was a vitalist, not a mechanist like Hobbes. For orthodox Christians there was a separate spiritual order capable of intervening in or operating on nature from without. For Hobbes there was no such spiritual order at all. For Stubbe, unlike both Hobbes and the orthodox, there was a spiritual order, not separate from nature, but conflated with it. For Stubbe spiritual forces not only worked in nature, but were at least potentially accessible to people – to 'the Liberators of their country' now and perhaps to others later. To this extent Stubbe's men, unlike Hobbesian men, were capable of being moved by something more generous than 'competition,' 'diffidence' and 'glory.'[59] Here was the metaphysical foundation for the good old cause, for civil liberty and liberty of conscience: men must have the freedom to witness to the spirit within them. Stubbe, however, did not go as far as Harrington and claim that men could bring themselves so much into harmony with the spiritual principles in nature as to build an immortal commonwealth in which all men could be admitted to citizenship. Politics for Stubbe were also a matter of contingency, necessity and calculation – and to this extent he was closer to Hobbes than to Harrington.

What we shall see is that the deistical natural religion which Stubbe began to devise in the late 1650s in connection with his efforts to bolster the good old cause and consolidate the gains of revolution is a subject he continued to pursue after the Restoration, and that his efforts along these lines lead us into some unexplored paths for charting the early history of rational religion in England. Stubbe's thought and career, which otherwise appear so disjointed, acquire a surprising continuity when viewed in this perspective and shed new light on the question we asked at the start, what is the positive linkage between the religious, political and philosophic radicalism of the mid-century turmoil and the emergence of a radical and rationalist religious tradition in England?

Meanwhile, now that we have surveyed Stubbe's republicanism, we are better able to return to the question introduced in the first chapter, of the character of his commitment to Hobbes's ideas. We know that he championed Hobbes's materialist critique of organized religion, particularly as it manifested itself in its Roman and Presbyterian Scholastic forms. We know also that Hobbes was sympathetic to radical Independency, and that thus on this score too Stubbe would be in something like agreement with him. But we suggested at the end of the first chapter that Stubbe's Independency would be different in content from Hobbes's. In 1659 Stubbe published what was an essentially Hobbesian attack on conventional Christianity called *A Light Shining out of Darkness*, which points up this difference in content at the same time that it reveals the debt that radicals like Stubbe owed to Hobbes. The relation of revolutionary radicalism to Hobbes's thought turns out again – this time in the religious sphere, as Quentin Skinner has shown in the sphere of political theory – to be more complex and ambiguous than we had thought.

One of Stubbe's aims in *A Light Shining out of Darkness* was to subject to criticism the claims of Presbyterian and Anglican clergy that their powers and privileges came from God's commands. Stubbe's *Light* was an attack by a radical Independent upon more conservative forms of religion, particularly the Presbyterians. As such it represents another of his efforts to defend the good old cause against its enemies. In this enterprise his principal tool was Hobbes's own materialist, historicist analysis of established religion, worked out in the last two parts of *Leviathan* and elsewhere. To this extent Stubbe's *Light* may be treated as a Hobbesist tract, reflecting the intellectual collaboration between Hobbes and Stubbe recorded in correspondence which begins in 1656 and ends in 1659.

In 1656 and 1657 their common enemy had been Wallis and the Presbyterians. In 1659 Stubbe was still engaged in polemics with conservatives, as his attack on Baxter indicates, although he had been forced to restrain expression of his animus against Wallis by the University authorities.[60] *A Light Shining out of Darkness* was a more general, less personal critique, though Wallis came in for special mention once. Stubbe's arguments, nevertheless, were those he and Hobbes had discussed two and three years before.

Hobbes's *Leviatham*, as we have seen, constituted, among other things, a frontal assault upon clerical pretensions to spiritual authority. Presbyterians, like Wallis, rested their ideology upon the notion that the clergy of their church were the representatives of God upon earth who received their authority remotely from God by Apostolic succession at the moment of their ordination by fellow clergymen. The usages of the church were, according to this view, also divinely instituted and could claim to trace their historical origin back to the earliest Christian – that is Apostolic – practice. Thus, the tithe, like clerical authority itself, was *jure divino*, prescribed by God and hence sacrosanct.

Hobbes's counterblast, delivered in the third and fourth parts of *Leviathan*, was twofold, metaphysical and Scriptural, and assimilated the Presbyterian position to Romanism – both were guilty of the same errors. First, there is a serious misinterpretation of Scripture. There is no Scriptural warrant for coercive clerical authority. In fact the opposite is true: Christ made clear that his kingdom is not of this world – not, that is, until the end of time when he will return to take up direct rule. If Christ's kingdom no longer exists in historical time, the clergy have no coercive power, 'but only a power to proclaim the kingdom of Christ, and to persuade men to submit . . . thereunto, and by precepts and good counsels, to teach them that have submitted, what they are to do, that they may be received into the Kingdom of God when it comes.'[61] In the meantime all coercive power, all temporal authority, is left by Christ, as revealed in the New Testament, to the civil sovereign, and the upshot is that the clergy, like everyone else, must take their orders from the state. Second, there is a tradition of metaphysical error, entrenched in the universities and hence taught to and spread by the clergy. Scholastic philosophy, deriving chiefly from Aristotle, supports the clergy's power because they draw from it superstitious notions with which to fill men's minds and thus achieve control. Chiefly to blame is the notion of the existence of incorporeal spirits. This notion leads clergy and people to believe in magical agencies that are without any basis in reality, but which nevertheless frighten and mystify believers and thus function to confirm clerical prestige and authority.

Hobbes delivered a more specific attack on the Presbyterians in a tract aimed at Wallis on which he and Stubbe closely collaborated. This tract, *Markes of the Absurd Geometry, Rural Language, Scottish Church-Politicks and Barbarismes of John Wallis*, extended the arguments already rehearsed in *Leviathan*. Against Wallis, Hobbes argued that the clergy do not obtain their power from God by a separate and peculiar institution. They are simply creatures of the state. The civil sovereign can make and unmake them at will to perform every clerical function – including the most sacred of all, the administration of the sacraments. Neither is there any substance to the clerical mystique drummed into people's heads by clergy preaching the hocus-pocus of false philosophy. All is clear, straightforward and completely Erastian,[62] These were the arguments Stubbe followed in *A Light Shining out of Darkness* three years later.

In the form of queries rather than outright assertions Stubbe used Hobbesian arguments to strike out at clerical, and in 1659 specifically Presbyterian, claims. Thus he questioned whether there is any Scriptural warrant for establishing a separate clerical caste with special powers and privileges. He thereby cast doubt on the Presbyterian argument for a ministry established by divine right (founded in Scripture).[63] Likewise, Stubbe scrupled at the notion, equally Presbyterian and Roman, of one true universal church served by a duly ordained ministry who thus are ministers not of this or that congregation but of the whole church.[64] In this critical enterprise he took a quasi-Hobbesist stance. Hobbes flatly denied the traditional argument from divine right that Christ had instituted a church and ministry separate from the civil authority. Stubbe deployed this argument not to deny but seriously to question conventional ecclesiological views. In this regard Stubbe's enthusiasm for Hobbes chimed with and probably in large part grew out of his radical Independency.

According to Stubbe, the only true church was the individual congregation constituted by its members. It was self-governing, elected its own minister and supported him by voluntary individual contributions. There was no separate priesthood or ministry; there was, instead, a priesthood of all believers. The binding force was not the church conceived of and functioning as a universal institution with a hierarchy and governing code.[65] Rather the activating principle was the holy spirit communicated directly to each believer. This form of church conformed to the practice of the earliest Christians which had been gradually corrupted, first by the conversion of numerous heathens who brought with them the distinction between priests and laity,[66] and then more completely from the reign of Constantine when the priests were granted greater and greater wealth, power and privileges by the emperors.[67] Thus things had remained for centuries, but the English revolution presented a new opportunity for the revival of the primitive, Apostolic church, the purifying of Christianity along the lines of radical Independency, for Stubbe the religious component of the good old cause.

By 1659 when Stubbe published *A Light Shining out of Darkness*, he was engaged in the defense of the good old cause against its conservative detractors. He looked forward, as we have seen, to the creation of an unequal commonwealth led by those whom he considered loyal enough to the cause to be entrusted with the task of building and preserving the republic. Among those whom he included in this mission were the newest sectaries of all, the Quakers. Feared and hated by social conservatives and conventional believers for their doctrine of inner light, their egalitarian ideas and their opposition to a separate clerical caste and tithing,[68] they would be natural allies in the defense of a cause, like the one Stubbe supported, that shared similar ideals – and so Stubbe regarded them.[69] He singled them out among others for inclusion among the 'Patriots' in the government of his commonwealth.[70] So it is not surprising that Stubbe took up the defense of Quakerism in *A Light Shining out of Darkness*. What perhaps is surprising is the vigor of that defense. He was obviously in more sympathy with Quaker ideas than political expediency dictated, and he was ready to vaunt Quaker claims even against fellow Independents, John Owen in particular, who took a hard line against this new movement that was spreading with such success through so many parts of England.[71]

What was it then, apart from political considerations, that attracted Stubbe to the Quakers? The answer is simple: he assimilated Quaker ideas to his own brand of Independency. From his point of view the Quaker inner light was exactly equivalent to the Independent doctrine of the holy spirit communicated directly to each believer. The two notions offered the same validation of religious experience, represented the same source of religious authority and justified a rejection of what was seen by Stubbe and the Quakers alike as the claptrap of conventional religious belief and practice.[72] According to Stubbe, Independents and Quakers shared virtually the same negative opinion of a separate ministerial caste created by an ordination supposed to derive successively from the Apostles, supported by a compulsory tithe and claiming exclusive authority to preach and interpret Scripture.[73] Stubbe obviously saw that the Quaker doctrine of the inner light that gave every believer the right, if not the duty, to declare the truth was very near to his own notion of the holy spirit informing the individual Christian and making everyone his own priest.[74] Stubbe's interpretation of Quakerism conformed to his own radical Christian vision in which he saw every worshipper freed from all earthly authority to realize his own spiritual destiny. His Christian was autonomous with respect to any worldly authority, and his view in this regard chimed with his republican political vision of a polity of autonomous and sociable men.

By now Stubbe had left Hobbes far behind. Now that we have examined his republican and sectarian views we can say more precisely how he departed from Hobbes. It was Stubbe's concept of the autonomous believer and citizen that was not Hobbesist. Both Hobbes and Stubbe (it almost goes without saying) would bind the Christian subject to the civil magistrate. According to Stubbe, however, this binding had serious limits which did not and should not apply in *Leviathan*. First the civil magistracy for Stubbe had to be created and preserved by 'the people.' Secondly that magistracy could not infringe the right of Christians to witness to the holy spirit acting upon them. Toleration was fundamental to the polity. Stubbe was an Erastian like Hobbes, but Stubbe's Erastian magistrate had to promote toleration, whereas Hobbes's did not have to do so and probably would not. Hobbes's ecclesiology emphasized the commanding role over religious affairs to be played by the civil sovereign.[75] He establishes the doctrine (as long of course as he does not violate the fundamental tenet that 'Jesus is the Christ')[76] and chooses the personnel – he can even perform the sacraments because there is no separate 'spiritual' jurisdiction presided over by a clergy with special 'spiritual' powers beyond the reach of his authority. Hobbes may very well have been sincere when he said that the best form of church polity lay in a kind of Independency, but as we suggested at the end of the first chapter, the tenor of this Independency would be different from Stubbe's version. Ideally, Hobbes's believers, each harkening to the spiritual voice within, would be quietists, and if they were not so instinctively, they would be made so by the hammer of the state. Each one or at least each congregation would be lost in its own world. The only public religious life would be orchestrated by the state.

Stubbe's Independency, we can now see, would be completely at odds with the quietistic Hobbesian vision: in Stubbe's spiritual universe men would be free to witness to the truth at the prompting of the spirit both publicly and privately. He said, for instance, in his defense of Quakers: 'As for my part, since I am not sensible of the convictions or emotions of the Spirit under which another lies, so I dare not condemn the Quaker, whether he reprove openly, or walk naked through the streets, denouncing woes and menaces: it is sufficient argument for me, that what God bids, is not undecent.'[77] For Hobbes, God (or Christ) bids the civil sovereign to determine what is decent, and most likely that would not include a Quaker walking 'naked through the streets, denouncing woes and menaces.' That sort of thing would lead to civil disorder and had in fact led to civil wars. For Stubbe, on the other hand, those wars, which were so negative in Hobbes's eyes, had produced the good old cause, releasing men to enjoy and exercise their civil and spiritual liberty – of which the 'naked' witnessing Quaker was an extreme but happy instance. In general Stubbe's appreciation of man's capacities was higher than Hobbes's (though not so high as Harrington's). Stubbe believed that man should be allowed, even encouraged, to demonstrate them in the public sector.[78]

The difference between Hobbes and Stubbe should now be clear. But this should do nothing to obscure the fact that Stubbe employed Hobbesian analysis and thought of himself as a Hobbesist. There is, moreover, another wrinkle on the question. As we shall see in the next chapter, after the Restoration Stubbe was accused of Hobbesism and continued to deploy Hobbesian arguments. Stubbe's 'Hobbesism' throws new light on an old historical question: the character and extent of Restoration Hobbesism. The issue has been previously dealt with by saying that while Hobbes's views were reputed to be widespread and were in fact widely feared, it is difficult to find more than isolated examples of actual Hobbesists.[79] Stubbe's case suggests that another approach to the question would be more workable: 'Hobbesism' referred not specifically and precisely to Hobbes's own views; it functioned instead as a catch-all pejorative for opinions of generally the same subversive character: in other words it may have been the threat that certain views presented rather than the views themselves that welded them together in the popular mind and the literate imagination and earned for them the blanket epithet of Hobbesism. If so, Hobbesism was probably much more widespread than we have thought. Certainly we must now add Stubbe to the list. The character of the Hobbesist outlook will also be different – more congruent to the social situation than was once thought.

3

Surreptitious naturalism: the invention of a new rhetoric

Hobbesist, Independent, quasi-Harringtonian Army republican, Stubbe represented a curious radical mix during the late 1650s. The mixture, if anything, was even more curious, if less radical, after the Restoration. After 1660 he retreated from his open advocacy of Independent and republican ideals and adopted a stance of outward allegiance to the established church and monarchy – so much so that the standard interpretation of his career during the Restoration sees him as a turncoat defender of conventional Christianity and monarchical government. The remainder of this book seeks to overturn that interpretation on the grounds that it mistakes Stubbe's public posturing for the full story. Stubbe, it is true, presented himself as being loyal to mitre and crown. But this public display served, intentionally I shall argue, to disguise (not to conceal) his radical views which, once they are laid bare, turn out to be remarkably consistent with many of his earlier (pre-1660) ideas. This reinterpretation not only makes Stubbe out to be a more consistent thinker; it also allows us to trace the survival of radical ideas coming from the 1650s into the hostile and repressive environment of the early Restoration. Indeed, before we are finished we shall be able to forge some new links between the philosophic and political radicalism of the 1650s and that of the 1680s and 1690s, which is perhaps the chief reason for undertaking to examine Stubbe's career in such detail.

Stubbe's radicalism as it emerged in the 1660s and 1670s was different from his earlier radical views. In the 1650s he had been a republican and an Independent. This was his design for the nation, and he had been open in espousing it. After 1660 this cause, the good old cause, was dead, and Stubbe was the first to acknowledge it. But this did not prevent him from holding radical views and purveying them. During the Restoration he adapted his views to changed circumstances, clearly recognizing that what he had once thought possible was not to be and that his views would have to be consistent with what was possible, given the new order of things. His gradualism and his realism regarding circumstances, underlying his revision of Harrington in 1659,[1] reasserted themselves after 1660. He remained critical and reformist. But his reformism was one thing before

1660 and quite another thereafter. Not only did the Restoration temper his radicalism; it also required him to look for new means of communicating his views. Crown and parliament set up a rigorous system of censorship.[2] Stubbe was no longer free to publish openly. So from at least February 1666, he began to experiment in the devices of satire and subterfuge in order to get his views into print. These experiments, by which he was able to publish his heretical and seditious opinions, despite the strictest censorship, also invite study and will form an important part of this and subsequent chapters.

Stubbe's writings during the Restoration have been taken at face value and so read as a conservative defense of church and monarchy. But beneath the surface appearances Stubbe was still maintaining a radical stance, though adapted to the limits imposed by the new political reality. What previous scholarly commentators have not seen, though it was not missed by some of Stubbe's contemporaries, was that a distinction must be drawn between the ideas Stubbe put forward during the Restoration and the manner, the style and the language he used to express them. When this distinction is made, Stubbe emerges as something much closer to his old (pre-Restoration) self than has been seen before. This analysis of Stubbe's early Restoration writings should also accomplish another, more general, purpose: it should teach us by example that we should be wary when reading Restoration tracts. First, as Stubbe's case will show, such tracts do not always mean what they pretend. Second, as his case will also show, it is not only a question of separating meaning from pretense; it is also a matter of finding the meaning lurking behind and even implicit in the pretense. This latter task is especially demanding, as it amounts to a process of decoding. The detective work that follows should thus prove instructive: it will throw Stubbe in a completely new light, and the resulting illumination will offer a new path into the difficult terrain of the early Restoration.

Stubbe was associated with the Vanian Army republicans, and when the Presbyterian reaction set in against the Army and its erstwhile creature the Rump in February and March 1660, Stubbe was among those who suffered.[3] In February he 'was complained of' in parliament for having defended Vane in print. The next month the Presbyterian Dr Edward Reynolds was restored as Dean of Christ Church and through his efforts Stubbe lost his Studentship in the College and his position in the Bodleian. Reynolds had Stubbe removed because of his attacks on Presbyterianism in *A Light Shining out of Darkness*. Reynolds probably had a peculiar animus against Stubbe because, if Wood is to be believed, it was he who was responsible for Reynolds's earlier ouster from Christ Church and Oxford.[4] In any case Stubbe's Oxford career was at an end, and though he would return there for visits and to hobnob with the dons he would never again hold a college fellowship or university post.

The next five years of Stubbe's life remain obscure, although what we do know about this period is important because it points to 1666 and beyond when Stubbe comes into his own again.

When he left Oxford, he moved to Stratford-upon-Avon where he practiced medicine. This is the first we learn of Stubbe the physician, although Wood says cryptically that 'he for some years had studied' medicine before the Restoration.[5] He was associated with the group of experimental philosophers at Oxford during the late 1650s who would go on to found the Royal Society after the Restoration, and among their interests were medical and physiological ones. He seems to have been particularly close to Robert Boyle and Dr Thomas Willis. He translated one of Boyle's early accounts of his experimental work into Latin, and saw one of the experiments conducted in Boyle's lodgings, in which blood was transfused into a dog.[6] His debt to Willis may have been still greater, as evidence suggests that he studied medicine under him.[7] Stubbe also undertook his own experiments on nitre, and these may have been performed in collaboration with Boyle and others who were also interested in the properties of nitre.[8] Stubbe's connection with these Oxford natural philosophers is interesting in light of what was said in the first two chapters. He shared their experimental interests but not their metaphysics or their religious and political views. While he was engaged in defending the good old cause, he was working with Boyle and Willis, neither of whom was a republican or an Independent. As we have seen, moreover, Stubbe's ecclesiological views were closer to those of Hobbes and Harrington than to the Oxford natural philosophers, including Boyle, who attacked them. Finally, Stubbe's vitalistic view of spirit embedded in nature and accessible to men had affinities with Hobbesian materialism and even closer ones with Harrington's idealism and immanentism and ran counter to the corpuscular philosophy of the Oxford experimentalists and of Boyle in particular, a philosophy designed in part to meet such dangerous views.[9]

Stubbe had been busy during his Oxford years; not only was he a classicist, a student of Hobbes's philosophy, a radical Independent and republican polemicist; he had also made himself a doctor of medicine. Unfortunately there is little record of this aspect of his career before 1660, despite the fact that medicine became the major source of his livelihood after the Restoration and that it played a major role in his intellectual life from then on.

Nor does the obscurity end there. Stubbe weathered the Restoration well enough, despite his identification with Vane, who was executed after 1660 for past political sins. Nor was it simply that Stubbe embarked upon a successful new medical career. He made his peace with the new regime and in doing so won some powerful new patrons in church and state. This process by which Stubbe adapted to new conditions between 1660 and 1662 will repay close study because it provides clues to his opinions regarding government and religion when he resumes his polemical activity in 1666. Even so the evidence is regrettably slim. One of his protectors was Dr George Morley, who was successively made Bishop of Worcester and Winchester and who during the first two years of the Restoration was a leading clerical supporter of royal schemes first for comprehension and then for indulgence of nonconformists.[10] From the first days of the Restoration Stubbe promised Morley 'an inviolable passive obedience' to the monarchy, and this was no doubt important in keeping him out of trouble with the authorities, though what Morley did is unclear.[11] It is known that after the bishops were restored and Morley became Stubbe's diocesan, he asked Stubbe to be confirmed in the Church of England, Stubbe agreed and the ceremony took place at Morley's own hands.[12]

Nor did Stubbe keep his new allegiance to Anglicanism quiet. In 1665 he published his own translation of a work by Joannes Casa, *The Arts of Grandeur and Submission: Or a Discourse Concerning the Behavior of Great Men Towards Their Inferiours, and of Inferiour Personages Towards Men of Greater Quality*. Stubbe dedicated it to Sir Charles Littleton, Deputy Governor of Jamaica from late 1662 to 1664, whom Stubbe would have known when he served as Royal Physician there during the same period.[13] The title itself is interesting in view of Stubbe's own position *vis à vis* the Restoration. More interesting still is his remark in the dedication regarding his reasons for becoming an Anglican: 'I . . . have joyned the Church of England; not only upon the account of its being publicly imposed . . . but because it is the least defining, and consequently the most comprehensive and fitting to be national.'[14] What is left out of this explanation is any consideration of piety: there is no hint of a spiritual motive for his communion. The motives are political. The state church is 'publicly imposed' and 'it is the least defining, and consequently the most comprehensive and fitting to be national.' These are negative reasons for his commitment to Anglicanism. What was important to Stubbe about Anglicanism, as he interpreted it, was not what it prescribed, but that it was 'the least' prescriptive and 'defining.' He went on in his dedication of *The Arts of Grandeur and Submission* to identify this irenic Anglicanism with 'what is ancient and Apostolic, as well as true.' True primitive Christianity is that which allows individuals the widest possible latitude of belief and worship; its hallmark is permissiveness rather than prescription. This reading of Anglicanism was far removed from the views of the Restoration church hierarchy. Just how far removed we shall see in this and subsequent chapters. But what is important to note here is that Stubbe's view of the restored church was remarkably similar to the civil religion he espoused before the Restoration, which he also claimed to be 'ancient and Apostolic.' What he was advocating both immediately before and after 1660 was a church which guaranteed toleration among Protestants.

Of course there was also an important difference between Stubbe before 1660 and Stubbe after. Before 1660 he had published openly and in detail his ecclesiological views. After 1660 his printed remarks became cryptic and fragmentary. Note, for example, the extreme circumspection of the language in which he framed his thoughts on the subject of the church in the dedication of his translation of Joannes Casa. Of the restored Anglican church he wrote that it was an institution 'wherein any unprejudiced person (not resolved to mistake particular men's actions or opinions for church-principles and errors) may observe all those circumstances to continue in order to the promotion of sober piety.'[15] In a very involuted way he was saying that 'sober piety' developed under circumstances of toleration rather than coercion. Yes, there should be an established church, but within it all men should be left to find their own way. Stubbe was willing to become an Anglican after 1660, but his view of what the church should be was different from what actually existed. On the surface it might appear that Stubbe had accepted conventional Anglicanism. He outwardly maintained that posture. But clandestinely he was true to the position he had argued before the Restoration. That position, it is true, could no longer be pleaded forcefully; it was confined to cryptic utterances and the occasional oblique reference, at least in print. But that language should not blind us to the fact that Stubbe had not given up on his radical civil religion, and, as we shall see, though he was not free any longer to publish his views, he found other, more covert, means of purveying them.

Not only did he associate himself in print with the established church; he also publicly declared his allegiance to the restored monarchy. In 1662 Stubbe published *The Indian Nectar, Or a Discourse Concerning Chocolata*, and in the preface he wrote:

The late changes in our nation have disengaged me from my former adherencies; and I have no longer a regard or concern for Sr. Henry Vane, or Gen. Ludlow, than is consistent with my sworn allegiance . . . And, though I have a very despicable opinion of the present age, yet I hope it will not be guilty of any such unworthiness towards our sovereign.[16]

Stubbe has turned his back on his former patrons. He detests 'the present age' but not the king. Later we shall see how he could make this distinction and what it meant. In this new dispensation, having discarded his old patrons, he had found some new ones, and powerful ones at that. He wrote of this new patronage: 'That you may know how great incentives I have to study, besides my own inclinations; there are more than ordinary interested in me, besides the King's Majesty . . . there is the Hon. Robert Boyle Esquire, Dr [Alexander] Frasier, physician to His Majesty, and several other honourable and learned personages.'[17] The tract in which this passage appears, *The Indian Nectar*, was dedicated to another physician and natural philosopher, Willis, under whom Stubbe had studied medicine at Oxford, and in the tract Stubbe mentioned others who sooner or later figured in his list of patrons, Thomas, Baron Windsor, the Governor-General of Jamaica from 1661 to October 1662, and Sir Henry Bennet, presumably the future Secretary of State and Earl of Arlington.[18] As the list indicates, Stubbe had attracted favorable notice at court and in court-linked scientific and medical circles. Robert Boyle was at the time (1662) active in government as a member of the Council for Foreign Plantations, Governor of the New England Company and one of the principal founders of the Royal Society of London.[19] Stubbe had also become known to the royal physicians, and one of them, Sir Alexander Frasier, was responsible for Stubbe's appointment as a royal physician in Jamaica, a post he was to take up in April 1662, when the expedition of which he was a member set sail.[20] He was also known to the king in other ways. In the *Discourse* on chocolate Stubbe said that he had prepared the drink for the king and queen.[21] The tract suggests still another reason for the interest taken at court in this former protégé of regicides.

The Indian Nectar is a discourse on chocolate written from the physician's point of view. Stubbe was a Galenist and argued that chocolate is of the utmost value in restoring and preserving the health by Galenical means. He maintained, according to Galenic doctrine, that good health results from the purifying of the blood. This process can take place by 'evacuations through the several emunctories of the body,' evacuations that take the form of sweat, urine, feces, spittle, catarrh, phlebotomy or 'moderate venery.'[22] Chocolate, Stubbe insisted, contributes to these various processes – so much so that 'there cannot be anything more apt to preserve health and vigour of spirit.'[23]

In particular chocolate works as a mild aphrodisiac and encourages 'moderate venery' – a subject Stubbe was more interested in pursuing than the other evacuative processes. Chocolate was widely held to be an aphrodisiac. The classic text giving rise to that opinion was Bernal Díaz's *The Conquest of New Spain*, in which Montezuma is described as drinking chocolate before he had sex in order to excite his lust,[24] a text with which Stubbe was acquainted.[25] Stubbe wrote: 'If it be the design of physick to preserve nature and free her from superfluous collections of humours; and nothing doth that better than *Chocolata*, as far as venery is but the collection and ejection of a superfluity gathered in and about the testicles: without doubt physicians cannot decline to recommend it.'[26] In particular Stubbe maintained that a healthy sex life and regular intercourse are the best possible treatment for 'madness' in 'young unmarried folks.'[27]

As it turns out, his aim in pursuing the subject was not merely professional. He used the occasion, as he had others before, to attack the Presbyterians. They, it seems, had condemned the drinking of chocolate because, they said, it encouraged luxury, sensuality and 'venereal inclinations.'[28] Stubbe answered by associating Presbyterian prudery in this matter with the Catholic monastic doctrine of mortification of the flesh.[29] Once more Stubbe assimilated Presbyterianism to Romish doctrine. In addition, the Presbyterians were hypocritical in their adherence to the doctrine, and to make the point Stubbe satirized what he regarded as their penchant for high living,[30] including a diet which, according to Stubbe, maximized sexual appetite: 'there is no venereal projects like to your constant diet.'[31]

Stubbe's Hobbesian critique of the Presbyterians in the late 1650s had allowed him to accuse them of popery in matters of ecclesiology. Now in 1662 his Galenism allowed him to equate Presbyterian and Roman Catholic views on sex. And in both cases the result was the same: Stubbe could go on to argue that true Protestantism spurns both the popish and the Presbyterian doctrines and returns to primitive Apostolic practice for inspiration and guidance, to Scriptural Christianity from which both Catholics and Presbyterians have fallen away. Rejecting Romish and Presbyterian mortification, true Protestants 'imagine that carnality may be subdued by other means, captivating the understanding into the obedience of faith, and subduing our wills, not breaking our backs; and denying our lusts, whilst we preserve a nature and temperament given us by God.'[32] Thus, original Christianity, identical with true Protestantism, as distinct from the false doctrine of the Presbyterians, countenances and even encourages the enjoyment of the world and 'moderate venery' even in 'young unmarried folks.' Stubbe saw Galenic medicine as offering the path to that enjoyment, sexual and otherwise, because it allows us to 'preserve a nature and temperament given us by God,' a nature and temperament by which we are meant to enjoy the world.

For Stubbe Galenism, primitive Christianity and his radical Protestantism are one. Galenic medicine provides the means by which 'we may enjoy in this world an undisturbed health and serenity of mind.'[33] This goal is 'conformable to God's word and the primitive practice.'[34] Scriptural warrant comes from two places. First, there is the fifth commandment: 'Honour thy father and thy mother, that it may be well with thee, and thy days may be long in the land, which the lord thy God giveth thee.'[35] Second, there is 'Solomon's wisdom,' which 'amounts to this . . . that it is good and comely and that there is nothing better for a man than that he should eat and drink and enjoy the good of all his labour.'[36] This identification of Galenical medicine with Scriptural Christianity is more evidence that even though Stubbe had become an Anglican, his Anglicanism departed sharply from conventional religion. There would be very few if any clergy who would agree with Dr Stubbe 'that there is nothing better for a man than that he should eat and drink and enjoy the good of all his labour.' There is no otherworldliness here, no mention of sin, repentance and redemption. Indeed the claim that 'a man . . . should enjoy the good of all his labour' is reminiscent of Digger sentiment and in particular Gerrard Winstanley's economic doctrine.[37] Stubbe does mention heaven, but then only to point out the similarity between felicity in this life and in the one to come: he does not see very much difference in the pursuit of happiness here and there.[38] Stubbe's is an exceedingly earthly, not to say earthy, religion. His Galenic Christianity is remarkably consistent with the religious opinions, informed by Hobbesism, which he adopted and preached before the Restoration. Then too he stressed what was Scriptural and pure, and his acceptance of Hobbes's metaphysic caused him to reject the notion of a separate spiritual realm and to collapse the spiritual into the material. We shall see that he did not retreat from his forward position after the Restoration, though he did not make his views explicit in this regard in the tract in hand. We shall see too that he was quite capable of mixing Galen and Hobbes, or Hobbes and Aristotle for that matter, in order to score polemical points in his ongoing argument against conventional Christianity. This Hobbesian–Galenical–Aristotelian mix will be especially important for understanding Stubbe's polemics against the Royal Society. The view he took in his discourse on chocolate may also be important for understanding his new patronage. Could it be that he found favor at court because his thisworldly outlook and particularly his anti-Presbyterian attack on prudery chimed with the attitude of a court given to more than 'moderate venery'?[39] If so, here would be a case of the French-inspired libertinism of the court after the Restoration linking up with the indigenous, radical Protestant libertinism carried forward from the Interregnum. In any case this new court patronage would serve him well for years to come.

Stubbe named Boyle as one of his patrons in 1662. They met in Oxford after Boyle moved there in 1655 or 1656[40] and Stubbe returned there from military service in Scotland. They both knew Thomas Barlow.[41] All three men, Stubbe, Boyle and Barlow, shared the view that the church did not exist and govern by divine right and that as a result the settlement of religion in England should include a modicum of toleration.[42] Stubbe's view of course derived from his radical Independency informed by a Hobbesian metaphysic and a Hobbesian reading of Scripture. Boyle and Barlow were neither Independents nor Hobbesians and were horrified by and rejected both.[43] They were concerned to see the Anglican church established on the most secure foundations and so rejected the argument from divine right of bishops or king as being too narrow, dangerous and divisive. They pitched their case, instead, on the welfare of England, the national good, which they identified with the interests of the literate and propertied men in society and specifically with the gentry, merchants and clergy. The national interest so defined required toleration of some Dissenters – all in fact who recognized no higher authority in this world than the state, so excluding papists who acknowledged the higher authority of the pope and hard-core antinomians and illuminists who claimed direct access to the spirit world. Together with Peter Pett, Boyle and Barlow argued their case for a religious settlement along these lines in print just after the Restoration.[44] And Boyle may have continued to patronize Stubbe in part because his views of the church and a church settlement agreed to some degree with theirs.

Boyle was also a Scripturalist in the sense that, like Stubbe, he wished religion to be Scripture-based. But Boyle's interpretation was radically different from Stubbe's. He would have been extremely hostile to the social implications of Stubbe's reading of 'Solomon's wisdom.' To Boyle's view man was not put here by God merely to 'eat and drink and enjoy all the good of his labour.' Instead there were rewards and punishments to be meted out hereafter, according to one's conduct in this life.[45] The egalitarian and anti-capitalist if not Digger overtones in the notion that 'a man . . . should enjoy all the good of his labour' would not have been lost on Boyle either.[46] Nonetheless, it was their agreement that Boyle obviously acted upon at the Restoration and not the things on which they disagreed. Boyle either overlooked them or hoped he could bring Stubbe around. Boyle was always very keen on educating men to his view.

Boyle would also have been interested in Stubbe for his scientific interests. Stubbe was a medic, and he was later to write that during his Oxford years, when he met and worked with Boyle, he had been 'addicted' to the new philosophy. Of course the reasons for that addiction were not what Boyle would have wished. Stubbe claimed to have been interested in science as a means to undermining conventional Christianity.[47] But Boyle was willing to patronize Stubbe, despite their differences. Stubbe for his part was glad for the patronage, though, as we shall see, there was to be an exchange between them over exactly the issues that had always divided them.

In April 1662 Stubbe sailed to Jamaica and stayed three years. We know virtually nothing of his time there. He was a royal physician, was often ill and seems to have entertained the idea of leaving Jamaica, going to New Spain and practicing medicine there.[48] He also sent reports back to Sir Robert Moray, one of the principal founders of the Royal Society, which consisted of an account of his observations of the animal and plant life of the island and which were subsequently published in the *Philosophical Transactions* of the Royal Society.[49] No doubt his illness caused him to return to England in 1665, where he lived first in London, then in Stratford and finally in Warwick. Once he had resettled in England his practice became routine. He spent most of the year in Warwick and during the summer went to Bath, where he treated the rich, the well-born and the fashionable who were there for the season and where, as we shall see, he did much else besides.

Up to this point we have watched Stubbe maneuvering cautiously – for survival, for patrons and for a new public voice – in the treacherous waters of the Restoration. But the picture suddenly changed in early 1666, when he emerged in print as an advocate of radical views. The occasion was provided by the short-lived career in England of Valentine Greatrakes.

Greatrakes had made a reputation in Ireland as a faith healer who could cure, among other ailments, scrofula, otherwise known as the king's evil for being susceptible of cure by the royal touch. Invited by Edward, Viscount Conway, to England to treat his wife, the Lady Anne, of severe and persistent headaches, he went to Ragley, the Conway seat, in Warwickshire in January 1666. Though his art failed on Viscountess Conway, he performed a number of cures in the neighborhood before being commanded by the king to appear at court. Once in London in April, he resumed his healing and attracted a large following.[50] But fame was not the only result. His career was the source of considerable apprehension on the part of the authorities and especially the clergy.

After the Restoration Charles II had revived the ceremony of the royal touch, and the king's power to heal was regularly invoked by the clergy as a sign that the king's authority came from God. The royal touch had become a court ritual shoring up divine-right monarchy.[51] Here was Greatrakes, a mere commoner (though a gentleman),[52] achieving the same results as the king by what was called 'stroking' – hence his reputation as 'the Stroker'[53] or 'the Irish Stroker.'[54]

There was then the strong hint of sedition in Greatrakes's success, and the scent was made stronger by the timing of his career as a healer. Greatrakes's cures were associated with religious enthusiasm. George Fox had claimed to perform miraculous cures for the king's evil, and Greatrakes had been an officer in Cromwell's army in Ireland.[55] Thus one of those who thought the cures masked sedition wrote: 'How dangerous it is to admit of impulses & visions, and how common it was with men of Mr. Greatrakes former way to obtrude, need no further proof, than Oliver's impulses, James Naylor, and other Quakers' visions, and light within, which would have superseded, if allowed, all religion, law, duty, right and wrong.'[56] Greatrakes, moreover, was in England at the height of the plague, when the king had suspended his own public healing ceremonies.[57] It was also a time of millenarian expectation. In Daniel and Revelation the number 666 bore apocalyptic significance. So the year 1666 was the date on which some, mainly sectaries, had pinned their hopes for the fulfillment of the Biblical promises.[58] One cleric claimed that because of this, the masses were highly suggestible and that it would thus be all the easier for the 'subtle' and the 'cunning' to turn Greatrakes's cures to seditious ends.[59] Finally, much of central London had only recently been burned to the ground, and it was widely held that the fire had been set by Catholics and sectaries acting either separately or together.[60] Thus, Greatrakes's cures, coming on the heels of the fire as they did, were seen as offering further ammunition to these subversive factions, especially the Catholics.[61]

Stubbe, living at this point in Stratford-upon-Avon, had become a physician to Lord Conway's household.[62] He was at Ragley when Greatrakes was there in January 1666, and observed him perform his cures.[63] The next month he wrote *The Miraculous Conformist*. The tract was dedicated to Willis and addressed in the form of a letter to Boyle, dated 18 February 1666. In it Stubbe argued that the cures were miracles, but were the result not of God's intervention in the world but rather of nature itself or more particularly 'the peculiar temperament or composure of his [Greatrakes's] body.'[64] He then proceeded to explain the cures by borrowing Willis's theory of fermentation worked out during the previous decade, a theory Stubbe probably learned from Willis himself when he was his student.

According to Willis, all bodies are made up of atoms; each atom in turn possesses one of five different chemical compositions. In animals certain combinations of these chemical compositions produce particular kinds of motion in the blood which Willis called fermentations. Diseases can be accounted for as being produced by 'effluvia' entering the body and disturbing these fermentation processes. The physician's job is to rid the patient of alien 'effluvia' and thereby restore the proper fermentation. The notion of restoration derived from the Galenic idea that what comprises health is a balance of the humors and that the physician's task is to restore this balance through purgation. But in Willis's theory the humors have been replaced by dynamic, material particles in the blood, atomic in structure and chemical in composition, and to this extent he was building on a new paradigm, that of the mechanical philosophy which made an enormous impact in Oxford beginning in the 1650s and to which he was a leading contributor.[65]

Stubbe explained Greatrakes's cures by assimilating them to Willis's theory of fermentation and disease:

God had bestowed upon Mr Greatarick a peculiar temperament, or composed his body of some particular ferments, the effluvia whereof, being introduced sometimes by a light, sometimes by a violent friction [stroking], should restore the temperament of the debilitated parts, re-invigorate the blood, and dissipate all heterogeneous ferments out of the bodies of the diseased, by the eyes, nose, mouth, hand, and feet.[66]

Stubbe claimed, moreover, that there was evidence of the peculiar material composition of Greatrakes's body:

Lord Conway observed one morning as he [Greatrakes] came into his Lordship's chamber, a smell strangely pleasant, as if it had been of sundry flowers: and demanding of his man what sweet water he had brought in the room, he answered none; whereupon his Lordship smelled on the hand of Mr Greatarick, and found the fragrancy to issue thence; and examining his bosom, he found the like scent there also . . . Dean Rust observed his urine to smell like violets, though he had eat nothing that might give it that scent. Sir Amos Meredith who had been his bedfellow, said, that in the night he had observed the like agreeableness of smell in Mr Greatarick's body, at some hours,[67]

Given the healing powers of this peculiar body, operating according to Willis's theory, Stubbe leaped to his heretical conclusion: 'it is nature cures the diseases,' and not some unseen spiritual agency coming from God.[68] True, 'God had bestowed upon Mr Greatarick a peculiar temperament,' but the healing power lay in his material body and not in any spiritual agency. And there was worse to come. Stubbe put Greatrakes's cures on a par with those of 'Christ and the Apostles,' thereby implying that these too should be understood as natural rather than supernatural processes: 'If he [Greatrakes] doth the things that never man did, except Christ and the Apostles, . . . judge what we are to think.'[69] Stubbe claimed, moreover, that 'undoubtedly God hath permitted all religions (though not the Protestants, till now) to have their real miracles, that men may learn to try miracles by the truth, and not the truth by miracles.'[70] Stubbe thus challenged both the doctrine that miracles were ceased and the doctrine that the only true miracles were the Biblical ones, which could then be taken as proof that Christianity was the one true faith.

The reaction was immediate. Word of Stubbe's tract had spread even before it was printed. There was prior word too of his intentions. Daniel Coxe, Boyle's close friend, wrote to him on 5 March 1666. Coxe had learned

by them who have reason to pretend to understand Dr. Stubbe's designs . . . that Dr. S. intends to demonstrate from what Greatrakes hath performed that the miracles of our blessed Savior were not derived from any extraordinary assistance of a Divinity, much less from the Union of the divine nature with Humanity; but that as G[reatrakes's] they might be merely the result of his constitution which same may be affirmed of others that have performed real miracles (as we simple people style them). And this he intends to address to your Honor . . . But we here have all such a strong persuasion of Mr. Boyle's good will & unfeigned love to Christianity that we cannot imagine he should patronize anything which hath such a direct tendency to atheism & doth most positively enervate the very basis of Christianity; & invalidate (at least seemingly) the strongest motive to believe the veracity of those excellent dictates which all that rightly improve their reason make the rule of their present life & the foundation of their hope for a future felicity exceeding imagination.[71]

Coxe was suggesting then that Stubbe's purpose was to attack the Biblical miracles in order to undermine the foundations of orthodox Christianity. Coxe went even further and claimed Stubbe's 'design . . . will exceedingly oblige those who, like himself, are so intent on the gratifications of sense or evil passions that they have not will . . . to think of a Deity or immortal souls or have so much philosophy as to reason themselves out of their religion, a fond persuasion wherein a company of pitiful, superstitious, credulous persons . . . are deluded.'[72] Coxe accused Stubbe, in other words, of mortalism and atheism. Stubbe's Hobbesian materialism, moreover, would lend support to the charge of mortalism. In conventional Christian doctrine the incorporeality of the soul went hand in hand with its immortality: if the soul is corporeal, how can it be immortal?[73]

But it was not only Hobbes who supplied Stubbe with the philosophical foundations for heresy. It is clear that in *The Miraculous Conformist* his principal sources were Willis and Galen. We have already shown Willis's influence; let us now explore Stubbe's debt to Galenism. Galen called the soul 'a temperament' and regarded it as a mixture of bodily qualities.[74] This view of course derived from Galen's humoral physiology and psychology: all physical and mental pathology could be explained in terms of the operation of the four humors or subtle fluids of which the body was seen to be composed – blood, choler, phlegm and bile or melancholy.[75] The humors of an individual were the product of diet, and these in turn affected reason and will.[76] Individual behavior depended then on bodily factors.[77] Galenism was always open to charges of materialism and moral determinism.[78] The suspicions of Latin Christians were aroused against it as early as the fourth and fifth centuries.[79] In Restoration England Galenical physicians were 'generally reputed no better than atheists.'[80]

While Galen did not completely dismiss the Platonic and Christian view of the incorporeal nature of the soul, he treated it 'as a doubtful hypothesis' and tended 'to consider even the rational soul as the temperament of the brain.'[81] A leading historian of the subject, Owsei Temkin, refers to Galen's reduction of mental and spiritual phenomena 'to material processes which, in turn, might be animistically conceived,' as a form of 'pagan naturalism.'[82] This comes very close to what Coxe accused Stubbe of maintaining, and Stubbe's Galenical language in *The Miraculous Conformist* clinches the case: Greatrakes performed his miraculous cures by virtue of 'the peculiar temperament' or 'composure of his body.'[83] Of course, as we have seen, Stubbe updated his radical Galenism by resort to the corpuscular theory of Willis, his contemporary and teacher. The medical theory came from Willis, the naturalism from Galen. Stubbe conflated the divine and the natural in the person of Valentine Greatrakes by interpreting Willis's theory in the direction of Galen's pagan naturalism, an interpretation with which Willis, a 'staunch' Anglican, would not have agreed.[84]

Once more, as in Stubbe's tract concerning the medicinal benefits of drinking chocolate, he linked his medicine to his Christianity. He made Greatrakes out to be a devout Anglican, 'the miraculous conformist,' and the most dramatic sign of his true Protestantism was his power to produce *miraculous* cures from *natural* principles. Only now, as not before, Stubbe revealed the precise materialism or 'pagan' naturalism that drew no clear distinction between God and nature and attributed all phenomena, spiritual as well as physical, to natural causes. Later in this chapter we shall explore the religious and political implications of this position and the religious and political motives that led Stubbe to adopt it.

Nor was Galen Stubbe's only source in medical literature for his 'pagan' interpretation of the cures. David Lloyd, who wrote an orthodox reply to Stubbe's tract, traced the origin of interpretations like Stubbe's to *De Incantationibus* by Pietro Pomponazzi.[85] This early sixteenth-century heretical Aristotelian sought to give naturalistic explanations for events that were conventionally attributed to supernatural interventions in nature by angels and demons.[86] In *De Incantationibus* Pomponazzi argued that 'certain gifted men, drawing on their own occult powers, can cure by the sheer power of will and imagination.'[87] Among the cures that could be explained in such terms Pomponazzi included the royal touch for the king's evil.[88] Here then is a very likely source for Stubbe's interpretation of Greatrakes's cures, made even likelier by the fact that Stubbe possessed copies of Pomponazzi's works, including *De Immortalitate Animae* (1534).[89] Pomponazzi, incidentally, had argued that Galen believed in the eternity of the world and the mortality of the soul.[90] Stubbe then stood in a long line of radical Galenists and Aristotelian humanists.

To support his own interpretation of Greatrakes's cures, Stubbe also cited *Disquisitionum Magicarum Libri Sex* by the late sixteenth-century Jesuit Martin del Rio,[91] a work giving authoritative expression to Catholic views on magic.[92] Lloyd pointed out, however, that Stubbe got Del Rio backwards by using him to support his interpretation, when in fact Del Rio inveighed against such naturalistic readings.[93] Lloyd's indication of the sources of Stubbe's interpretation shows that he was basing his arguments on sixteenth-century natural magic. Stubbe, the radical Protestant, paganizing Galenist and Hobbesian, found authority for his views in the natural magic of the late Italian Renaissance. Here is another connection between the fifteenth- and sixteenth-century magical and Hermetic traditions and the subversive religion of the late seventeenth-century English radicals. Stubbe in this respect prefigured John Toland and his circle after the Revolution of 1688–9. Toland was much indebted to the late sixteenth-century Hermetist and heretic Giordano Bruno for his religious views.[94]

Stubbe of course had addressed *The Miraculous Conformist* to Boyle, and on 9 March 1666 Boyle responded privately by letter – with characteristic *sang-froid* but with unaccustomed haste (he had received Stubbe's 'account of Mr. Greatrakes' stupendous performances' only the night before).[95] He detected the subversive implications of Stubbe's opinion of Greatrakes's cures and proceeded with great care to refute his arguments. Both the haste and the care indicate that he took his opponent in deadly earnest.

Boyle agrees with Stubbe that miracles are still possible and did not 'cease with the age of the Apostles.'[96] So he is willing to be convinced that Greatrakes can perform miracles 'especially in an age where so many do take upon them to deride all that is supernatural; and whilst they loudly cry up reason, make no better use of it than to employ it first to depose faith and then to serve their passions and interests' – perhaps a cryptic attack on Hobbes.[97] But, according to Boyle, Stubbe goes too far when he seems 'to make a parity' between Greatrakes's cures, even if miraculous, and the miracles of Christ and the Apostles.[98] Boyle thinks 'it more fit to look upon this gift of Mr. Greatrakes as a distinct and inferior kind than to degrade the unquestionable miraculous gifts of the Apostles . . . to the same level with his.'[99] The fact that Greatrakes cannot cure in every case, Stubbe argues, does not make the cures he performs something less than miracles. They are still miracles because the Apostles themselves did not always perform miraculous cures.[100] But this is to distort the meaning of Scripture, Boyle says: 'As to what you say about Trophimus, whom St. Paul left sick at Miletus . . . it concludes not that St Paul could not cure him, unless you can make it appear that he endeavoured it, as you confess Mr. Greatrakes did to cure the excellent Lady Conway and others.'[101] Thus, not only is Stubbe's argument for 'a parity' defeated but the reverse (*pace* Stubbe) is neatly asserted. When the Apostles 'were sent forth and commissioned by Christ, . . . we never read that they attempted a cure which they could not effect.'[102] Not only this, 'but their performances were divers of them of a much higher nature than Mr. Greatrakes.'[103] Here Boyle reaches the nub of his opposition to what he regards as Stubbe's apparent view:

And if I could imagine that any discerning men were in danger of thinking that because you have made it plausible that some of your Thaumaturgus's cures are performed by . . . some kind of complexional efficacy, I should add that I think such a suspicion exceedingly ill-grounded because there are divers phenomena in the miracles of our Saviour and his Apostles that do not at all agree with so injurious an hypothesis as that would be.[104]

Now Boyle rehearses the ways in which the New Testament miracles are superior to Greatrakes's cures:

Our Saviour could communicate the power of working miracles to others at his pleasure (which I think you do not believe Mr. Greatrakes can do to you), as in the case of St. Paul; divers of his miracles were done on absent persons, as that on the Centurion's dying servant and others. The mute fishes obeyed him, and that so strangely that being at a distance one of them brought St. Peter not only himself, but a determinate piece of money. His power reached not only to living creatures, but inanimate ones, as the sea and the wind; the former of which supported him when he walked on it, and both the former and the latter obeyed him. His power, and that of his Apostles (which will not, I suppose, be ascribed to a peculiar temperament), reached not only to the curing of the sick, but the raising of the dead, . . . and divers of the Apostles' cures were done without any contact at all but barely by their word;

by which also they could do harm as well as good, and bring diseases and death as well as chase them, which will not, I presume, be ascribed to an exuberance of health (or *plusquam perfect* tincture, as the chemists speak).[105]

Not only does Stubbe seem to argue for 'a parity' but he also strongly suggests that Greatrakes's cures come not from God but from nature itself, which thus leaves the divine origin of the New Testament miracles open to question. Since in the orthodox view the miracles confirm the Scriptures as divine revelation, an attack on the supernatural origin of those miracles throws the unique sacred authority of the Bible itself in doubt. Boyle will thus have nothing to do with Stubbe's opinion 'that God had permitted all religions to have their real miracles.'[106] For him the Biblical miracles are precious evidence, more convincing than parallel phenomena in other religions, of the truth of Christianity – so precious in fact that he doubts whether Christian doctrine by itself, without the support of the miracles, would 'sufficiently assure men' of its truth.[107]

Boyle sees Stubbe's tract as particularly dangerous because it furnishes ammunition to 'those enemies to Christianity . . . that granting the truth of the historical part of the New Testament (which relates to miracles) have gone about to give an account of it by celestial influences or natural (though peculiar) complexions or such conceits, which have quite lost them, in my thoughts, the title of knowing naturalists.'[108] Boyle has in mind persons whom he does not identify, living in his own time, who may read Stubbe's tract. Obviously Stubbe's view of Greatrakes's cures is very close to that of 'those enemies to Christianity' whom Boyle mentions. Stubbe attributes Greatrakes's miracles to his 'peculiar temperament' embedded in nature, and they, Boyle says, speak of 'natural (though peculiar) complexions.' So close are the two views that Stubbe is in danger of being identified with 'those enemies to Christianity.' There were those like Coxe who did make him out to be the enemy. Boyle does not go quite so far in his reply to Stubbe.

At the time of the Greatrakes furor Boyle was especially concerned about such 'enemies to Christianity.' In an important discourse written in 1665 or 1666[109] and published twenty years later as *A Free Enquiry into the Vulgarly Received Notion of Nature* (1686), he claimed that there is (presumably in England):

a sect of men, as well professing Christianity, as pretending to philosophy, who (if I am not misinformed of their doctrine) do very much symbolize with the ancient heathens, and talk much indeed of God, but mean such a one as is not really distinct from the animated and intelligent universe, but is on that account very differing from the true God that we Christians believe and worship.[110]

Was this 'sect' identical with 'those enemies to Christianity' whom Stubbe's tract would oblige? It is plausible that this was so because the 'sect' in question, though calling itself Christian, worshipped nature rather than a supernatural god, and 'those enemies to Christianity' gave natural accounts of miracles which to orthodox Christians constituted supernatural events. Both groups in other words relied upon naturalistic explanations to the exclusion of the supernatural; they shared a bias towards naturalism.

Whether these groups were identical or not, Boyle stopped just short of identifying Stubbe with 'those enemies to Christianity' who rendered such naturalistic accounts of divine miracles. Throughout his long, closely argued reply to Stubbe, Boyle made a distinction between what his correspondent said and what he intended, while making it clear that what he said, whether he meant it or not, played into the hands of 'those enemies to Christianity.'[111] Boyle detected the subversive implications of Stubbe's view but bent over backwards to say that they might not be his 'deliberate tenets' so much as the unintended byproduct of the speed with which he wrote the tract, 'some unstudied expressions of your *raptim scripta.*'[112] Boyle offered Stubbe a way out, saying that he was 'very willing to leave you the liberty of explaining yourself in anything wherein the impetus you tell me you writ with may have had an influence on your pen.'[113]

But Coxe's prior letter to Boyle spelling out Stubbe's subversive 'designs' and the care with which Boyle's reply refuted Stubbe's 'unstudied expressions' suggest that Boyle knew that Stubbe meant what he said. Nor were Boyle and Coxe alone in seeing through the duplicity. As Boyle said to Stubbe, referring to his heretical past, 'you can scarce doubt but that it has made many persons indisposed to put the best construction upon what you write.'[114] On the same issue at exactly the same time Henry More was less oblique:

I perceive by a letter from London that Dr. Stubbe his paper is out about Mr. Greatrakes, touching which the resentment of serious men is such as I suspected it would be. For they look upon his management of the matter not so advantageous for religion, etc. But I think he is universally noted for what he seems not overambitious to conceal.[115]

Stubbe's previous association with Vane and 'the good old cause' rendered suspect whatever he said. But the point is too that what he now wrote raised the specter of his past. Nor was it only what he wrote, but the way he wrote it. In the minds of 'many persons' his meaning was subject to 'constructions,' and, according to Boyle, Stubbe's opinions in *The Miraculous Conformist* could be interpreted in two ways – as either 'some unstudied expressions of your *raptim scripta*' or 'your deliberate tenets.' Although Boyle chose to treat those heterodox statements as so many 'unstudied expressions,' he probably recognized them for what they were, namely, Stubbe's 'deliberate tenets.' More's remark bears this out: 'Mr Boyle resented Dr. Stubbe his letter very ill, I perceived by what he said to me.'[116]

Stubbe had come into his own by early 1666. In *The Miraculous Conformist* he had found his Restoration voice; he had hit upon a way of masking his intentions, of contriving utterance to disguise meaning, of concealing 'deliberate tenets' behind apparently 'unstudied expressions.' It was a way of irony, satire and subterfuge, and it allowed him to say heterodox things which he could not otherwise have got away with. There was a problem of course: the 'unstudied expressions' might be so convincing that the 'deliberate tenets' would be missed. But that would be a problem for the future. As Boyle's reply shows, the device worked when applied in *The Miraculous Conformist*: the 'unstudied expressions' were effective; they masked 'deliberate tenets' without obliterating them; the subversive meaning lay beneath the surface but not so deeply beneath that it disappeared altogether. Indeed the words conveyed or at least adumbrated that meaning.

Several unanswered questions remain. First, why did Stubbe choose to address the tract to Boyle? The obvious answer of course is that Boyle had been his patron for several years. Stubbe acknowledged this patronage in the tract.[117] But another reason suggests itself. Boyle's own corpuscular philosophy sought to give mechanical explanations of physical processes without resort to spiritual agencies operating in nature, the so-called occult qualities associated with Scholasticism. As a result, Boyle had always to guard against being misconstrued as some kind of materialist because he was a corpuscularian. There were those who pushed his philosophy in that direction, and he continued to defend it against such threats. In fact, as we now know, he meant it to answer and silence such threats.[118] Stubbe was now engaged in reinterpreting the corpuscular philosophy associated with Boyle and the Royal Society in a naturalistic direction. As we have seen, he dedicated *The Miraculous Conformist* to Willis, who was a Fellow of the Royal Society, and then proceeded to give a naturalistic explanation of Greatrakes's cures by using Willis's theory of disease, which rested in part on the corpuscular philosophy. Stubbe must, therefore, have thought that the corpuscular philosophy lent itself to his own naturalistic understanding of the world and for this reason chose to dedicate his tract to Willis and address it to Boyle. It is difficult to believe, however, that Stubbe, canny as he was, did not know the difference between his own radical views and the more conservative ones of Boyle, Willis[119] and the Royal Society, and so it must be assumed that in invoking the names of such luminaries, he was not being entirely artless. Disingenuousness would also explain why Stubbe did not send the 'letter' to Boyle before it was printed. He must have known what Boyle's response would be. As Boyle said, once he had read the tract:

it is no small trouble to me . . . that I did not see the manuscript before it came abroad. For if I had seasonably seen what you wrote about miracles, I should freely have dissuaded you from publicly addressing to me what I cannot but much dissent from; and perhaps I should have been able to prevail with you to omit all that part of your epistle.[120]

Finally, the fact that Stubbe addressed the tract to Boyle chimed with its tone and style. The use of language to disguise meaning was a device of subterfuge. The address to Boyle was another kind of cover. Both allowed Stubbe to obtrude heterodox views into print in a time of stringent press censorship. Stubbe is his own best witness in this regard. Introducing that part of the tract where he offered his naturalistic explanation of Greatrakes's cures, he wrote to Boyle,

since the freedom you allow me with you permits me to speak anything, I shall, without derogating from the power of God, and with all due veneration to so extraordinary characters of his goodness, propose unto you some thoughts which occurred to me hereupon: as confused as they are, they may administer to others some occasion of greater enquiries.[121]

He professed piety in the acknowledgment of God but went on to offer a completely naturalistic account of miracles: implicitly God was in danger of being absorbed into nature, the supernatural into the natural order, though Stubbe never spelled this out in so many words. But of course this was just the point: his meanings were left implicit; the words were open to more than one interpretation, and this allowed his public to read between the lines. He proposed some thoughts: 'confused as they are, they may administer to others some occasion of greater enquiries.' The confusion was contrived, another pretense and deception to allow what was said to be said at all and so to provide 'some occasion of greater enquiries.'

Stubbe had chosen *his* occasion well. Greatrakes's cures provided the springboard for his covert attack on miracles and a separate spiritual order. The address to Boyle insured maximum impact at the same time that it served as protective cover. 'Deliberate tenets,' moreover, could not be clearly distinguished from 'unstudied expressions.' But there was more than just word play and *jeux d'esprit* involved here. At issue for Stubbe (and this we shall see more clearly in the next two chapters) were two opposed views of the relation of learning, especially natural philosophy, to religion and society. The experimental, corpuscular philosophy was meant to foster open-ended inquiry into nature in the interests of truth and the advancement of learning. As worked out principally by Boyle during the 1650s and adopted and made official by the Royal Society after the Restoration, this natural philosophy was also meant to promote order and prosperity: by answering papists, silencing heretics and quieting sectaries, by promoting agriculture, trade and industry, by expanding the overseas empire and contributing to domestic peace – all in the interests of church and king, revived Anglicanism and the restored monarchy.[122] Men from all backgrounds and every rung in the status ladder but servants and the indigent were supposed to be recruited to the task.[123] Boyle was active in this recruitment process and probably patronized Stubbe for this reason.[124] Stubbe himself suggested as much.[125] He was a perfect test case. A former radical revolutionary brought around to the mission of the Royal Society, he and his talents would be put to good use in the service of the restored order he had sought to overthrow. As Boyle's protégé, he would be expected for his part to contribute to this latitudinarian enterprise by corresponding with the Society on matters of natural philosophy and medicine.

So when he took up his pen, wrote an account of Greatrakes's cures, a natural history so to speak, and addressed it to Boyle, he was on one level playing his part. But this was another instance of mocking pretense. His 'thoughts' that 'may administer to others some occasion of greater enquiries' are not what Boyle and the Society had in mind: the fundamentals of orthodox Protestant Christianity were not to be meddled with; 'free inquiry' (to use Boyle's phrase) was not meant to reach so far.[126] On the contrary, natural philosophy, the proper study of nature, was supposed to confirm the faith, not undermine it. So at a deeper level Stubbe was challenging the Society on its own terms, using its ideal of open-ended inquiry to call into question the conventional Christianity to which its natural philosophy had been fastened and which it was meant to serve. Stubbe, in other words, was attempting in *The Miraculous Conformist* to break down the alliance, forged in the 1650s and institutionalized in the Royal Society after the Restoration, between latitudinarian Anglicanism and the corpuscular and experimental philosophy. In this enterprise, moreover, Stubbe was not above deploying the Society's own views against it: indeed this seems to have been one of the major tactics of his campaign. The device was especially valuable because it allowed him to appear to be serving the Society's legitimate goals, when in fact he was training its own guns against it. Here again Stubbe proceeded by feigning innocence, masking his subversive intentions in the cloak of legitimacy.

Here is an important clue to reinterpreting Stubbe's attack on the Royal Society, begun two years or so after the publication of *The Miraculous Conformist*. In chapter 5 we shall see that this later attack was consistent in both objectives and tactics with the cryptic message of the earlier pamphlet. His paganizing naturalism, composed of perhaps equal parts of Galen and Hobbes, underlay both the earlier and later thrusts. Stubbe spoke with one radical voice during the Restoration, though the message had to be masked in subterfuge.

The final question is: what exactly were his radical intentions, rendered so skillfully in *The Miraculous Conformist?* In *The Miraculous Conformist* Stubbe harked back to his pre-1660 position when he argued, in Galenic fashion, that Greatrakes's miraculous cures came from 'the temperament and composure of his body': nature. Miracles were not supernatural but natural phenomena. Implicit in this account was the view that there is no separate spiritual realm but only the world of physical nature, a view that recalls Stubbe's earlier Hobbesian materialism. Hobbes himself of course had held that God is separate from nature.[127] But his critics were quick to raise the question that if all is matter and spirit is disallowed, how is it possible for God to be separate from physical nature? Stubbe was unclear in this respect as well. He seemed to allow for a God distinct from the material universe but, given his view of miracles, to disallow any separate spiritual realm. Whether Stubbe followed Hobbes in preserving an ambiguous distinction between God and nature or whether he subsumed God into nature, it was common in the Restoration for critics of those who identified God with nature to charge their opponents with 'Hobbesism.' Such 'Hobbesism' was in fact closer to Spinozism – or in Stubbe's case radical Galenism, but it was common in the Restoration to lump Spinoza and Hobbes, and hence their followers, together.[128] So Stubbe was a representative of Restoration 'Hobbesism,' understood in this sense, and, as we shall see, this was the way he was read by his contemporary opponents, although the term which Temkin applies to Galen's thought 'pagan naturalism,' probably comes closer to describing accurately Stubbe's position.[129]

The Miraculous Conformist should thus be read as a 'Hobbesist' tract, and there is more in it that identifies it with Stubbe's pre-Restoration line of thought.

For Stubbe Greatrakes was a throwback to primitive Christianity, the Apostolic days of the church. It was widely noted at the time that Greatrakes appeared to be a pious Anglican, ever careful, as he was, to refer his acts of healing to God's power and glory, and he characterized himself as a devoted, tolerant and charitable son of the established church.[130] Stubbe made much of these virtues and associated them with his miraculous gifts. The resulting composite picture of him – tolerant, generous, witnessing to God according to his gifts, which in his case consisted of the miraculous power to heal – was of a Christian remarkably reminiscent of the first age of primitive purity. 'In fine,' Stubbe wrote, 'without prejudicing this age. . . , he seemed to me by his faith and by his charitableness to include in his soul some grains of the Golden Age and to be a relic of those times when piety and miracles were sincere.'[131] Before 1660 Stubbe had argued for a return to primitive Christianity. Now in 1666 he is espousing the same ideal.

The agreement, furthermore, between the tract in hand and his earlier view is more telling than that. According to Stubbe then and now, there is no *separate* supernatural order; the divine is immanent in the universe and directly accessible to mankind without clerical mediation. Under the primitive dispensation a separate clergy claiming exclusive control of spiritual power had been and, if restored, would be redundant. For Stubbe Greatrakes's cures were so many emblems of this pure Christianity, this lay religion in which spiritual power is democratized because immanent in nature. For Stubbe, Greatrakes was *The Miraculous Conformist*, 'a relic of those times when piety and miracles were sincere' (and every man his own priest) and an omen that such a church might be restored. Not only then is *The Miraculous Conformist* Hobbesist in the sense that the spiritual world (if not God himself) is subsumed into the material order; it is also Hobbesist in the conclusion it draws from this, namely, in its denial of the clergy's claim to possess a monopoly of spiritual authority on earth.

Of course Stubbe again departed from Hobbes, as he did before 1660, on the question of what he would put in place of the church as now constituted. Stubbe would have a church in which every man pursued his own spiritual course, witnessing to God as the spirit moved him, according to his gifts. If Greatrakes was an example, this would include the power to perform miracles. Hobbes would not have gone so far; indeed he would have shuddered at the thought. For him the age of miracles had ceased.[132] For Stubbe, if Greatrakes was any sign, it had only to be begun anew.[133]

Here is one measure of the distance between Hobbes's own mechanistic metaphysics and Stubbe's vitalistic naturalism. For Hobbes all was matter in motion; men as a result were driven by nothing more than passion and self-interest and had in fact to be coerced into finding and following their enlightened self-interest. For Stubbe the divine was embedded in nature and directly accessible to the individual such that men could act responsibly for themselves, as for instance in matters of faith, and might even be capable of committing themselves to a larger social good, as for instance Greatrakes's healing career had shown.

The good old cause had ended in failure in 1660. But for Stubbe its religious component at least – a national settlement at once Apostolic, Erastian and libertarian – could still be salvaged in some fashion. We shall see in more detail in the next chapter what he had in mind. For the moment it is enough to recognize that he had not abandoned his revolutionary religious ideal. He remained true to it, though he had to find new, surreptitious means of putting it in print. *The Miraculous Conformist* should be seen as one of the cleverest and most effective of these, at once bold and coy, rife with implicit meanings, exactly suited in its style to the radically altered conditions under which its message had now to be preached.

The cryptic meaning of Stubbe's tract may not have been restricted only to religion – it may also have carried an equally subversive political message. We have already seen that Greatrakes's cures were interpreted as seditious, or at least potentially so by some, and that those who read them in this way pointed an accusatory finger at Catholics, millenaries and sectaries.[134] But one of these accusers also implicated republicans. David Lloyd spelled out the republican overtones of Greatrakes's success as a healer:

And certainly (might a melancholy, or a discontented man think) any man may work upon the imagination, as well as princes; and finding it feasible by one or two experiments, he with other cunning people's suggestions, might set up a healing power, as well as the king, levelling his gift, as well as they would his office, with a design that when it appeared he could *do* no more than other men, he should *be* no more than other men: yea, and when parity of reason led them to attempt in other diseases what with some success they had begun in the King's Evil, they might not only outdo his Majesty, but be in a fair way to give laws to the world.'[135]

If it could be shown that Greatrakes could perform the same cures as the king, not only would one of the props be pulled out from under divine-right monarchy, Greatrakes's cures would also suggest that if the king possessed no special powers that at least other gentlemen did not have, the monarchy was without justification, should be pulled down and a republic – presumably of gentlemen like Greatrakes himself, if not others – put in its place. By gentrifying the royal touch Greatrakes was at least by implication establishing the metaphysical grounds for an attack on monarchy and the advocacy of a gentry-dominated republic.

This was Lloyd's reading of Greatrakes's healing mission – it was fraught with republican sedition as well as subversive heresy. Lloyd did not go on to single Stubbe out for drawing these republican conclusions from Greatrakes's career. Nor is there any evidence in Stubbe's tract that he was drawing these republican conclusions from Greatrakes's cures. According to Anthony Wood, however, Lloyd wrote his tract after *The Miraculous Conformist* had appeared and in answer to it,[136] and it is true that Lloyd devoted two pages of his tract to *The Miraculous Conformist*. He laundered out the heresy implicit in Stubbe's tract by pretending that his arguments showed that Greatrakes was an imposter rather than a real miracle worker – exactly the opposite of what Stubbe in fact claimed.[137] Given the fact that Stubbe was a former champion of republicanism, and widely known to be so, it is at least highly plausible that when Lloyd spelled out the republican implications of Greatrakes's cures in his answer to Stubbe's tract, he did so because Stubbe was in fact interpreting those cures in a republican direction, perhaps even using them to make republican propaganda. This inference is strengthened by the fact that, as we shall see in subsequent chapters, Stubbe still harbored republican sentiments, and was seen to do so, though he expressed them in a characteristically, and necessarily, cryptic way in the new political climate of the early Restoration.

4

'Mahometan Christianity': Stubbe's secular historicism

> . . . so that there is no hopes that popery can be kept out, but by a company of poor people called fanatics, who are driven into corners as the first Christians were; and who only in truth conserve the purity of Christian religion, as it was planted by Christ and his Apostles and is contained in Scripture.
>
> Henry Neville, *Plato Redivivus*

Up to this point I have analyzed the development of Stubbe's ideas chronologically and according as they appear in print. But I must now deviate from that rigid chronological treatment in an effort to throw some light upon Stubbe's fundamental political and religious ideas as they developed during the Restoration, which in turn will illuminate major issues dealt with in both the last chapter and the next. To do this I must examine a document out of strict chronological sequence, Stubbe's *An Account of the Rise and Progress of Mahometanism*. It was not written before 1671, when Stubbe mentioned his intention to set down his thoughts on the subject.[1] So he had entertained the ideas that it contains before he wrote them out, and indeed they chime with views he held before and after the Restoration which we have already met with.

Stubbe's *Account* existed only in manuscript copies for two centuries before it was published for the first time in 1911. The editor of this edition, Hafiz Mahmud Khan Shairani, has recognized the work as constituting one of the earliest appreciations of Islam we have in English, remarkable for its lack of Christian bias and its intuitive and sympathetic grasp of the meaning of Muslim faith and practice. By attention to internal evidence he has also suggested that *An Account* was written between 1671 and Stubbe's death in July 1676. The editor does not go further, however, and offer evidence for the attribution to Stubbe except to point out that the first known copyist of the manuscript, Charles Hornby, 'supposed' it to be by Stubbe when he copied it in 1705.[2] Nor has the most recent commentator on the discourse shed more light on its authorship. He too follows the supposition of Hornby and others without providing any corroborating evidence.[3]

It is now possible to say with reasonable certainty that the work is in fact by Stubbe. The evidence comes from one of his other works, *An Epistolary*

64

Discourse Concerning Phlebotomy (1671), in which in the midst of a treatment of the history of plagues Stubbe said:

I believe the disease small pox to be novel and of no longer date than the Sarracenical revolution: I could instance in the nature of such great alterations, that they have been preceded and accompanied with many petty changes in other things: and if ever I have so much vacant time as to make political reflexions upon the rise of Mahomet, I may declare much to this purpose.[4]

Thus we know that Stubbe had it in mind in 1671 to write an account of 'the rise of Mahomet,' which is one of the main themes of the treatise attributed to him, as the title itself makes clear. But that does not exhaust the evidence for his authorship. He went on in the same passage partially quoted above to suggest what his account of 'the rise of Mahomet' would include should he ever find the time to write it. He would put the origins of Islam into historical context. Thus he would show, so he said, 'that the Christians were . . . ignorant, . . . debauched, and perfidious, and addicted to legends more than to the sound doctrine of the Gospel, at that time, that most of the fables in the Alcoran were accommodated to . . . the times, more than to truth (and so Mahomet told them) and that he pretended to revive ancient Christianity.'[5] If we turn to *An Account of the Rise and Progress of Mahometanism*, we find each of these three themes woven into its fabric. Let us look at each of them in turn, as they appear in *An Account*. First the work does treat of the decadence of the Christian churches at the time of 'the rise of Mahomet,' and a case is made for a connection between the two: the decline of Christianity spurs the advance of Islam.[6] Second *An Account* stresses that Mahomet often employed popular fables in the Koran rather than stating the truth because they were so much believed in by the masses that for him not to have brought the fables to bear on his message would have put his new religion at serious risk.[7] Indeed *An Account* states that Mahomet deliberately introduced 'those superstitious usages' into the Koran to make his new religion more attractive to readers.[8] Last *An Account* maintains that much of Mahomet's success lay in his revival of primitive (Arian) Christianity which had been lost sight of by this time because of the dominance among the Christian churches in many places of a corrupt Trinitarianism.[9] Thus on all three scores *An Account* matches Stubbe's brief description in his *Discourse Concerning Phlebotomy* of what he would do if ever he sat down and wrote out his thoughts on 'the rise of Mahomet.'

On these grounds I think we may conclude that Stubbe was the author of *An Account*. The next task, now that authorship has been established, is to determine why Stubbe was led to write such a remarkably astute and unbiased account of a non-Christian religion in a world, that of Restoration England, seething with religious passion and controversy,[10] a task which obliges us to summarize and analyze the arguments of the text itself.

Stubbe's book, as the title indicates, is a history of religion, and he makes clear at the beginning of the second chapter that his approach to his subject breaks radically with tradition.[11] He rejects supernatural and providential-ist explanations as being irrational and unwarranted clerical inventions. He relies, instead, entirely upon human, material and accidental factors. His is a naturalized and secularized account in which there is no place for the intervention of outside spiritual forces – 'miraculous accidents, unim-aginable effusions of the Holy Ghost, and such like, which no reason can comprehend nor example parallel.'[12] From the start and throughout his history he is consistent with his 'Hobbesian' outlook; he is a 'Hobbesian' secular historicist.[13] But this does not mean that his history strives to be values-free: it is in fact values-laden, the more so because he is so insistent upon treating religion in secular, historical terms rather than the clerical, providentialist ones of conventional historiography.[14] Thus for Stubbe, anticlerical historicist that he was, the history of the early Christian church becomes the story first of its progressive corruption and second of the return to something like its primitive purity by Mohammed, the founder of Islam!

Within this general interpretative scheme Stubbe sees the whole history of religion from the origins of Christianity to the foundation and expansion of Islam as constituting a series of 'great revolutions,' enormous transform-ations in culture and society. (He uses the term 'revolution' in an extremely modern sense.) His history is an epic of those revolutions, an epic divided into four parts, each initiated by a separate 'revolution.' These changes came, in Stubbe's account, through historical agencies rather than supernatural ones.

The first of these revolutions was 'the reception of Christ' by some Jews as the Messiah. Here as in all subsequent cases the way was prepared by 'circumstances.'[15] In this case the imperial government imposed heavier taxes beginning ten years after the birth of Christ, and Stubbe gives a sensitive historical analysis of what he took to be the results:

then the sense of their miseries made the people more credulous, & whether they more easily believed what they so earnestly desired might happen or that the malcontents (taking the advantage of their uneasiness) did then more frequently & diligently insinuate into the multitude that opinion, it so happened that there arose about that time sundry false Messiahs, & the world was big with expectation raised in every country by the Jews (who had received the intelligence from their common metropolis Jerusalem) that the great prince was coming who should establish the Jewish monarchy & bring peace & happiness to all the earth.[16]

After the crucifixion and resurrection Christ's followers and Apostles continued to spread the faith, made vivid by the Pentecostal miracles, that he was indeed the Messiah 'whose second coming would complete the happiness of all nations, as well Jews as Gentiles.'[17] The gospel news spread through much of the Roman world because the Jews themselves had spread, settled and prospered throughout the empire: 'This being the condition of the Jews and all the [Jewish] nation (however dispersed) being prepared beforehand to entertain any tidings of a Messiah who should advance the throne of David to a universal monarchy, 'tis not to be wondered that Christianity was so soon spread over the whole earth.'[18] 'The principal tenet' of these earliest Christians then was the millenarian belief in 'the temporal reign of the Messiah & the union of the Jews & Gentiles under one most happy monarchy.'[19]

Stubbe is equally insistent upon what these Christians 'in the most primitive times'[20] did not believe:

But that they did never believe Christ to be the natural son of God by eternal generation or any tenet depending thereon or prayed unto him or believed the Holy Ghost or the Trinity of persons in one deity is as evident as 'tis that the Jews & they did expect no such Messiah, and the introducing such doctrines would have been capital among them as tending to blasphemy and polytheism.[21]

Because the first converts were Jews or Judaizing Christians, moreover, 'the whole constitution of the primitive church government relates to the Jewish synagogue.'[22] Each congregation was distinct from every other, 'as independent as were the Jewish synagogues everywhere.' Each congregation also had its own governors, 'its peculiar bishop or angel of the church and ruling presbyters.'[23] Thus there was no hierarchy, no subordination. 'The presbyters,' moreover, 'were not priests but laymen set apart to their office by imposition of hands; no temples, no altars, no sacrifices were known in those days, nor was the name of priest then heard of.'[24] Among this collection of equal congregations there was a great diversity; the early church was a loose collection of sects, 'each retaining their own opinions mixed with the doctrine of the Messiah,' which was the one thing that bound them together.[25]

The Judaizing Christians were avid proselytizers, and they made their task simple by offering a streamlined religion to the Gentiles. Doctrine was 'principally contained in the grand tenet that Jesus was the Messiah of the Jews, who was to unite Jew and Gentile under one temporal monarchy.'[26] To prepare for that event Gentile converts 'were to repent of their sins, renounce idolatry and entirely to obey the seven commands of Noah.'[27] This last reference to 'the . . . commands of Noah' and the view of church government recall Stubbe's pre-1660 position. One of the chief sources for this position was also the same: John Selden.[28] Stubbe has amended his views in important ways since 1660, as we shall see. The sharp emphasis upon the Arianism of the earliest church is one such dramatic change.[29] But his position still rests in many respects upon his revolutionary ideal of Erastian Independency and a minimal, natural Christianity, 'the religion of Noah,'[30] and he clearly identifies this pure Arian faith with that of the first Christians.[31] Critical historian and materialist that he is, however, he does not paint a uniformly glowing and idealized picture of this primitive church. First, the early Christians were poor and ignorant and harbored an 'enmity to all ethnick learning.'[32] Second, and because of this ignorance, the first Bible, the Greek Septuagint, was highly inaccurate. The Apostles, save Paul, and their followers did not know Greek, and yet it was into Greek that their message was translated 'so that all the sacred books of the New Testament (except what bears the name of Paul, who indeed did understand Greek) may be justly supposed to be but translations or counterfeits performed by unknown persons.'[33] Even Paul, despite his Greek, cannot be trusted because of 'his juggling carriage and his trimming,'[34] becoming 'all things to all men that he might by all means save some.'[35]

The second of Stubbe's four pivotal transformations, the next 'revolution' in the history of the early church, occurred in the early second century. Some Jews in Jerusalem and Alexandria rose up against the Romans under the leadership of 'another Messiah . . . who styled himself Benchocab or the son of the Star.'[36] The emperor Hadrian retaliated by crushing the rebellion in both cities. 'This revolution had a mighty influence upon Christianity.'[37] The Christians cut themselves off from the Jews and the figure of Christ and pretended 'only to a spiritual Messiah, since they could not have preserved themselves but by so doing.' Indeed they went further and developed those tendencies that 'the vulgar' Gentile converts to Christianity had already manifested, 'attributing a divinity to Christ upon the account of his extraordinary acts and miracles' and syncretizing 'some passages in the New Testament with the Platonic philosophy' to produce 'the doctrine of the Trinity.'[38] In Stubbe's view this syncretism was for the worse; the resulting doctrines led to 'confusion' and to the invention of further 'uncouth words,' like 'essence, person, consubstantiation, eternal generation, etc.'[39] In an effort to 'comply with paganism' the Christians also began to use priests and to resort to temples, to invent a whole spiritual order, in other words, and to endow certain men with the power to be its earthly guardians.[40] These developments among Christians were hastened by 'the frequent persecutions by the Roman emperors against them, who looked upon them as no good subjects, since they expected a temporal Messiah and . . . disclaimed all subjection to the pagan magistrates.'[41] So successful were the Christians at conforming themselves to paganism and the laws of 'the pagan magistrate' that they appealed increasingly to the imperial troops. Ever the Hobbesian secular historicist, Stubbe explains why:

The discipline of the Roman legions being extinct and the armies composed most of foreigners, men of mercenary spirits and no friends to the established religion, these soldiery beheld opulent priests and vestals, together with their colleges with an envious eye and cared not if a new religion were introduced, so that they might share the spoils of the old.[42]

The third one of Stubbe's four revolutions was Constantinian. That emperor enhanced the church's authority to augment his own. He obliged the clergy by endeavouring to reduce Christianity to 'one uniform doctrine' – hence the Nicene Creed. He increased the power of bishops so that they could serve as 'spies and checks upon his governors.' He elevated the bishops of Rome and Alexandria 'to a kind of princely dignity, that they might gain the greater veneration among the people and equal the splendor of the pagan priests,' especially as those cities 'were the two places that had most influence upon his empire.'[43] He paganized the ecclesiastical government by establishing a clerical hierarchy which matched the hierarchy in pagan cults. Equally paganized were the Christian rituals, now performed by priests before altars and in buildings resembling pagan temples.[44] Despite their outward success the Christians were divided among themselves, and, 'by mutually exposing each others lives and doctrines, all the parties became equally contemptible and ridiculous.'[45] Among these sects there was a major division between Arians and Trinitarians – the former noted for their numbers, wealth and learning and the latter, being 'enemies to all human learning,' for their ignorance and superstition.[46] The Trinitarians gained the upper hand during the reign of Justinian who, because he defeated the Arian Goths, persecuted Arianism 'and by severe laws established and enforced the Trinitarian religion.'[47] This victory also represented the defeat of Arian learning and the triumph of pagan superstition. Stubbe's description of the Roman Catholic Church established by Justinian is worthy of Hobbes and doubtless owes not a little to *Leviathan*:

Christianity was then degenerated into such a kind of paganism as wanted nothing but the ancient sacrifices and professed polytheism, and even as to the latter there wanted not some who made three gods of the Trinity, others made a goddess of the Virgin Mary, the reverence to the saints differed little from that of the pagans to their heroes and lesser gods.[48]

He also makes the Hobbesian point that authority divided between church and state, such as was brought about by the Constantinian revolution, leads to endless civil turmoil.[49] He outdoes Gibbon on the legacy of that revolution: 'when Christianity became generally received, it introduced with it a general inundation of barbarism and ignorance, which overran all places where it prevailed.'[50] From ashes, however, the phoenix is born.

While most of Christianity was sunk in superstition and internecine war, Mohammed accomplished the fourth revolution, the invention, establishment and expansion of Islam.[51] Stubbe devotes most of his manuscript to explaining this process, and the account is once more set within the framework of his Hobbesian historicism. He portrays Mohammed as an extremely shrewd operator, as Christian apologists had traditionally done. But for Stubbe, unlike them,[52] Mohammed's relentlessly calculating intelligence is something not to be scorned but admired because it allowed him to contrive a religion that exactly suited the circumstances of place, time and tradition. He borrowed the Arian Christianity of the first centuries, now for the most part abandoned by Christians themselves in favor of a corrupt Trinitarianism. He found this original Christianity surviving among Judaizing Christians who over the centuries had settled in Arabia itself. They had fled there in small bands, along with Jews and motley others, to escape successive waves of persecution within the Roman empire.[53] Mohammed's genius was to slap the Arian beliefs of this remnant of Apostolic Christianity on top of the pagan superstitions of the desert tribesmen, among whom he sold his new religious package. They were allowed to go on in the practice of their ancient rituals, but these were given new meanings in keeping with the spirit of the new religion.

The resulting syncretism, consisting of belief in God and worship of him through prayer and voluntary almsgiving (which went to the poor rather than to a parasitic clergy) is remarkably close in some respects to Hobbes's prescriptions for a rational religion given in *Leviathan*, though the almsgiving is Stubbe's (and Mohammed's) own touch.[54] In other respects Mohammed's creed diverges from those Hobbesian prescriptions in the direction, interestingly enough, of the early English deism of Edward, Lord Herbert of Cherbury and his follower, Stubbe's exact contemporary, the radical Whig Charles Blount. As we shall see, Blount's and Stubbe's paths will cross again. For the moment let us compare Stubbe's account of Mohammed's simple creed, Hobbes's natural religion and the deistical confessions of Cherbury and Blount.

Islamic doctrine consists of belief in one God and Mohammed's prophetic mission. God is to be worshipped through daily prayer at set times, almsgiving, a pilgrimage to Mecca and fasting.[55] Stubbe specifies further, God is omnipotent, his attributes are incomprehensible, and 'his providence disposeth of all affairs below, . . . according to the decrees of his eternal predestination.'[56] Muslims also believe in 'the immortality of the soul, the resurrection of the body, and the Last Judgement.'[57] There is also a precise system of rewards and punishments, meted out in the afterlife:

those who are preserved . . . from sin, do after death live in happiness until the resurrection and day of Judgement: . . . those who are more or less wicked, must in the grave and in a kind of purgatory undergo some torments until the last day, and then with more or less difficulty they shall be saved; but that nothing of evil how little soever shall escape unpunished, nor anything of good how small soever pass unrewarded.[58]

There is no hell: everyone will be saved but made to suffer according as they have sinned. Curiously the Roman Catholic notion of purgatory is invoked as a device to reconcile universal salvation and moral responsibility in what is otherwise an extremely radical creed.

Not only does Stubbe describe this primitive Christianity revived by Mohammed. He also pronounces very favorably upon it:

This is the sum of Mahometan religion, on the one hand, not clogging men's faith with the necessity of believing a number of abstruse notions which they cannot comprehend, and which are often contrary to the dictates of reason and common sense; nor on the other hand loading them with the performance of many troublesome, expensive and superstitious ceremonies, yet enjoining a due observance of religion, as the surest method to keep men in the bounds of their duty both to God and man.[59]

No wonder Stubbe did not see fit to publish *An Account*: in it he turns true religion inside out. Trinitarian Christianity is dismissed as hopelessly corrupt and false in favor of Islam, which is represented as the religion of Christ and the Apostles.

There are some striking similarities between Stubbe's 'Mahometan Christianity' and Hobbes's natural religion set out in chapter 31 of *Leviathan*. There Hobbes says that men can reasonably acknowledge God's existence as creator and governor of the universe and that he should be worshipped further through prayer and thanksgiving.[60] Men are not to inquire into the nature of God because finite beings cannot comprehend the infinite.[61] Such efforts in the past have led to 'volumes of disputation' rather than truth – to heat, not light.[62] Hobbes also speaks of God's 'natural punishments.' To wit: 'he that will do anything for his pleasure, must engage himself to suffer all the pains annexed to it.'[63] Hobbes and Stubbe have both produced a pared-down faith. In both what is emphasized is man's acknowledgment of God's existence and the necessity of worshipping Him. For Hobbes rewards and punishments are embedded in nature, the act of living; for Stubbe they are postponed until death, punishments being meted out in purgatory. Both creeds, however, reject, as Stubbe puts it, 'a number of abstruse notions' and 'the performance of . . . superstitious ceremonies.' Hobbes's system is a religion conformable to man's 'natural reason only, without other word of God.'[64] Stubbe's doctrine consists of the beliefs of 'the most primitive' Christians, revived by Mohammed.

At this point Stubbe and Hobbes part company because Hobbes adds to his natural religion some points deriving from Scripture, that 'other word of God' beyond human reason. Scripture tells Hobbes that Jesus is the son of God. Hobbes is not, like Stubbe, an Arian, though he is also not a Trinitarian in the conventional sense.[65] Stubbe, moreover, speaks of God and nature interchangeably,[66] while Hobbes makes a clear distinction between them.[67] For him there is no divine power in nature, although, if all is matter, as he also maintains, the questions of what and where God is, are left open. But that is probably just as Hobbes would have it. Beyond acknowledging God's existence and honoring him through prayer and thanksgiving, finite men cannot comprehend the infinite and therefore should not inquire.

Because of these differences between Hobbes and Stubbe, there are more striking similarities between Stubbe and the early deism of Charles Blount. Here is one formulation of a natural religion published by Blount:

Natural religion is the belief we have of an eternal intellectual being, & of the duty which we owe to him, manifested to us by our reason, without revelation or positive law: The chief heads whereof seem contained in these few particulars.
1. That there is one infinite eternal God, Creator of all things.
2. That he governs the world by Providence.
3. That 'tis our duty to worship & obey him as Creator and Governor.
4. That our worship consists in prayers to him, & praise of him.
5. That our obedience consists in the rules of right reason, the practice whereof is moral virtue.
6. That we are to expect rewards and punishments hereafter, according to our actions in this life; which includes the soul's immortality, and is proved by our admitting providence.
Seventhly, that when we err from the rules of our duty, we ought to repent & trust in God's mercy for pardon.[68]

Blount's formulation shares with Stubbe's 'Mahometan Christianity' all of the points that Hobbes's natural religion does, and more besides. Both Stubbe and Blount are Arians: Christ is not God, as he is for Hobbes. For both also, unlike Hobbes, the soul is immortal, and rewards and punishments are to be meted out in the afterlife, although on this point Blount's creed represents a halfway house between Hobbes and Stubbe, as it allows for 'natural punishments' (in Hobbes's sense) distributed in this life as well.[69] Blount acknowledges his indebtedness to Cherbury's natural religion but never mentions Stubbe. These strong similarities between Stubbe's 'Mahometan Christianity' and Blount's natural religion argue, however, for a close connection between the two thinkers, especially as they were contemporaries. As we shall see, such a connection can be established by the evidence. For the moment it is enough to assert, on the basis of the evidence already adduced, that Stubbe must now be reckoned as one of the founders of English deism, though his creed wore the guise of 'Mahometan Christianity.'

But his manuscript includes more than deism. Stubbe is also concerned in his *Account* to show Mohammed's political genius, much of it stemming from the uses he made of the religion. Thus he contrasts the religious policy of Islam with that of the Christianized Roman empire. In the latter for political reasons the emperors from Constantine onwards had allowed the clergy to claim a spiritual authority separate from their own civil authority, and this had led to ignorance, superstition, contention and a weakening of the empire. Mohammed, on the other hand, placed control of religion in the hands of the civil ruler and the result was the opposite. Stubbe does not draw out the contrast but merely lets the reader arrive at the intended conclusions for himself: 'What a discourse might be made upon his [Mohammed's] uniting the civil and ecclesiastical powers in one sovereign!'[70] This of course is Hobbes's prescription, set out in the last half of *Leviathan*, and the influence of that book on Stubbe is again unmistakable. The Muslim creed itself works to the same purpose: 'Their articles of faith are few and plain, whereby they are preserved from schisms and heresies.'[71] And this in contrast again to corrupted Christianity whose clergy have invented a number of conflicting opinions that issue in disputation and war.[72]

Descending to particulars, Stubbe explains the ways in which the doctrines of 'Mahometan Christianity' make at once for public morality and shrewd politics. Regular prayer five times a day, washing before prayer and abstinence from wine keep natural human sensuality within proper bounds.[73] In this regard Stubbe rings one change on Hobbes. Where he says that man's appetites are insatiable,[74] Stubbe says rather that they merely become so once indulged and that a remedy thus lies in limiting satisfaction to 'what is absolutely necessary.'[75] This was what Mohammed taught his followers, and the result was not only 'most healthy' but also produced the best subjects and soldiers.[76] Mohammed was interested in inculcating a personal morality that would serve the religion. Since God meant for the Muslims to expand in order to extirpate idolatry and spread the true faith,[77] that morality was the one which would produce the best soldiers – hence the emphasis upon Spartan virtues, the austere life. Mohammed of course was shrewd enough to make up for this by holding out the promise that in paradise all appetites might be indulged to the full: his afterlife was exceedingly sensual.[78] In the meantime, however, Muslims had to put the brakes on the senses. Another course that worked in the same direction was the requirement that every Muslim makes a pilgrimage to Mecca and observe the movable fast of Ramadan. Mohammed insisted upon

these two points upon a prudent foresight that they would be of great use in a military empire such as he designed, to the support whereof valiant and hardy soldiers were necessary and that nothing could more conduce to the successive generation and education of such than these two institutions; for how active, laborious, & abstinent must the women as well as the men render themselves, to be able to endure the fatigue of the pilgrimage or the hunger of the fast.[79]

Another form of sensuality which Mohammed also hoped to curb was private wealth which grew as the empire expanded. Thus to prevent Muslims from being 'debauched by riches,' he obliged them 'to give alms to the needy.' Here again the motive was political: 'and this is inculcated . . . that they might not grow effeminate through luxury or mutinous by means of their riches.' Almsgiving was another route to martial and civic virtue, and Stubbe refers to it as 'a kind of Grecian levelling law.'[80] Indeed the forbidding of usury would encourage charity: Muslims 'might more readily relieve their necessitous brethren either by giving or lending frankly, when they had not that way of making advantages of their money.' The result would be an empire 'great and lasting' because the subjects would be neither 'too poor and needy' to be inclined to rebellion 'nor exasperated against each other by reason of some growing too great by their oppressions and extortions on the rest.'[81] Mohammed also enjoined the work ethic in order to guarantee that charity did not encourage idleness among the poor and that wealth did not effeminate the rich.[82] Mohammed's empire would thus consist of subjects toughened by work, fasting and prayer and united by a simple faith and the elimination of the idle poor equally with the idle rich.

Sensuality was discouraged, but polygamy was legalized. According to Stubbe, showing remarkable detachment, this was not contradictory because polygamy is not 'a piece of sensuality in the Mahometan religion.'[83] On the contrary, it was Scriptural and Apostolic; Mohammed picked it up with so much else, from the Judaizing Nazarene Christians and made it a part of policy, seeing that it would be 'exceedingly subservient to the multiplying of subjects which are the sinews of empire.'[84]

In two other respects Islam in Stubbe's hands turns out to be superior to conventional, priest-ridden Christianity. First Mohammed, conquer though he did, refused to force his religion upon subject peoples but rather extended toleration to theirs 'provided it were not idolatrous' and that they pay 'a moderate tribute.'[85] Once more the result was extremely politic: 'The security which he gave to the Jews and Christians that they might live quietly under him without molestation brought a great deal of riches into the publick treasury, and those securities were observed with so inviolate a faith that it was a great invitation to the next neighbours to come under his government.'[86] So favorable are the conditions of Muslim rule, Stubbe maintains, that Christians in contemporary Europe would prefer, if given the choice, Muslim rule to their own: 'And it is indeed more the interest of the princes & nobles, than of the people, which at present keeps all Europe from submitting to the Turks.'[87] Second, Stubbe admits that the Muslims practice slavery by making slaves of subject peoples. But he goes on to say that the slavery that Europeans impose in the New World (which he would have observed firsthand in Jamaica) is much worse. Europeans see that it is contradictory to be a slave and a Christian at the same time. So in order to maintain slaves and 'to secure . . . the benefit of their labor,' the slaveowners 'debar them and their posterity from the benefits of the Gospel . . . and thus by shutting them out from that which we think the only door to salvation, we do (as much as in us lies) put their souls in as bad a condition as their bodies, which is a cruelty that Turks and pagans would be ashamed of.'[88]

Stubbe also praises the sort of government Mohammed established. It was rule by one man but it was not government by a monarch, an emperor or an army general. Rather it was government by a prophet, an inspired leader. As such his power was absolute but not tyrannical because he ruled by a natural prudence that freed men from superstition, injustice and onerous exactions, and instead nurtured learning, tolerance and prosperity: 'he is so far from depriving any Ismaelite [Arab] of his liberty, that he would set even a bird free if he saw him encaged, and so remote from ambition and avarice that the greatest pleasure he takes in having anything is that he may give it away to some more indigent Moslemin.'[89] Absolute power was harnessed to absolute virtue and the result was salutary – not oppressive but liberal and liberating.[90] This prudent use of absolute authority was meant to insinuate itself into men's affections and convince their reason, 'not to impose upon their understanding or force their will.'[91] The behavior of the prophet, moreover, was the key because he became the inspired example to follow and to emulate. He was all 'valour and piety.'[92] His success did not lead him to abuse his power but enabled him 'to do more good, bestow more alms, and more to advance the glory of God.'[93] He was the model of the good Muslim – Spartan, to moderate private wealth and reduce poverty, and tolerant. Since Mohammed's creed was 'Mahometan Christianity' deriving from the Apostolic Christians, the government Mohammed set up in conformity to that creed might also be taken for a Christian ideal – a government based upon natural prudence to match 'the religion of Noah' and of nature.

The reader has perhaps already discerned that Stubbe's *Account* of 'Mahometan Christianity' is not merely a historical exercise. It is also meant to serve as a standard against which to measure current Christian practice and the current conduct of Christian princes – and no doubt Charles II and the English church most of all. Nor do church and state fare very well in the comparison. Stubbe's *Account* is not merely descriptive and explanatory of the past; it is a prescriptive critique of contemporary religion and government. Hobbes's ideas play their part. England would be better off if religious authority were vested in the civil sovereign, as under Islam. Just as Mohammed did, moreover, the sovereign should enforce a rational religion, a 'Mahometan Christianity' which would represent a return to the Apostolic church. Again just as Mohammed did, the sovereign should allow for toleration of opinion beyond the enforcement of this doctrinal minimum, this rational religion of nature. And again this would be to follow the practice of Apostolic Christians, as Stubbe had set this out in radical Independent terms before the Restoration.[94] So his account represents Hobbes mixed again with the ideals of radical Independency. What is missing in his *Account* is his earlier explicit republicanism. A scheme giving the people the power to rule themselves has been replaced by government by an inspired leader. But even in this respect there are remnants of the pre-Restoration ideals. Stubbe's republic was to be ruled by the virtuous who were seen to be inspired men in the same sense that Mohammed was – at once dedicated, worthy and shrewd. The new prophetic rule and the old republican and civic ideal were both intended to set up governments in which virtue would rule; power would be harnessed in both to virtue; and the result would be to create not only virtuous rule but also virtuous men and women, public virtue and a virtuous state, if not republican virtue. The emphasis in Stubbe's *Account* upon almsgiving and the resulting levelling up and down is probably also a holdover from his pre-Restoration attack on tithing and his republican egalitarianism. Certainly he had argued before 1660 that the Apostolic Christians had looked after the poor and that this should inform current practice.[95]

At least one observer, the Reverend Joseph Glanvill, had learned of Stubbe's 'Mahometan Christianity' by 1671 and associated it with what Glanvill regarded as Stubbe's questionable view of monarchy.[96] We shall return to Glanvill in the next chapter. For now it is enough that this association is evidence, in addition to what *An Account* itself provides, that it represents a clandestine attack upon established religion and government and a call for the reform of both. It does not advocate violent revolution, a return to civil war and the good old cause, but it is radically reformist – so much so that it was not printed but circulated among friends and fellow freethinkers. In its implicit attack upon church and state it brings to bear many of the political and religious ideas that had previously informed Stubbe's radical Independency and republicanism. It represents a restatement of those ideas and ideals in light of Restoration circumstances, an accommodation of them to those circumstances.

Stubbe wrote his *Account* in the very period, perhaps the same year, that Charles II asserted what he claimed to be the royal prerogative in ecclesiastical affairs and issued his Declaration of Indulgence (1672). Stubbe was writing position papers and propaganda for the court supporting the Indulgence in 1672–3.[97] Was his manuscript related then to this royal attempt at toleration? Certainly the Indulgence was an exercise in Erastian tolerationism of the kind that Stubbe advocated in *An Account* as constituting the ideal religious policy. In chapters 5 and 6 further evidence will be adduced to indicate the close connection between the manuscript and the reformist message that Stubbe preached in court circles and elsewhere after 1670, if not earlier.

Nor is Stubbe's manuscript the only example of an attempt to bring Muslim ideas and institutions to bear on English affairs in the 1670s.[98] There was considerable interest at court in the 1670s and 1680s in things Islamic, from coffee to costumes to religious doctrine. Viscount Conway, who was a Privy Councillor for Ireland at the time, commissioned his brother-in-law, Sir John Finch, Ambassador to Constantinople, to write a series of reports concerning Muslim customs and culture with a view to suggesting the ways in which they might be applied in England to the reform of political and religious institutions. In 1675, Sir John complied after some delay, and the letters exist in manuscript in the British Library.[99]

It is also especially interesting that Viscount Conway, who had requested Finch's reports, was the principal patron of Henry Stubbe. Could it be that he also commissioned Stubbe to write *An Account* for his instruction? The evidence does not say. But certainly he would have taken an interest in Stubbe's project, if he knew about it, though how sympathetic he would have been is another question. No doubt Finch's reports would have been more to the taste of the Tory Viscount than Stubbe's 'Mahometan Christianity' with all of its heretical associations, though Lord Conway may have been amused by the conceit if not edified by the example.

Now that we have explicated the text of Stubbe's *Account* and explored at least some of its meanings we are much better placed to deal with the most baffling and perhaps the most important – certainly the most notorious – chapter in his career: his famous attacks on the Royal Society. The episode occurred in the period from 1669 to 1671, the years immediately prior to the period of the composition of *An Account*. But Stubbe already had in mind the idea for the manuscript during the period of those attacks, and most important of all his 'Mahometan Christianity' was intimately bound up with them. Indeed they cannot be properly understood without taking Stubbe's manuscript into consideration, which is why it has been treated before the attacks, though it was written immediately afterwards.

5

Aristotle on the ale-benches

I will add, the little credit the Church of England has amongst the people; most men being almost as angry with that popery which is left amongst us (in surplices, copes, altars, cringings, bishops, ecclesiastical courts, and the whole hierarchy; besides an infinite number of useless, idle superstitious ceremonies; and the ignorance and viciousness of the clergy in general) as they are with those dogmas that are abolished.

Henry Neville, *Plato Redivivus*

With the publication of *The Miraculous Conformist* in 1666, Stubbe resumed a polemical career in which he speaks with his old anticlerical 'Hobbesist' voice, though no longer freely but in a code full of cryptic meanings. We are now in a position to examine the principal sequence in his career as an early Restoration polemicist, his famous attacks on the Royal Society, delivered and published between 1669 and 1671. In these he defended Aristotle, Galen and Scholastic learning against the new philosophy of the Royal Society, as it was put forward by Thomas Sprat and Joseph Glanvill. The standard accounts of the controversy have interpreted him as a conservative defender of church and monarchy, wedded to the old Scholastic 'humanism' against the new scientific 'naturalism' and fighting a rearguard action against science and progress.[1] Were this view correct, Stubbe would have had to make a considerable about-face between early 1666 and 1669 when the controversy began. As it turns out, however, the standard view is mistaken, and Stubbe's attack on the Royal Society is consistent with his earlier commitments and particularly with his stance adumbrated in *The Miraculous Conformist*. The standard account of Stubbe and the Royal Society went wrong in part precisely because it ignores this important context and background, the continuity of his thinking. Stubbe's polemic against the Society is immersed in an even wider context that will be set out before the attack itself is considered.

It has been claimed that Stubbe was working for others in attacking the Society. At the time fingers were pointed at the clergy in the universities, the apothecaries, the Royal College of Physicians and the aged Aristotelian Robert Crosse.[2] There may be some truth in all of these claims, but the one for which there is clearest evidence, and that offers the greatest insight, is the link to Crosse. He had once been an Oxford don, 'a great tutor and Aristotelian, and much noted in the university for a learned man.' He was 'puritanically inclined' and 'sided with the Presbyterians' during the Civil War, was a member of the Westminster Assembly and in 1648 was tendered the Regius Professorship of Divinity at Oxford. He refused it but 'had soon after the rich vicarage of Great Chew in Somerset' near Bath, which he kept until his death in 1683.[3]

When we meet him in 1668, he is at odds with Joseph Glanvill, a fellow cleric, who had been Rector of Frome Selwood in Somerset since 1662 and was appointed Rector of Bath in 1666. Glanvill had already published two books arguing that the experimental and mechanical philosophy promoted by the Royal Society had, in many ways, superseded Aristotle and traditional learning.[4] For his efforts on its behalf he had been elected Fellow of the Society in 1664.[5] He was also drawn into a local controversy with Crosse, the unregenerate Aristotelian, who claimed that Scholastic philosophy was the foundation of true religion and learning and that the attempt made by Glanvill and the Royal Society to set Aristotle aside in favor of the new mechanical philosophy would lead to atheism and popery.[6]

It was not merely an arid, academic dispute between two rustic clerics, however: it was in fact symptomatic of the times and especially of the religious crisis in Somerset. Crosse's charge of atheism and popery levelled against Glanvill is particularly revealing of the issues. During the Restoration fear of popery was intense. Nor was this fear restricted to the threat of an outright Catholic takeover. Popery had a more insidious meaning. The fear extended to a suspicion that the established church was popishly affected because prelacy, ritual and persecution had been re-instituted.[7] This suspicion, moreover, was exacerbated by the threat posed by Louis XIV and the question of the king's religion. Nor were these merely high-level political concerns; they reached down into the localities and nowhere more than in Somerset, which was an important pocket of nonconformity after 1662. Dissenters were numerous, powerful and vocal in both Bristol and the country districts. Quakers were especially active and well organized.[8] The Conventicle Act (1664) was flouted by open attendance at meetings in private houses and barns fitted out like churches.[9] After the Act expired in 1668 there was a two-year breathing space before it was re-enacted, which further increased dissenting activity.[10] The Dissenters could be counted upon to be especially sensitive to the issue of popery. For them the established church itself was suspect not only because of its structure, doctrines and ceremonies, but because it had systematically excluded them and opposed toleration.

Crosse, it appears, though himself a persecutor of Quakers,[11] did not address his attacks on Glanvill and the Royal Society merely to the church or the conforming community. There is clear evidence that one of the meetings in which he levelled his charges was attended by Quakers.[12] One of Glanvill's chief concerns, moreover, was that Crosse had carried the attack to the wider public: 'he told his tales to every country-farmer and acquainted every mechanick [artisan] with his mighty deeds and purposes: so that for a short time, there was no other subject handled on ale-benches and in coffee-houses in all his neighbourhood.'[13] It also upset Glanvill that he preached his message in Glanvill's own parish.[14] Crosse had taken the dispute outside the church and addressed farmers and artisans in streets and places of common resort. This offended Glanvill's sense of propriety and social status, as the following remark also indicates: 'But I perceive my adversary is for fighting in dirty lanes and among the coal pits [where he would find peasants and "mechanicks"], like the Irish among the bogs. Let him enjoy the empire of learning in those places.'[15] Glanvill makes it clear that he will aim instead at capturing clerical opinion.[16] Crosse's message then would have reached Dissenters and ordinary people, and charging atheism and popery as it did, it would have been bound to affect and stir them.

This too would have preyed on Glanvill's fears, given his own predicament which was also that of the established church in Somerset. In 1667, before the expiry of the Conventicle Act, Glanvill claimed that the populace had virtually abandoned the authorized services for attendance at conventicles held in barns which they 'make up . . . into the formalities of churches, with seats for the convenience of speaking and hearing.'[17] His report is confirmed by those of other Somerset clergy, especially Dr John Beale, who was Rector of Yeovil and, like Glanvill, an active Fellow of the Royal Society and proponent of the new philosophy.[18] More worrisome still, the local JPs failed to inforce the Act. Beale, for example, writing of Glanvill to Joseph Williamson in the office of the Secretary of State, says: 'he has long applied for a remedy to his neighbor justices, but without success, and instead of affording protection, they have been offensive and exposed him to the rabble.'[19] Some JPs even kept conventicles in their houses.[20] Among the Dissenters were also included some of the wealthiest Bristol merchants, and they, Beale claimed, were sheltered by connections at court, which meant that they could bribe those who might otherwise prosecute them for violating the Clarendon code.[21]

In Somerset the lines were drawn between orthodoxy and Dissent just as they had been at the outbreak of the Civil War. As Beale says: 'The gentry, as well as the ignorant and ill-affected, help to beget the jealousy of popery, and are apparently fallen back to 1642.'[22] The particular issue dividing the two parties was toleration. Writing of the Dissenters, Glanvill says: 'They say they shall have liberty of conscience and that the government, which cannot stand much longer, durst not do otherwise than permit them their freedom.'[23]

Dissenters would have listened to Crosse with receptive ears. The established church, as Beale indicated, was a popish symbol for them, and to the extent that Crosse identified Glanvill and the Royal Society with orthodoxy, his charge of popery would have stuck. Nor was Crosse alone in making the identification. Beale writes of other 'shallow zealots and stauncher Calvinians' who 'asperse the Royal Society' on the same Scholastic grounds as Crosse used.[24] Crosse then had a ready audience.

The question is why did Crosse, an Anglican priest, take the issue to the people and preach his message even among Dissenters. We must recall that he had been a Presbyterian member of the Westminster Assembly, who had obtained his living at Chew Magna in the late 1640s. Perhaps he had never ceased being a 'stauncher Calvinian' himself and resented Glanvill appearing on the scene with his new-fangled philosophical notions and his easy, latitudinarian Christianity.[25]

In any case, Glanvill and Beale's concern was more than intellectual: their defense of the Royal Society against the Aristotelianism of Crosse and his erstwhile supporter Stubbe was bound up with the social and religious issues facing them as Anglican clerics in Restoration Somerset. That defense was part of their attempt to cope with a local crisis of authority into which the new philosophy and the Royal Society had themselves been intruded as issues.

Glanvill and Crosse met and disputed in early 1667.[26] At that meeting Glanvill was tarred with the brush of atheism.[27] He replied in print in 1668, when his *Plus Ultra* was published. Crosse also tried to resort to the press but his manuscript was denied a license to be printed.[28] In the dispute between Glanvill and Crosse the charge of atheism had specific meaning defined by the situation.

Not only was Somerset a vital pocket of Dissent; there were also those whom the orthodox branded as atheists, probably because they attended no church at all or entertained such extreme heretical notions that they did not appear to be Christian. Beale has it that 'Bristol, Somerset, Gloucestershire and Devon [are] all far gone' towards atheism.[29] A churchwardens' presentment for one Bristol parish in 1669 reveals that there was at least one family in the parish who were recognized to be 'notorious separatists' and 'atheists.'[30] Finally, there were in Somerset and adjoining counties Hobbesian materialists, especially, if Glanvill is to be believed, among 'most of the looser gentry and the little pretenders to philosophy and wit,' who would generally have been regarded as atheists of sorts.[31]

Among these latter the dispute between Glanvill and Crosse was interpreted in a Hobbesian vein, as one grounded in clerical self-interest on Crosse's side and on Glanvill's in a stupid adherence to the Christian notion of a spiritual order populated by witches and demons. The conclusion reached by such interpreters also seems remarkably Hobbesian. The evidence for this Hobbesist reading of the dispute comes from a piece of doggerel which Anthony Wood claims was the work of 'wags at Oxon.'[32] There is indication in it, however, that it reflects local Somerset opinion.[33] In the poem Crosse is made to decry, in terms distinctly bawdy and libertine, the displacement of Aristotle by the mechanical philosophy whose representative he makes to be Descartes:

> You young men are contemptuous
> For you brave Aristotle scorn
> Strive to lift up Descartes horn
> For shame bent so presumptuous
>
> Can that Monsieur uphold our Church
> He'll doubtless leave her in the lurch
> And basely clap our Mother
> Which if fanatics chance to spy
> Behold the Scarlet Whore they'll cry
> And let alone the other[34]

Here is the argument that Stubbe also used: the abandonment of Aristotle for the new philosophy would weaken the intellectual foundations of the Anglican church and pave the way to popery. There is also the hint in the second stanza that the Cartesian philosophy itself is popish in tendency.

Next the verse has Crosse make the Hobbesian point that clerical power and property rest upon the clerical monopoly of Scholastic learning and the foolish reverence for it fostered by the clergy among the people. If so, the conclusion is obvious: Aristotle should not be challenged.

> Hath so much bacon so much cheese
> So much land and so much lease
> Been got by predicable
> And must you us and it expose
> To be contemn'd by churches foes
> And laughed at by the rabble.[35]

The suggestion is that the church's enemies take Glanvill's attack on traditional learning one step further to attack clerical wealth and privileges. Such an attack was no doubt grounded on the Hobbesian assumption that Scholastic philosophy was little more than a cover for clerical greed and pretension.[36] The passage also suggests that the conflict between old and new learning contributed to popular anticlericalism.

When Crosse has finished, Glanvill speaks and stands self-convicted of the intellectual arrogance of his new-fangled philosophical ideas, an amalgam of Neoplatonic and Epicurean views:

> When souls did preexist
> I saw the atoms frame the world
> And how the globuli were whirled

And caught them in my fist
Then I discern'd the regiment
Of daemons in the firmament
And all their gallant orders
Knew their intrigues, their ranks, their laws
Whose feet were cloven, who had claws
Who judges, who recorders.
This noble science I have shewn
In print which ne'er before was known[37]

But some very ordinary people, 'dirty coalmen,' take issue with Glanvill's notion of the spiritual order:

Although some dirty coalmen
Who ne'er conversed with the Devil
Have to my tenets been uncivil
And say they do but fool men.[38]

Once more the Hobbesian point is made: the spiritual order is a clerical invention designed to keep men superstitious and so subject to clerical authority. The verse ends on an Erastian note:

Now bless our king
His foes down fling
That he may long reign here-a
For these two philosophic elves
Like bloody Gibelines and Guelph
Divided have our Shire-a.[39]

The Erastian sentiment is probably inspired by Hobbes. The reference to Crosse and Glanvill as 'philosophic elves like Gibelines and Guelph' is almost certainly a take-off on the passage in *Leviathan* where Hobbes says: 'The ecclesiastics, when they are displeased with any civil state, make . . . elves, that is, superstitious, enchanted subjects, to pinch their prince, by preaching sedition.'[40]

Crosse managed to draw Stubbe into this controversy in the summer of 1669,[41] when he would have come to Bath for the season, having recently established a medical practice in Bath and the neighborhood. Despite the fact that he became Crosse's advocate, he was never merely his mouthpiece. From the beginning Stubbe regarded Crosse's Aristotelian views as outdated and had reservations on this score about linking up with him in the first place.[42] Nor did they ever succeed in burying their differences – by 31 January 1670, they had fallen out in public.[43] This should have been the first, salient clue to subsequent interpreters of Stubbe's involvement that he was not a conventional defender of Aristotle, Galen and the Scholastic tradition.

Once Stubbe decided to enter the fray, he barnstormed Somerset with his message for more than a year before he committed anything to print,[44] although the delay may have been due in part to the licensers.[45] Not only did Stubbe take up Crosse's antipapal rhetoric; he also adopted his methods, to which Glanvill is again eloquent witness. Of Stubbe's technique he writes:

He travelled up and down to tell his stories of the Royal Society and to vent his spite against that honourable assembly. He took care to inform every tapster of the danger of their designs and would scarce take his horse out of an hostler's hands, till he had first let him know how he had confuted the virtuosi. He set his . . . tongue at work in every coffee-house and drew the apron-men [artisans] about him, as ballad-singers do the rout in fairs and markets.[46]

Glanvill stresses that Stubbe, like Crosse, took his message to ordinary people, the poor, the not-so-poor and the illiterate in places of common resort, inns, coffee houses and alehouses. Among these audiences were probably the 'dirty coalmen' referred to in the contemporary doggerel on the dispute between Crosse, Stubbe and Glanvill. The latter, as we shall see, accused Stubbe of using the dispute as an avenue for purveying the very Hobbesian notions which the doggerel attributed to the 'coalmen.' No wonder Glanvill was worried about Stubbe and Crosse's tactic of preaching to ordinary people.

There had been an expansion of coffee houses and alehouses since the Reformation and especially during the seventeenth century, when new drinks like coffee and chocolate began to make their impact.[47] The church was worried by this expansion after the Restoration. Glanvill himself decried coffee houses in print in 1673 in *The Character of a Coffee-House*, in which he described such an establishment as 'a lay-conventicle' where 'each man seems a leveller, and ranks and files himself as he lists, without regard to degrees or order.'[48] Glanvill here put his finger on the more general fear of churchmen. These secular establishments were places where the authority of the church did not reach, and yet they were places to which people were inevitably drawn – to eat and drink, to play and revel, to talk, argue, exchange views.[49] Worse still, they attracted men of every status, even the poor, whom the alehouses especially catered for.[50] The fear then was that such places were indeed lay conventicles, levelling in tendency, where all men were priests and one man's opinion was as good as another's. In such an environment heresy, irreligion and sedition, Glanvill and others maintained, might and would flourish.[51] Hence Glanvill's concern that Stubbe preached his message in such places.

Not until 1670 and 1671 did Stubbe reach a wider audience through the printed word, to which we can now turn.[52] The principal objects of Stubbe's scorn were Glanvill's *Plus Ultra* and Thomas Sprat's *History of the Royal Society*. The latter work, though written by Sprat, was masterminded by

Wilkins, a Secretary of the Society at the time, and supervised by a committee of the Royal Society, and thus represented an official account of its origins, purposes and Baconian program.[53] These works by Sprat and Glanvill explored a common theme, the progress of knowledge and particularly the superiority of the new experimental philosophy of the Royal Society to the Aristotelian philosophy of the past. Glanvill and Sprat agreed that the experimental program of the Society represented a surer way to the discovery of useful and practical knowledge than the traditional method based upon the philosophy of Aristotle, adopted in the Middle Ages and only recently displaced by Bacon, Boyle, and the experimentalists of the Royal Society. Sprat went even further and argued that the experimental philosophy was not only basic to the pursuit of science but also provided the foundations for true religion, domestic peace and national wealth and power. It was a formula at once applicable to the reform of science and society.

The patient, cautious, industrious inquiry required in the conduct of experimental science would have a ripple effect in society at large. Most of all the pursuit of science would enhance national wealth and power. It would also create new industries and hence increase employment, thus reducing the number of the idle poor. To the extent that men were set to work, the threat of subversion from below would be overcome, and men would bury their differences in favor of the economic opportunities that science creates. Finally, the scientific temperament, modest, humble and skeptical, would produce good manners and foster true Protestant Christianity, to Sprat's mind identical with Anglicanism, because modesty and humility would cure sectarian enthusiasm and cautious doubt would prevent men from giving wholesale submission to papal authority. This was the natural religion of the Royal Society – liberal, tolerant, moderate, and visionary, millenarian even, in the sense that experimental science was seen as offering a path to Jerusalem.[54]

It is not clear, and may never be, what provoked Stubbe to enter the fray and deliver the most violent and publicized attack on the Royal Society that it has ever incurred. Stubbe himself claimed that he was stirred to write his attacks because Glanvill and Sprat had impugned 'the Aristotelian and Galenical way' of practicing medicine on which his own considerable reputation as a physician rested.[55] Whether we shall ever know why precisely Stubbe initiated his attacks, he soon found his stride, developed a standard body of arguments and wrote and published, with the help of London supporters, a half dozen or so tracts expounding his position.[56]

Stubbe's argument was pitched on two grounds. First, contrary to Glanvill, he claimed that Aristotelian natural philosophy, particularly when applied to medicine, far from being bankrupt, was superior to the so-called experimental philosophy of the Royal Society. Glanvill's deprecation of Aristotle, Stubbe claimed, was due to his ignorance of ancient philosophy rather than to the superiority of the moderns.[57] But he maintained that there was a more serious case to be made against Glanvill and Sprat, and this led him to his second argument.

Not only was the comparison between the ancients and the moderns invidious and hence harmful to medical science. To the extent that such a view took hold and displaced the traditional Scholastic curriculum in the schools and universities, it would prove the undoing of church and monarchy. Specifically, England would fall prey to the heretics, especially papists, Socinians and atheists, and Stubbe's worst and principal fear was that the papists would win out and popery, the embodiment of Antichrist, prevail.[58] Stubbe derived his argument for the potential triumph of popery from the strategy of the early seventeenth-century magician Tommaso Campanella, for the re-Catholicization of Protestant Europe, especially England and Holland. Campanella claimed that Catholicism might be reintroduced via natural philosophy which would divert men's attention from religion and allow the papists to intrude their faith among men thus preoccupied with science.[59]

Stubbe invoked Campanella's strategy because he claimed that Sprat's *History* would have the same effect, though in print at least he left open the question of whether or not this was Sprat's intention. Sprat argued in *The History* that the Royal Society should accept to membership men of all religious communions, including Catholics, because it was not interested in what divided men, but in scientific collaboration which in the long run in any case would lead them to bury their differences and live together in peace and prosperity.[60] In reply to Sprat's argument Stubbe writes:

what benefit and advantage popery may derive from this, that our nobility and gentry, our divines and laity, laying aside all memory of the French and Irish massacre, and Marian persecutions, the gunpowder treason, the firing of London, and forgetting all animosities and apprehensions of future dangers, converse freely with and write obligingly to them [i.e., Catholics], testify a great esteem of them, and from the disuse of all harsh but too true censures, come at length to lay aside all rancor . . . ; I say, how great benefit popery may draw hence, I cannot well comprehend.[61]

Stubbe was claiming that in effect, if not intentionally, Sprat's *History* represented Campanella's scheme revived: 'how would Campanella have clapped his hands for joy to see this happy establishment [the Royal Society] which he so long ago projected in order to the converting of England, Holland, and other heretical countries?' Stubbe asked rhetorically.[62]

The danger posed by the experimental philosophy of the Society was not limited to science and medicine. Knowledge and learning, Stubbe and Sprat agreed, played a vital role in determining the character and fate of religion and polity, and Sprat's formulas, according to Stubbe, would undermine both in favor of popery. The natural religion of the Royal Society must not be allowed to prevail. The traditional Aristotelian curriculum must be preserved in the face of it because, Stubbe argued, Scholastic philosophy not only provided the best medical knowledge; it also protected church and state against their enemies, papists, atheists and Socinians. To quote Stubbe: 'the politics of Aristotle suit admirably with our monarchy . . . The ethics there [of Aristotle] are generous, and subservient to religion, and civil prudence, and all manner of virtue: the logic and metaphysics [of Aristotle] are . . . entwisted with the established religion, and . . . requisite to the support of it against Papists and Socinians.'[63] Stubbe then presented himself as being opposed to Sprat and Glanvill's reading of the mission of the Royal Society because they would subvert church and monarchy; he also presented himself as being equally committed to the philosophy of Aristotle for the support it gave to medicine, established religion and government.

On this basis Stubbe has been uniformly interpreted by scholars as a conservative defender of the status quo in science, learning and religion. Herschel Baker in an influential book published in 1947 and R. F. Jones in his classic study, *Ancients and Moderns*, are chiefly responsible for inventing this interpretation. Baker describes Stubbe as 'that irascible and unlovely conservative . . . seeking to check the tide of science and "progress".'[64] Jones for his part speaks of Stubbe's 'conservative spirit, with its genuine fear of change.'[65]

I intend in the remainder of this chapter to challenge this interpretation by offering a new reading of the evidence, a reading which, instead of making Stubbe a conservative, renders him into precisely the opposite – a philosophical and religious radical – and sees a consistency between this stage in his career and his earlier polemical involvement, both before 1660 and most recently in the Greatrakes controversy.

In the midst of that furore Stubbe produced a tract, *The Miraculous Conformist*, defending the authenticity of Greatrakes's cures. One detects the remnants of Stubbe's pre-Restoration radicalism and republicanism in his argument in the tract that the power to heal is inherent in nature, hence accessible to men like Greatrakes and not limited to Christ, the Apostles or the king. How then does one square Stubbe the heterodox critic of divine-right monarchy in 1666 with Stubbe the defender of church and state against the likes of Sprat and Glanvill three years later? There are two possibilities. Either Stubbe changed his mind between 1666 and 1669 or his defense of church and state in 1669 is not what it appears and has been interpreted to be. There is no evidence for the first supposition – that he changed his mind. But there is considerable evidence for the second, and this entails reading his tracts against Sprat and Glanvill more closely than before and then examining Glanvill's response to them.

When this closer reading is performed, a picture emerges that throws considerable doubt on the standard interpretation of Stubbe's attacks because it is revealed that, although he defends church and monarchy, his view of both is so far from the accepted one that it would give more conventional apologists little or no comfort. Certainly if measured by the yardstick of his own time, he is a long way from the conservatism that Baker and Jones impute to him. Let us then take that yardstick and hold it up to Stubbe's views, as these are revealed in the tracts on the Royal Society.

Writing in 1670 about why he undertook his attacks, he says:

I had . . . powerful inducements . . . ; and those are the exigencies of the English monarchy, whereunto . . . it is the prudence of every particular person to contribute all he can to the support of it, against all such intendments as may . . . introduce popery on the one side . . . and against all anarchical projects or democratical contrivances, whereof a debauched and ungenerous nation is not capable.[66]

Clearly he has discarded his republican commitments of the 1650s, and equally clearly he sees popery to be a real threat, as many people did, by 1670. Stubbe now looks to the restored Protestant monarchy to provide a defense against both popery and democracy. But he pitches his argument on the secular grounds of prudence rather than the religious grounds of duty and devotion to a king who rules by divine right. This latter was the official and conservative view at the time, the view preached from Restoration pulpits not to be upset until the events of 1688–9, whereas Stubbe's prudentialism would have sounded suspiciously Hobbesian to a sensitive Restoration ear.[67] Hobbes's works had put forward in bold form a de facto theory of sovereignty which held that men subject themselves to their rulers not for religious reasons but out of prudent self-regard.[68] Fortunately, there is contemporary confirmation of this Hobbesian reading of Stubbe's meaning. Glanvill detected Stubbe's prudentialism and attacked him for the rejection implicit in it of the religious argument for obedience.[69] Stubbe's prudentialism may also have been partly what Glanvill had in mind when he associated Stubbe's views with Hobbes.[70]

Stubbe says other things about monarchy, which Glanvill does not pick up, that would have given equal offense to official and pious opinion. He claims that Aristotle's politics 'suit admirably with our monarchy' because they are opposed to 'seignioral and absolute' rule.[71] This may be an oblique reference to the idea of mixed monarchy, a constitution in which sovereignty resided in the king, the Lords and the Commons – in other words, in parliament, understood as consisting of three coordinate estates, rather than in the king alone. This idea was current during the civil war years and the 1650s, but was proscribed by the court after 1660, re-emerged during the Exclusion crisis as a Whig doctrine, and was singled out for condemnation during the royalist reaction following the defeat of

Exclusion.[72] Stubbe's acceptance of parliamentary sovereignty, if this was his view, would also explain why he rejected 'paternal right' and 'primogeniture' as grounds for 'sovereignty.'[73] His position in 1671 is distinctly anti-Filmerian and what would a decade later be called Whig. At the time his rejection of the idea that sovereignty lies in hereditary kingship would also have raised the specter of Hobbes.

After the publication of his principal attack on Sprat's *History, A Censure upon Certain Passages contained in the History of the Royal Society*, he is accused of having libelled the king.[74] What is it in the *Censure* that provoked that response? One cannot be certain, but there is a section which must have raised more than a few eyebrows. Stubbe accuses Sprat of justifying absolute monarchy or despotism[75] and goes on to state his own view of government, which gives every subject the right to submit the commands of his earthly rulers to the scrutiny of his conscience in order to determine whether or not those commands violate the will of God.[76] What Stubbe in fact does is to rehearse sixteenth-century resistance theory deriving from Calvin and elaborated by his, chiefly Huguenot, interpreters. I know of only one other printed apology for this theory so early in the Restoration.[77] It was not an apology calculated to please the authorities in 1671, and yet it is slipped into a tract ostensibly written to defend the Restoration settlement. Either Stubbe did not know what he was doing or he knew all too well and was attempting to cover his tracks by saying one thing and meaning another or by saying contradictory things at the same time in such a way as to mask subversive meanings by professions of allegiance, in a word, by resorting to subterfuge. Whether Stubbe knew what he was doing or not, his brief apology for resistance theory – and much else – does not fit the standard account delivered by Baker and Jones.

One Fellow of the Royal Society in particular, Edward Chamberlayne, came in for Stubbe's censure. Chamberlayne had recently argued that because England was so rich in agriculture, the yeomanry became prosperous without effort and hence lazy and disrespectful of 'nobility, gentry, and clergy.'[78] Chamberlayne's argument in this regard reflected a more generalized conservative opinion put forward during the Restoration that, contrary to more recent views, there could be such a thing as a 'surfeit of peace and plenty,' a surfeit because prosperity beyond a point would spoil the lower orders, making them restive, discontented with their legitimate rulers and ready for insurrection.[79] Chamberlayne proposed to solve this problem by increasing taxes, which would 'necessitate the common people to be industrious in their callings, and so to mind their own, as not to disturb the state and church affairs.'[80] Other Fellows of the Royal Society, including Boyle, expressed similar views.[81] Stubbe would have none of this: it is not, he says (*pace* Chamberlayne), 'the interest of our monarchy that all the commonalty be kept poor and in a complaining condition,' a statement in agreement with his mildly levelling views expressed in *An Account of the Rise and Progress of Mahometanism.*[82] There is more than a trace of identification with the little men in Stubbe's cryptic message. Thus he also defends tradesmen against a scheme put forward by the Royal Society to supervise the granting of patents.[83] He sees this project as the first step towards its regulation of trades and its control over university preferments, finally ending in the suppression of intellectual and commercial freedom, another mark of popery. He asks tradesmen to consider the consequences and looks to parliament as the proper protector of the liberties threatened by the Society. He has great confidence that parliament will take up his cause, as elsewhere he says, 'when I bring the case [against the Royal Society] before the Commons, I am sure I shall here be powerfully abetted, and the Society will have the worse.'[84] These are perhaps further indications that he held to the view, heretical during the Restoration,[85] that parliament was sovereign and not the king.

The attack on the patents scheme and the widely held conservative view enunciated by Chamberlayne represent an assault on an idea central to the message of Sprat's *History*: that the Royal Society welcomes the participation of all grades and constituents of society (save servants and the indigent), including farmers and merchants as well as Chamberlayne's 'nobility, gentry, and clergy' and that in the Society these groups will work together, pooling their interests and talents, to solve England's problems and lead the country to peace and prosperity for everyone who makes a contribution. It was a mighty vision of national unity and Stubbe was contradicting it. The Society might call for unity of interest and national purpose. But if Chamberlayne's attitude towards the yeomanry, his scheme for taxing them, and the patents proposal are any indication, the national interest was so defined by the Society that 'the nobility, gentry, and clergy' stood to gain at the expense of tradesmen and small farmers ('the yeomanry'). The dispute between Stubbe and the Royal Society has suddenly been transmuted into politics, and Stubbe (contrary to what Jones and Baker might have thought, had they noticed) was not on the conservative side.

Rather he was taking the side of small farmers and tradesmen against the Royal Society. It is interesting that these are exactly the groups to whom he made his appeal against Glanvill and Sprat in Bristol and rural Somerset. Could it be that there was a political message contained in those attacks? The fact that he saw parliament, at least in his printed attacks, as the defender of popular liberties against the Society strengthens that possibility. Beale's view of the relation of the mission of the Royal Society to society at large is also interesting in this connection. At the time Beale argued in a series of letters to the Society that one principal means of achieving the Society's goals was through agricultural improvement. As he says, 'one manor well improved, may be truly better worth than the same and two more such that are at the common tenants usual mercy.'[86] As the disparaging reference to 'common tenants' indicates, agricultural improvement in Beale's mind was synonymous with enclosure of which he says: 'All our helps in agriculture will hardly equal this design, either for improvements or plenty, for increase of the people or of provision. How to devise this and to avoid insurrections is the main point, which I conceive to be easily feasible, as anon I will offer.'[87] The problem with enclosure, as Beale indicates, was always the tenants and copyholders. But so carried away is he with the benefits that his concern for them is limited to the question of 'how . . . to avoid insurrections.' Out of such stuff local politics could be made, and it is possible that Stubbe, in Beale's own shire, was doing so. This possibility is somewhat strengthened by the fact that 'insurrections' against enclosure were not uncommon in Somerset before and after 1660. These anti-enclosure riots were staged, and led, by rural artisans who were among the people to whom Glanvill claimed Stubbe was making his appeal.[88] Could it also be that in Stubbe's attacks on the Royal Society we have an early example of a 'court–country' split? The Society chartered and patronized by the king would represent 'the court,' and Stubbe's defense of small farmers and tradesmen, together with his appeal to parliament as the defender of popular liberties, would represent 'the country' opposition. This is plausibly, if not conclusively, the case, strengthened by Stubbe's role as a propagandist for the 'country' opposition during the mid-1670s, to be explored in chapter 7.

Stubbe's heterodoxy manifests itself in his religious views as well as his political ones. True to say, he does argue that orthodox Anglican doctrine is so bound up with Aristotelian logic and metaphysics that any departure from the latter in the direction of experimental philosophy and what he calls 'mechanical education' would jeopardize the established church.[89] In particular such a departure would weaken the church's ability to defend itself against attack from papists, Socinians and atheists because the church would lack the clergy skilled in the Scholastic mode of disputation needed to put up a good fight.[90] But his argument is curiously left-handed. While claiming that religious education should be founded upon Aristotelian philosophy, he does so because such 'instruction would represent those ceremonies and habits [of the church] as decent, orderly and rational which would otherwise seem uncouth and phantastical.'[91] In other words, the bare bones of established church doctrine might not be palatable – 'would otherwise seem uncouth and phantastical' – without a mantle of Aristotelian metaphysics thrown over them – not the message one would expect to get from a defender of the orthodox faith. Nor is this all the evidence that gives the lie to Stubbe's supposed orthodoxy.

In his *Censure* of Sprat's *History* Stubbe claims that Sprat's view of religion unwittingly supports the ancient Arian heresy which denies Christ's divinity and hence the Trinity and which in its modern form is known as Socinianism. Sprat has argued against the linkage between Aristotelian philosophy and Christian theology by saying: 'Religion ought not to be the subject of disputations: It should not stand in need of any devices of reason: . . . nothing else is necessary but a bare promulgation [of Christian doctrine], a common apprehension, and sense enough to understand the grammatical meaning of ordinary words.'[92] Stubbe seizes upon this passage and maintains that the upshot of Sprat's argument, were it to take effect, would be for Christianity to become purely Scriptural, which would be a victory for Socinianism, that Sprat's *History*, in other words, by insisting that religion be severed from metaphysics and allowed to rest on 'the grammatical meaning of ordinary words,' as found in the Bible, would give encouragement to the Socinians.

Stubbe claims to be defending the established church from Arians and Socinians as well as papists by preserving Aristotle from the depredations of Sprat and Glanvill. But there is an implicit assumption in his suggestion that Sprat's insistence upon a Scriptural religion based not upon Aristotelian philosophy but rather 'the grammatical meaning of ordinary words' in the Bible would hand religion over to the Socinians. The assumption is that the Bible does not support the weight of Aristotle imposed upon it, that on its own it is an Arian document, that in effect the doctrines of Christ's divinity and the Trinity (not to say any others) are not Biblical but Aristotelian, that orthodox religion is unscriptural and true (Arian) Christianity is heretical in orthodox terms. These of course are the points that Stubbe made in his *Account of the Rise and Progress of Mahometanism*, written at approximately the same time as his attacks on the Royal Society. Once more Stubbe is pretending to argue for orthodoxy but is in fact insinuating something – this time the identification of Scriptural religion with Socinianism – which would leave orthodoxy aghast. Listen to the subterfuge in Stubbe's own words:

It is but too apparent that those in our days who join with the Arians in decrying new words and such as are not in Scripture, who think that Christianity ought not to be confined to any methodical creeds or articles . . . ; 'tis manifest that they look with indifference on the things signified by those words and forms; 'tis manifest that they overthrow the constitutions of the Church of England, whose *Articles* make use of those significant terms, transmitted from the Fathers to our Schools; and subvert the basis of our religion, as it is represented in our laws.[93]

It is the repeated use of the phrase ''tis manifest' that gives Stubbe away. Manifest to whom, the orthodox might well ask? Manifest to me, Stubbe would reply, because he comes to the issue already convinced of something no orthodox Christian would ever admit, namely, that the 'ordinary words' of the Bible do not support such doctrines as Christ's divinity and the Trinity, that on its own terms divested of the metaphysical superstructure raised upon it to sanction such doctrines, the Bible is an Arian document.

The point is driven home in what Stubbe next says. He quotes Sprat on 'The grounds whereon the Church of England proceeds . . . : and they are no other but the rights of the civil power, the imitation of the first uncorrupt churches, and the Scriptures expounded by reason.'[94] Stubbe's comment follows: 'This expression is dangerous as it is worded because the Socinians may derive advantage from it and the orthodox may think and find themselves injured (especially in these times, when the Socinians multiply upon us) by it amongst the unwary.'[95] Ostensibly opposed to Socinianism, he is spinning out the Socinian implications embedded in Sprat's position, and of course those implications represent an exact summary of his own clandestine views reported by Coxe to Boyle and put forward in the manuscript *Account of Mahometanism* – Erastian Independency, toleration enforced by the civil sovereign and a doctrinal minimum, natural religion, 'the Scriptures expounded by reason.' One means still available for publicizing those views and getting them into print was to represent them as 'dangerous,' while making it clear that they were, nonetheless, in 'imitation of the first uncorrupt churches.' Better still was for Stubbe to find such 'dangerous' views, deriving from unimpeachable origins ('the first uncorrupt churches'), expressed in the semi-official *History of the Royal Society* and, naughty though it was, to acknowledge *The History* as the source. Stubbe was truly having it both ways – embarrassing the Society and its historians and at the same time advertising his own 'dangerous' views under the cover of pretended orthodoxy.

Nor was this the only evidence indicating that Stubbe was himself an Arian. In 1666, when he produced *The Miraculous Conformist*, arguing against the king's monopoly of the so-called royal touch and against the Christly and Apostolic monopoly of power to perform Biblical miracles, he had been accused of some form of Arianism. Not only was he consistent in his views but in his methods of expression. He had invented the cryptic utterance in *The Miraculous Conformist*; in the tracts against Sprat and Glanvill he perfected pretense and subterfuge. Those tracts were not a departure from, but a further development of, his radical ideas and the technique for publicizing them under difficult conditions. He was still a radical polemicist, but he had also become a master of deceit.

A question immediately arises: if Stubbe thought that Aristotelian philosophy supported false theological doctrine, why would he go to such lengths to defend Aristotle as a servant of the church? Again the clue is provided by one of his polemical tracts against Sprat and Glanvill entitled *The Plus Ultra Reduced to a Non Plus*. There he says that the primitive church divided into two factions,

Arians and Catholicks: that the Arians were Aristotelians is to me as evident as that Mahomet taking the advantage of that faction and of the brutal lives and ignorance of the Catholicks depending upon the Patriarch of Constantinople did advance the sect of Christians called Mahometans; and his successors the caliphs did wholly employ themselves to improve the doctrines of Aristotle and the Peripatetics. So that Aristotelianism, Arianism, and Mahometanism issued out of the same parts of the world, viz. Alexandria, and the adjacent countries.[96]

Little enough might be made of this rather incidental comment in which Aristotle, Arianism and Islam are thrown together in a bewildering intellectual hotch-potch. Little might be made of it, that is, were it not for Stubbe's *Account of the Rise and Progress of Mahometanism*. That treatise can be made to throw considerable light on the curious nature of his commitment to Aristotle and the question of his Arianism.

In his treatise Stubbe traces the origins of Islam to the Arianism of Hellenistic Alexandria. This Arian Christianity, Stubbe argues, was true primitive Christianity.[97] So Stubbe is claiming something that would make the hair of the pious stand on end, that the pure Christianity survives, if at all, in contemporary Islam.

What then of orthodox Christianity, the religion asserting Christ's divinity and the Trinity, where did that come from – or, as Stubbe might ask disingenuously, where did Christianity go wrong? It was corrupted from two sources – first an inundation of pagan converts and second the emperor Constantine. The converts, being pagan, needed to be convinced by arguments familiar to their heathen heads, and so in order to accommodate them Jesus was said to be divine and the Trinity was invented – all with help from Platonism and a corruption of Aristotle.[98] Thus, as we have seen, Stubbe can argue in Arian fashion that orthodox Christianity is false to the extent that it departs from Scripture in the direction of a debased Aristotelianism. Constantine and some of his successors did their part too in leading Christianity astray: they made the church rich and powerful by allowing it to enforce uniformity and to persecute schismatics.[99] Worst of all, the Catholic clergy claimed independent spiritual authority and justified it by resort to the notion of an Apostolic succession which was supposed to allow divine authority to be communicated to successive generations of clergy. Again this communication of spiritual power rested upon a Platonic and Aristotelian metaphysic of the spirit which was both unscriptural and fraudulent.[100] Almost certainly Stubbe's understanding in this regard derived from Hobbes and specifically the fourth part of *Leviathan*, where he argued that the clerical claim to spiritual power is a pretense rooted in Scholastic philosophy.[101] In this regard Stubbe's Restoration Arianism was connected to his earlier quasi-Hobbesian Erastian Independency – and the linkage was firmer than this.

By contrast to the unscriptural and ignorant orthodox Christians or Catholics, as Stubbe calls them, primitive, Scriptural Christianity survives and flourishes first in Alexandria and adjacent parts, and then, because Mohammed takes it up, it thrives wherever Islam spreads.[102] Such

Christianity is at once Arian and properly Aristotelian.[103] The Arian faith consists of a simple creed based upon belief in one God and in his justice in dispensing rewards and penalties in the afterlife exactly appropriate to one's conduct on earth.[104] The religion is free of abstruse notions like Christ's divinity and the Trinity that must be shored up by a false and weighty metaphysic.[105] Beyond this doctrinal minimum one is free to worship and think as one chooses. There is no separate clerical caste claiming independent spiritual authority, again justified by a false metaphysic. To the extent that there is a leader of the church he is identical with the civil sovereign – a Hobbesian touch.[106] This freedom from abstruse doctrine, clerical pretension and false metaphysic means that science and learning can thrive, all under the aegis of Aristotle and his commentators.[107] Here is the true Aristotelianism, to which Stubbe subscribes, as distinct from the debased version of the Catholics.

This view of the primitive church is what causes Stubbe to accuse Sprat of being a bad historian, ignorant in particular of early church history.[108] As Sprat sees it in *The History of the Royal Society*, echoing the standard Anglican view,[109] the primitive church was bogged down in controversy and heresy until Constantine came along: 'and so at last by the help of many general councils, got them [the heresies] extinguished (if I may say they were extinguished, seeing in this age wherein we live, we have seen most of them unhappily revived).'[110] Sprat also takes an entirely negative, monolithic and unhistorical view of Aristotelianism: it is not only unhelpful in the study of nature; it is and always has been unhelpful to religion. 'How small assistance it brings, may be seen in those points, in which its empire seems most to be placed, in God's decrees, his im-materiality, his eternity and the holy mystery of the Trinity: in all which are brought into a more learned darkness by it.'[111] This view of Aristotle fitted in with Sprat's anti-Scholasticism. His historical schema saw good Constantinian Christianity being restored after centuries of Scholastic darkness by the twin forces of the Renaissance revival of learning and the Protestant Reformation.[112] From hence sprang science. This schema was of course a Protestant humanist commonplace.[113] In a parting thrust at the Aristotelians, Sprat says of the Muslim Arabs (who were followers of Aristotle) that they have been 'almost always perversely unlearned.'[114]

Stubbe's historical schema of the primitive church could not have been in sharper contrast to Sprat's view. According to Stubbe, Constantine did not save the primitive church from error but paved the way for its further corruption by granting wealth and privilege to the clergy. They in turn grew intolerant and misinterpreted Aristotle to bolster their position, inventing a separate spiritual order and making themselves its sole earthly representatives and guardians. All of this ran counter to primitive Christianity in which there was no clergy and men were free, beyond a doctrinal minimum, to worship and to think as they pleased. The so-called heresies that Sprat deplores thus become in Stubbe's hands signs of the vitality of the primitive church and of the intellectual freedom associated with it. True, Constantine 'got them extinguished,' but with that the rot set in. Moreover, the so-called divine mysteries, like the Trinity – 'the spiritual and supernatural part of Christianity,' as Sprat calls them[115] – were unknown in the primitive church before Constantine. So Sprat is wrong when he says that Aristotle did not serve those mysteries: he was corrupted in order to serve them. Finally, Sprat is simply unaware of the survival of primitive Christianity first at Alexandria and later under Islam. If he had been, he would have discovered both that primitive Christianity was Arian and libertarian and that as such it went hand in hand for centuries with true Aristotelian science and learning, in contrast to the centuries-long ignorance and intolerance of the Catholics, propped up by their false version of Aristotle.

So we are ready to answer our question: Stubbe can defend Aristotle at such lengths as he does, despite the identification of a certain kind of Aristotelianism with false theological doctrine, because the Aristotelianism to which he is ultimately committed is not that of the Catholics but is rather the one identified in his mind with Arian belief. As such it chimes with his view of true Christianity – first a civil religion with the secular authority at its head enforcing a doctrinal minimum, a set of essential beliefs, and allowing toleration beyond that and, second, a civil religion in which there would be no separate clergy claiming their own exclusive spiritual authority to preach, teach, discipline and punish.

One might well ask now why did Stubbe take such pains to defend the established church supported by what he regarded as the debased Aristotelianism of the Catholics which so appalled him? The answer of course lies in the context. During the Restoration he was not free openly to publish his Arian views; they had to be consigned to a clandestine manuscript, *An Account of the Rise and Progress of Mahometanism*, quietly circulated among friends.[116] In his public advocacy he had to be cautious, hence his resort to subterfuge. There is another, more interesting, reason for his willingness to defend conventional (corrupted) Aristotelianism: the Catholic threat. That was real too, at least in men's minds and paranoid fantasies, and he may have been quite sincere when he argued that Englishmen would have to dispute with Roman Catholics on the latter's terms, which meant knowing the Catholic Aristotle, if they were to stand up to the popish threat.[117] If Stubbe believed in anything, it was the force of circumstance. His *Account of the Rise and Progress of Mahometanism*, as we have seen, is a secularized history of the church in which religion, instead of depending upon divine interventions for its success or failure, grows out of circumstances and a genius in men, like Mohammed, for inventing a

religion that takes account of circumstances.[118] If Stubbe saw religious
history in these terms, then he no doubt applied the same understanding to
the religious situation in Restoration England. He was a de facto Anglican
just as he was a de facto royalist. Circumstances dictated religious belief, at
least in its outward profession, just as they did political obligation. Against
the Catholic threat he can thus argue for preserving a Catholic
Aristotelianism. Should that threat pass, then perhaps men can be brought
around to the true, Arian Aristotle. This is the view, it seems to me, implicit
in his sustained attacks on Glanvill and Sprat.

There is evidence in Glanvill's response to support this conjecture and
indeed the whole interpretation of the attacks offered here. With the
assistance of Beale and Henry Oldenburg, Secretary of the Royal Society,
Glanvill produced an important tract in 1671, replying to Stubbe's
attack.[119] Stubbe had argued that 'prudence' dictates that 'every . . .
person . . . contribute all he can to the support' of the restored monarchy
because it protects England against 'popery on the one side' and on the
other 'against all anarchical projects or democratic contrivances, whereof a
debauched and ungenerous nation is not capable.'[120] The reasoning seems
innocent enough on its surface, but Glanvill detects subversive undertones:

'Tis prudence to endeavour the support of the monarchy now as things are, not
duty. The want of virtue and generosity makes the nation incapable of democracy
for the present: but when 'tis reclaimed from its debauches and grown generous (as
it was in the time of M. Stubbe's former patrons) then democracy will be the only
proper government. Monarchy may serve for a debauched and ungenerous nation,
but democracy is the government of the virtuous and generous.[121]

Glanvill, no doubt with help from Beale and Oldenburg, has an uncanny
knack for exposing Stubbe's insidious irony and duplicity. As he says in
reference to the passage of his just quoted: 'thus Stubbe cunningly
recommends himself to his democratical friends even when he is pretending
friendship to monarchy.'[122]

Stubbe supports his ostensible opposition to 'democratic contrivances'
with a marginal note in which he cites certain late Renaissance Italian
treatises addressing the issue of political corruption that renders republican
virtue impossible. He cites the statement of the case by Virgilio Malvezzi,
Trajano Boccalini and Paolo Paruta. Stubbe owned the works of these
thinkers, all Tacitists, and used them to explain the failure of the good old
cause and the restoration of monarchy.[123] He ends his list of citations with a
Latin text:

Ut verissime dixerit Cosimus Medices Cardinali Salviato, in tanta opum inaequalitate,
morumque corruptione, Florentinam Repub. non esse amplius libertatis capacem,
quae optari potius quam sperari debeat.[124]

[As Cosimo Medici truly said to Cardinal Salviato, during so much inconstancy and corruption of manners, the Florentine Republic being no longer capable of liberty, it is to be wished for rather than expected.]

Glanvill will not let Stubbe get away with this either and says of the Latin text, 'there is a quotation in the margin of the same page to assure his kindness to democracy, even when 'twas prudent to make a shew for monarchy.'[125] Glanvill is nothing if not dogged in his exposure of Stubbe's artifice. Thus he freely translates and interprets the Latin text as follows:

You see, O ye Patriots of the Good Old Cause, M. Stubbe is constant to you; Democracy is the only Liberty, 'tis the government to be desired, though little to be hoped for in such a corruption of manners: your slave doth but jest with monarchy and shew his prudence in flattering it a little, till a good occasion shall serve for him to return again to you, his patrons and benefactors.[126]

We shall see more clearly in the next chapter what Stubbe's political views were, as adumbrated in his attack on the Royal Society. We shall then be able to gauge the accuracy of Glanvill's 'exposure' and see that, although he seriously overstated his case against Stubbe on this score, Stubbe did retain a very qualified commitment to his pre-Restoration political ideals.
    Glanvill has not finished exposing Stubbe and turns next to what he has to say about the Royal Society:

he falls upon His Majesty's institution [the Royal Society] out of a pretended concern for monarchy and religion. The king, he fancies, hath erected a Society that will undermine monarchy; and those bishops and divines that are embodied in it are managing a design to overthrow religion: therefore M. Stubbe stands up on a mighty zeal and defends monarchy against the king and religion against the divines, no doubt with a purpose to do a mischief to both.[127]

Here again Glanvill has penetrated Stubbe's disguise. He goes on to say that Stubbe's *Legends No Histories*, the tract he is most concerned to answer, would have been more openly subversive than it is if it had not been for the London censors:

I was lately told by a Licenser, one of my Lord of London's Chaplains, that it was well for him that those things were blotted out for he assured me they were such as deserved the gaol and a pillory at least. For he impudently upbraided the king with the example of Queen Elizabeth in forbidding the king of France to build ships; jeered the illustrious Duke of York about his sea-engagements with the Dutch: and twitted His Majesty with the management of that [second Dutch] war.[128]

According to Glanvill, not only are Stubbe's attacks on the Royal Society subversive, he has never given up his seditious principles and has pursued a consistently subversive career since the Restoration. To prove his point he provides a précis of the heresy embedded in *The Miraculous Conformist*:

Christ Jesus and his Apostles appeal continually to their works, those miraculous ones they performed, as evidencing the divineness of their commission and the truth of their doctrines; and M. Stubbe tells us that all religions have had their real miracles; and so let them dispute or fight it out as they can, miracles must be tried by truth, not truth by miracles. . . . And when he hath taken away the testimony of the spirit in miracles, he knows well enough what will become of Christianity: This he endeavours here by many very odd suggestions. M. Greatarick did things miraculous, and these he performed by the temperament and composure of his body, so that healing miracles are the effects of the effluvia of a particular ferment, and so Christ Jesus shewed nothing of divinity in curing diseases by his touch. Yea, M. Greatarick is mated with him and the Apostles.[129]

Here Glanvill has caught Stubbe's subversive Galenical naturalism and goes on to subject other works by Stubbe to similar analysis.[130] He also exposes Stubbe's commitment to 'Mahometan Christianity,'[131] and associates this view with Stubbe's 'Hobbesism.'[132]

There is evidence, moreover, that Glanvill knew something more of Stubbe's commitment to 'Mahometan Christianity' than he had revealed in cryptic passages in his attacks on the Royal Society. In Glanvill's *Further Discovery*, one of his two published answers to Stubbe, he says of his antagonist: 'I am glad you have so good an opinion of St Paul, as to compare yourself with him. Pray how long hath the Apostle been so much in your favour?'[133] Stubbe in his *Account of the Rise and Progress of Mahometanism* associated St Paul with the corruption of primitive Christianity.[134] Thus, either Glanvill had seen something Stubbe had written to this effect, even perhaps a version of *An Account* itself, or Glanvill had otherwise learned of Stubbe's views in this respect. Whichever it was, he knew something more of Stubbe's 'Mahometan Christianity' than he had revealed in print.

Glanvill's reading of Stubbe's career provides further evidence for the interpretation set forth in this work and runs directly counter to the standard view developed and put forward by Baker, Jones and others.

Glanvill was well placed to know his enemy and hear his views on such topics as 'Mahometan Christianity'. He had observed him at close quarters in Bath and Oxford. In Bath Glanvill had supped at the same gentlemen's tables with Stubbe, overheard and engaged him in conversation. One Bath physician, Robert Peirce, had a house close to one of the baths, where the well-to-do could stay, eat and entertain. One gentleman, Sir James Long, kept a table in Peirce's house where guests came and talked 'freely.'[135] This Sir James is very probably the same 'Sir J.L.' at whose 'table' Stubbe and Glanvill met at least once.[136] In one of the latter's printed attacks on Stubbe he records the conversation that took place on that occasion:

M. Stubbe . . . give my leave to ask you a few questions. . . . Your great pretences are the interests of monarchy and religion . . . Can you call to mind who told me at Sir

J.L.'s table at Bath that being sick, he prepared himself for death with Lucretius . . . , and being asked, whether he had not the Bible to help prepare him, made a pish of it, and said that he had not seen a Bible in seven years before and that it was good for nothing but to make folks humorous?[137]

This was but one of several times in Bath and Oxford when Glanvill heard Stubbe say blasphemous and atheistical things. Glanvill goes on in the same vein, putting rhetorical questions to Stubbe:

Do you remember who talked of several hundred Gospels that were of old, and made those we have to owe their credit to chance, in a discourse to me and two others of Oxford? . . . Do you remember who affirmed to me in the presence of Sir E.H. and other gentlemen that there is no more reason to believe there is a God than to believe there is none; that he believed it because he could not help it; and could not help because he was carried by an unaccountable impulse; that the arguments to prove a deity, drawn from the wisdom, beauty, order and usefulness that is in the frame of the creation, signifie nothing because we cannot tell what is wisdom, beauty, or order?[138]

This last comment is particularly suggestive. Probably once more following Hobbes, Stubbe rejects the argument from design on the grounds that finite man cannot fathom the nature of the infinite.[139] To Glanvill, Sprat and the Royal Society this would be taken as a particularly sinister view. The Society posits a universe designed, like a mechanical clock, by God and claims that the experimental philosophy can unravel that design to show men God's hand at work in the world and human history. The messages are clear, the lessons easy. All is order, peace and harmony – or can be if men will commit themselves to the experimental science and natural religion of the Royal Society.[140] Such a natural religion assumes that a supernatural God acts in the material world either directly or through spiritual agents to make things run as they do. To Stubbe, the opponent of the traditional, Christian dualism of matter and spirit and the exponent of a thoroughly secularized church history, this is to set up a false metaphysic that pretends to instruct men in divine mysteries, God's inscrutable dealings with the world. This is, furthermore, to repeat the errors of the Catholic clergy under Constantine who established their authority at the expense of corrupting the primitive church in part by resort to false metaphysics. The argument from design in the hands of the Royal Society is an instrument of popery in the same sense. It claims to discover God's plan in nature and history; it rests on the assumption of the existence of a separate supernatural order and its operations in the world. For Sprat and Glanvill the new philosophy cultivated by the Royal Society represents the final stage of the Reformation and holds out the possibility of the triumph of Protestantism over popery. For Stubbe, on the other hand, the linking of that philosophy to conventional religion is a step backward, a regression towards popery, because it perpetuates the notion of a separate spiritual order and the existence of a clergy to preside over it, superstition and clerical power – indeed, superstition falsely legitimating clerical power.

Stubbe gave his attack on design argument a particularly insidious twist. A completely mechanically designed universe, he claimed, left no room for miracles and so provided another instance of the way by which the natural philosophy of the Royal Society led to irreligion. He tried, moreover, to enlist the support of Henry More for this view. More, the influential Cambridge Neoplatonist, had been a proponent of Descartes's philosophy during the 1640s. But over the next decade he became aware of what he regarded as the atheistic implications of the Cartesian dualism: spirit and matter were conceived of as being so separate that the material world could be explained in completely mechanical terms without resort to spiritual causes. According to More and his school, Cartesianism put the doctrine of divine providence at serious risk and hence endangered true religion. In response More and his fellow Cambridge Neoplatonist Ralph Cudworth developed the idea that there is in nature an intelligent spiritual principle, plastic nature or world soul that carries out God's ordinary providence.[141] Stubbe seized on this notion as a means of attacking the mechanical philosophy of the Royal Society.[142] Their mechanistic view tended to exclude the miraculous from the universe; More's plastic nature, on the other hand, saved miracles by providing a spiritual agency in nature for performing them. Stubbe of course did not point out that his own view of miracles, adumbrated clearly enough in *The Miraculous Conformist*, saw them as coming from nature itself rather than from a supernatural God: the spiritual inheres in the material. So what he was attempting to do was to appropriate More's plastic nature, just as he had earlier appropriated Willis's theory of disease, to his own Galenical and 'Hobbesian' notion of spirit in matter. No doubt this is why Boyle conducted an ongoing dialogue with More directed against his view of spirit in nature: Boyle saw the subversive implications embedded in it – implications which the likes of Stubbe were only too willing to draw out.[143] More for his part would have nothing to do with what he regarded as Stubbe's misappropriation of his own views and collaborated with Glanvill in answering Stubbe.[144] Like Glanvill, Beale and Oldenburg, More also seems to have seen through Stubbe's ploys, at least the one in which he figured. Of Stubbe's attempt to harness More's philosophy to his covert design, More remarked to Lady Conway: 'I think Dr Stubbe because he fancies me pious thinks I am a fool. When our Savior Christ bids us be as wise as serpents as well as innocent as doves.'[145]

From Stubbe's perspective the Royal Society promoted popery by two means, one of which he spelled out in print and the other he left to subterfuge and communicated clandestinely. Publicly he declared that the Society was following Campanella's strategy for subverting the Protestant Reformation and re-Catholicizing Europe. Cryptically, both in print and manuscript, he suggested that the natural religion of the Society conduced to popery in another, more subtle, way: to the extent that the Society subscribed to the traditional Christian mysteries and used the authority of its philosophy to support them, to that extent it shared in the superstitious faith of the Catholics and was popish in tendency.[146] The natural religion of the Society, in other words, was scarcely superior to the debased Aristotelianism of the Catholics with respect to dispelling false belief and discerning religious truth. Stubbe's strategy in this regard was in line with the widely held view that there was much in Anglicanism that was infected with popery.

The only remedy lay in a proper understanding of Aristotle, the historical Aristotle rather than the corrupt Catholic version. This proper understanding would support pure Christianity, which was an Arian civil religion shorn of 'uncouth and phantastical' doctrines, shorn too of a separate clergy claiming independent spiritual power.[147] The recovery of the true philosophy, the real Aristotle, would point the way to this true Arian faith.

From at least early 1666 and the publication of his cryptic attack on the royal touch and by implication Christ's divinity, Stubbe had engaged in pro-Arian polemic. Nor did his attacks on the Royal Society represent a retreat into orthodoxy. On the contrary, they, like his earlier tract, *The Miraculous Conformist*, could be read as masked statements of his Arian views. Such was the way the polemic had to be conducted in the 1660s, and Stubbe was an expert. He upheld Aristotle against the Royal Society and thus could claim to be defending England, church and monarchy, from popery. But for Stubbe popery had a double meaning (this was of course a seventeenth-century commonplace): popery was the Roman church itself, but it was also superstitious Christian or pseudo-Christian doctrine, which might infect any communion. To the extent that popery meant the latter, and could lead to the former, Stubbe's defense of Aristotle represented an attack on the established church because his Aristotle, the true Aristotle, was consonant with an Arian view of the Godhead. But this could not be made clear in print; it could, however, be read between the lines. So, by defending Aristotle, Stubbe could conceal his real convictions, while not being untrue to them, indeed − better than that for his purposes − he could feign orthodoxy, while insinuating heresy. It was not a cover-up but an attempt at cryptic utterance, less subterfuge than disguise.

Glanvill, as we have seen, was concerned that Stubbe was taking his message to the plain folk of Somerset, and there was good reason for that concern. First, Stubbe was effective; Glanvill is witness to that: 'Stubbe railed lately at Bristol against the R.S. Dr Sprat, & me; he hath made most of the common sort of that town believe that the Society is a company of atheists, papists dunces & utter enemies to all learning.'[148] There was, moreover, much in Stubbe's message that would have appealed to Dissenters. In Somerset they were particularly actively opposed to the local authorities in church and state, priests and JPs, between 1669 and 1671, when Stubbe 'travelled up and down' the shire 'to tell his stories of the Royal Society.'[149] The Conventicle Act had lapsed in 1668 and Dissent came more into the open than before. When the Act came into effect again in May 1670, it galvanized Dissenters in Somerset to united action. One man reported to Williamson, for instance, a few days after the Act took effect: 'The face of things here looks scurvily and the factions all unite and speak very hard words, which I think to be treason in parables.'[150] The Dissenters in this atmosphere would have been sensitive to Stubbe's charges of popery and irreligion directed against the Royal Society. They would have been even more sympathetic because Beale, who was a party to the dispute on Glanvill's side, was identified by Somerset Quakers as one of their leading clerical persecutors in the shire.[151] Clerical persecution was commonly seen by Dissenters committed to toleration as tantamount to popery. If Stubbe allowed his own pro-toleration and libertarian views to be known locally, he no doubt gained an even wider following. Certainly his views conformed neatly to those which the Bishop of Bristol, Gilbert Ironside, was in 1669 most intent on ferreting out. On his instructions the churchwardens in each parish were meant to determine answers to the following questions among others:

Have you any [in the parish] that affirm that the civil magistrate ought not to prescribe anything to ecclesiastical persons in or about the worship of God, but that their duty only is to protect and defend the said persons? Have you any in your parish that affirm that the Church of England, as now by law established, is not a true and Apostolic church, reproaching the same as Antichristian?[152]

Whether Stubbe preached such notions is not known. But he certainly held them in the form of his 'Mahometan Christianity.' Glanvill is witness, moreover, to the fact that he was given to saying heretical things in public, at least at gentlemen's tables. Glanvill also knew something of Stubbe's 'Mahometan Christianity.'[153] Finally, it is clear that he addressed Dissenters. At one meeting where he and Crosse held forth there was a 'moderator,' identified only as 'yong R. Speed.'[154] This was probably Richard Speed, mariner, a relation of Thomas Speed, the head of one of Bristol's leading Quaker families,[155]

In this connection it is interesting that Stubbe and his radical religious ideas were known to at least one Bristol Quaker leader, George Bishop. In *A Looking-Glass for the Times* (1668) Bishop acknowledged Stubbe's *Light Shining out of Darkness* as the source of many of his own Quaker ideals.[156] In that work Stubbe had compared the Quakers to the primitive Christians.[157] Bishop died in September 1668, almost a year before Stubbe began attacking

Sprat and Glanvill in Bristol, Bath and rural Somerset. But Bishop's tract, published in 1668, and conversations no doubt smoothed the way to Stubbe's reception among Bristol Friends, especially as Bishop's reputation was enormous.[158] It is also worth noting that certain aspects of Stubbe's 'Mahometan Christianity' would have resonated with Quaker ideals. Besides the anticlerical and tolerationist themes, which would have had a wide appeal among Dissenters, Stubbe's emphasis upon charity to the poor, 'levelling,' sobriety and moderation – perhaps even the antislavery – could be expected to appeal specifically to Quakers, if not to other Dissenters.[159] One wonders, though, what Quakers and others would have made of his advocacy of polygamy.

The logic for the connection between the issue of the Royal Society and the question of toleration was impeccable: it had only to be made. The Royal Society, according to Stubbe, was leading England down the road to popery. Its natural philosophy did not represent true Protestantism but rather Christianity wedded to superstition, false doctrine and priestly power. This much we know Stubbe said in Somerset, and it would have been cause enough for concern to Glanvill and Beale as both clerics and Fellows of the Royal Society. Did he go on publicly to argue on the basis of his 'Mahometan Christianity' for a church under the control of the civil authority, swept clean of clerical pretension and tolerating all believers consenting to an Arian doctrinal minimum – a church returned to Apostolic purity? We cannot say for certain that he did, but it seems highly likely. If not, it was at least implicit in what he said and published and, at that, just beneath the surface.

It is, therefore, highly plausible that Stubbe used his public attacks on the Royal Society as occasions for agitating for toleration among Somerset Dissenters, especially Quakers, among whom he was already known, and that in doing so he preached his ideal of 'Mahometan Christianity.'

If Somerset Dissenters listened receptively, Stubbe was also well received in quite different quarters – Restoration Oxford – and there by two groups. 'Wags at Oxon,' Wood says, penned the Hobbesist doggerel on the dispute between Crosse and Glanvill.[160] Beale may have had in mind the same people when he wrote to Evelyn that Stubbe's raillery 'is more to be entertained by the dregs of the multitude and the Oxonians, with high applause.'[161] Glanvill also claimed that Stubbe's attacks gratified the other wits and drolls who ridiculed the Royal Society, and Oxford seems to have had its share of these.[162] Ridicule of the Royal Society would run on into the 1680s, a major example being some of the plays of Thomas Shadwell, whom Beale would later compare to Hobbes and Stubbe.[163]

Stubbe also found support in other circles in Oxford. He dedicated his *Legends No Histories* 'To the two famous universities of this land, Oxford and Cambridge, the chancellors, vice-chancellors, heads of colleges and halls, professors, fellows, and students in the same.'[164] He makes his reasons for the dedication clear in what follows:

All that are sensible of those studies by which the morality, religion, and civil policy of this nation hath been carried on happily before these impertinents & innovators; and how this nation is declined and debauched from everything that is serious and sober now, are convinced of the justice of my complaints, and how necessary it was that somebody should attack them; but it is for you to determine of the validity of my charges and of those proofs with which I come to implead them.[165]

He sought to gain the approval of the universities for his defense of Aristotle against the depredations of Glanvill and Sprat. To the same end he dedicated another attack, *A Censure upon Certain Passages Contained in the History of the Royal Society*, published in 1670, to John Fell, Dean of Christ Church and Vice-Chancellor of the University of Oxford.[166] As bastions of Aristotelian learning the universities could be expected to be receptive. At Oxford in the summer of 1669, moreover, an attack on the Royal Society had been mounted by Robert South, Orator of the University, at the dedication of Christopher Wren's Sheldonian Theater, and it was rumored that Fell had instigated it.[167] No doubt Stubbe, close at hand in Warwick and Bath, took the measure of this attack within the University and calculated that he could win support there. Nor was he wrong. John Wallis, Oxford professor, leading Fellow of the Royal Society and watchdog over its fortunes, went to considerable trouble to confirm a rumor that Dr Thomas Pierce '(our President of Magdalen College here) had sent to Mr. Stubbe for his good service, a piece of plate: &, that it might be the more acceptable, by a gentleman of quality.'[168] Wallis added that he had heard other unconfirmed rumors of similar gifts from London and Oxford presented to Stubbe as rewards for his attacks.

The attack on the Royal Society from within the universities was made in terms very similar to Stubbe's. The universities were still bastions of Aristotelian learning.[169] Those who attacked the Society on behalf of the universities did so, like Stubbe himself, as defenders of a curriculum based upon traditional Scholastic teachings. Fell, Obadiah Walker, the Master of University College, Oxford, and Meric Casaubon, Prebendary of Canterbury and son of the great classical scholar Isaac, were all ardent Aristotelians dedicated to preserving the Scholastic curriculum from the dangers posed by the science of the Royal Society.[170] It is not that they were hostile to natural philosophy.[171] It is rather that they regarded the natural philosophy associated with the Royal Society as being inimical to the goals of sound university education, goals they thought best achieved by adherence to a traditional curriculum.

The fullest defense of the curriculum came from Casaubon, whose *A Letter . . . to Peter du Moulin* was published in Cambridge in 1669.

Casaubon's views were echoed by Fell and Walker.[172] To Casaubon the chief objective of learning was 'to be well satisfied of the truth of Christianity upon a rational account,' and the best means of achieving this objective was provided by university education as this had been established in Protestant Europe during the Reformation.[173] Unhappily this Protestant educational reform was now being threatened by the sects and by the new mechanical philosophy of Hobbes and Descartes. Both the sects and the mechanical philosophers had the same reductive effect upon learning. The sects put their trust in Scripture alone and 'the design of both [Descartes and Hobbes] is and hath been . . . that all other books and learning should be laid aside as needless but what came from him [sic] or was grounded upon his [sic] principles.' Descartes had said: 'Cogito, ergo sum.' Casaubon read this as signalling a dangerous reductivism, all the more so because 'in such request.' The mechanical philosophers and the sects were responsible for 'the decay of learning,' and the result would be that 'the truth, in point of religion and divine worship, . . . must suffer.'[174] The damage will be so great that 'it will be very indifferent unto most men which they embrace, the Bible . . . or the Alcoran.'[175]

To Casaubon, as to Fell and Walker, the knowledge that the mechanical philosophy provided was too narrow, too strictly utilitarian, to constitute an adequate educational foundation for Protestant Christianity. Stubbe in his attacks on the Royal Society took up this theme. He used it to reinforce his argument that the natural philosophy of the Society played into the hands of papists and atheists.[176] It deflected attention away from the important matters of morals, religion and government into a concern for toyish experiments. It trivialized knowledge and spread among the sons of the nobility and gentry an ideal of virtuosity rather than of solid virtue. As he said: 'we are degenerated from the school of Aristotle to that of Epicurus, from all moral gallantry and virtue, to a most impertinent and effeminate virtuosity.'[177] This message resonated with what the academic critics of the Royal Society were saying. In fact so close is Stubbe's argument to theirs that one suspects him of tailoring it to win their support, especially in the universities. Here is another example then of Stubbe's duplicity. He joined the defenders of the traditional Aristotelian curriculum in their attack on the natural philosophy and latitudinarian Christianity associated with the Royal Society. But this liaison between Stubbe and the likes of Fell and Casaubon was tactical, at least on his part if not on theirs, because there is no evidence that they shared or even knew about his Arian Christianity. For the moment, however, he could make common cause with them and use their own commitment to Aristotle to embarrass the Society without revealing his commitment to a much more radical understanding of both Aristotle and Christianity. To some extent he could play both ends against the middle: he could feign orthodoxy, while punching holes in the alliance

being forged between the new science of the Royal Society and latitudinarian Christianity, an alliance that Stubbe seems genuinely to have
believed would further corrupt Christian doctrine. As we have seen,
moreover, there may have been another purpose behind his deception:
traditional, Aristotelian learning might serve its turn, protecting the church
against worse dangers, until such time as the true Aristotelian and Arian
Christianity could be revived.

One can only conclude that Stubbe was willing to obtain at least tactical
support wherever he could find it – from traditional clerics at Oxford, rustic
Dissenters in Somerset, prosperous Quaker merchants in Bristol, 'the
common sort of that town,' and 'the dregs of the multitude' wherever.[178] Of
course the rhetoric of his attack made such disparate support possible. His
attack on popery and defense of traditional learning allowed him to cast a
wide net. The subversive meanings were kept implicit, to be insinuated
rather than stated openly, though in Bristol and rural Somerset he probably
went further than he did in print. In conversations with Glanvill and others
like Sir James Long at Bath we know he did. Perhaps this explains why
Glanvill and Beale, both clerics in Somerset, were so shrewd in *A Praefatory
Answer* at decoding Stubbe's messages. This same code would equally
explain why others, like those at Oxford, were taken in. The rhetoric of
Stubbe's attacks allowed men to find in them an apparent defense of state
and church and to be deceived thereby into overlooking the rest. Glanvill
even accused Stubbe of deliberately writing with that aim in mind:

I am persuaded that M. Stubbe intends no more in his present pretences for
monarchy than to jeer it and to try whether the friends of the government are such
pitiful ignoramus's as to be satisfied . . . If there be any he can content so, there is no
doubt but he will laugh with his democratical friends.[179]

If he could no longer attack the theocratic monarchy directly, he could at
least 'jeer it' by feigning loyalty, while insinuating heresy, thus deceiving
'the friends of the government.'

Through his attacks he maintained correspondence with his old patron
Boyle and seems to have kept on even enough terms with him,[180] though
Glanvill claims that Stubbe thought ill of Boyle's experimental work but
'will spare him because he hath obliged him.'[181] He also seems for obvious
reasons to have won or kept the support of powerful members of the Royal
College of Physicians, including Charles Scarborough and another old
patron of his, Sir Alexander Frasier.[182] Boyle apparently reported to Stubbe
that Charles II was displeased with his attacks, and on 18 May 1670 Stubbe
wrote a long letter to Arlington explaining himself in the matter, and
begging that his patronage and that of the crown should continue, and, as
we shall see, it did.

To Arlington in self-defense Stubbe drew a distinction between heresy and schism.[183] Heresy was the maintenance of unchristian tenets, while schism was separation from communion. The former was evil and deserved to be punished, but not the latter. Milton drew the same distinction in print three years later.[184] How does this distinction relate to Stubbe's attacks on the Royal Society? For Stubbe, I think, Catholics were true heretics and Dissenters were mere schismatics. In the controversy with the Society he attacked Catholicism and the preachments of Sprat and Glanvill, which smacked of it and tended to it. These were the true objects of his scorn. Schism or separate communion was acceptable, assuming that the separatists upheld true Christian doctrine. Indeed the existence of multiple communions side by side conformed to primitive practice; this was the model of the early church, than which nothing could be purer. Stubbe's distinction between heresy and schism in his letter to Arlington is, I think, to be taken as another covert reference to his Protestant tolerationism and the ideals of his 'Mahometan Christianity.' He did not spell this out to Arlington, who was after all a Catholic of sorts; instead he left the distinction between heretics and schismatics largely unexplained.

In all Stubbe seems not to have suffered for his attacks. Subversive they may have been, but that was by implication. In Stubbe's printed attacks after all it was the Royal Society itself that was made to seem subversive and others, some in high places, went along with that. But this support from traditional clerics does not gainsay the argument that Stubbe was a radical, albeit operating in disguise.[185]

Stubbe was the first to point out in anything like a sustained and systematic way that the new philosophy, as institutionalized in the Society and proclaimed by its spokesmen, had been harnessed to a particular religious and political outlook that served the interests of the established church and state and meant that some groups would benefit from science and others would not or would benefit less. Not only of course did Stubbe say this was so; he also challenged this position because he was committed to another view of science that was based upon heretical and radical values and would serve other groups and interests. He took his views, moreover, to the country, to people in coffee houses and on ale-benches, 'the dregs of the multitude,' as Beale called them. 'He made his learning mercenary and cheap to every ordinary and ignorant fellow,'[186] and this was particularly alarming to his enemies.

The dialogue between 'Stubbians' and members of the Royal Society would be revived during the 1680s and continue in new forms after the Revolution of 1688–9.[187] Stubbe's own writings, though not his printed attacks on the Royal Society, would play a part in that continuing confrontation.

6

Court pen: 'ancient prudence' and royal policy

> So although the designs both at home and abroad for altering our religion, would be very little formidable to a well-founded government; yet in such an one as we have now, it will require all our care to obviate such machinations. Another reason is the little zeal that is left amongst the ordinary Protestants; which zeal uses to be a great instrument of preserving the religion established; as it was here in Queen Elizabeth's time.
>
> Henry Neville, *Plato Redivivus*

Up to 1672 we have watched Stubbe continue to write and publish views subversive of church and crown. In his contest with the Royal Society he saw parliament as the protector of popular liberty against the incursions of court-sponsored institutions like the Society. He even looked to parliament as the potential champion of his assault on the Society. So, if anything, his opinions might be identified with the country opposition to the court. Certainly the king, we know, was displeased with Stubbe because of his attacks on the Society, and we find Stubbe, in the midst of those attacks, writing a letter to Lord Arlington, begging him not to terminate his patronage because of them. In that letter Stubbe presents himself as the loyal defender of church and crown against their real enemy, namely, the Royal Society. Here was yet another case of Stubbe's rhetorical duplicity because it was in fact the other way around. It is true that Stubbe did support one conception of church and crown, but it was not one that was likely to give clergy and king much heart. He managed to pull off his deceit because he kept his real views concealed behind professions of loyalty, while confiding them to a manuscript circulated among friends and presumably like-minded men.

None of this quite prepares us for the fact that in 1672 and 1673 Stubbe is employed by the court to write propaganda supporting government policy. We know from the letter to Arlington, dated 18 May 1670, that Stubbe even then was patronized by the court. But what he did in the pay of the crown is not clear before the spring of 1672. In the months following, he wrote two books defending the two major decisions made by the court that year – the Declaration of Indulgence and the declaration of war against the Dutch – decisions taken on 15 and 27 March respectively. These two books established Stubbe as the chief government propagandist for the third Anglo-Dutch War and the assertion of royal prerogative in granting an indulgence to Dissenters and Catholics. In 1672 Stubbe had become a government hack. Does this mean that he had abandoned the critical stance to church and monarchy – cryptic though it was – that he adopted after the Restoration? To do justice to the question we must first examine what he now said in favor of the monarchy in light of the context in which he said it, and so we turn now to Stubbe in 1672, wielding for just that year a strictly court pen.

The royal Indulgence and the Dutch War both began in mid-March 1672. The Dutch government had propagandized its cause in England long before that and continued to do so afterwards, aiming especially to alienate Dissenting opinion from the government and the war effort.[1] Even during the war itself the Dutch printed and sent into England by surreptitious means pamphlets arguing their case against the English government, and steps were taken to intercept this clandestine traffic making its way from Harwich to London.[2] The Dutch did have a case. After all, the English were at war, thanks in large measure to the Treaty of Dover (1670), on the side of absolutist and Catholic France against Protestant and republican Holland, a fact guaranteed to be especially alarming to Dissenters. The official Dutch reply to the English declaration of war came in April 1672, and took the form of an anonymous pamphlet entitled *Considerations upon the Present State of Affairs of the United Netherlands*. The only English translation of this work to turn up so far exists in manuscript among the papers of Joseph Williamson, Arlington's secretary at the time. It is endorsed by Williamson as being 'out of a Dutch print April 1672,'[3] which leaves open the question of whether this manuscript was a translated copy of the edition in Dutch, which we know to exist, or a copy of an English language edition of which there is no record. But it was this tract that Stubbe was commissioned to answer. So in all probability, whether there was an English language edition or not, its contents became known in England. Stubbe duly performed his task, producing *A Justification of the Present War against the United Netherlands*, licensed and published in mid-June 1672. That summer he wrote another propaganda piece for the government on behalf of the war effort and the royal Indulgence. The job was completed before the murder of the De Witts (20 August 1672), and *A Further Justification of the Present War against the United Netherlands* was published early in 1673.[4] Stubbe was not the only propagandist for the war, but he was the most prolific.[5]

In the process of writing the second book Stubbe worked closely with government officials, especially Sir Joseph Williamson, to whom he explained the plan of the book (perhaps to obtain government approval) and who in turn answered his request for book illustrations.[6] Williamson had made a collection of anti-British Dutch propaganda, including medals and engravings, and Stubbe drew from it to show how the Dutch government misrepresented the English.[7] Stubbe was not only the most prolific government propagandist, but his work was intended to come as close as possible to presenting the government's case exactly as it wished. The art of official, printed and illustrated propaganda was new in England; Henry Stubbe was among its first practitioners.

Both of Stubbe's books deal with the same theme, as their titles suggest. They were intended to complement each other, the first being an answer to the Dutch *Consideratien* and the second, *A Further Justification*, intended by Stubbe to present the government's case to the English people, just as *Consideratien* had presented its case to the Dutch, in order to whip up public sentiment for the war and the royal Indulgence.[8] Stubbe's second book is more valuable, and longer, than the first, because, besides answering the Dutch, it attempts to convince Englishmen, especially Dissenters, of the merit of government policy. As such it is aggressively assertive in making its claims and to that extent very revealing.

In *A Further Justification* Stubbe addresses himself to two groups in particular within the political nation, Dissenters and churchmen, especially the Anglican clergy. The problem of the Dissenters in relation to the war was especially urgent, as we have seen, and Dutch propaganda was aimed particularly at them. The Dutch image of the English, Stubbe says, is that of a nation in which 'the King, City, and Country' are divided into 'so many different and irreconcilable interests.'[9] This image of weakness has caused the Dutch to commit those acts particularly at sea which have forced the king to declare war.[10] This image also allows the Dutch to think that because they are a Protestant republic they will find support for their war effort among English Dissenters who suffer under the restored monarchy and yearn for a return to the days of Cromwell.[11]

Stubbe urges the Dissenters and the potentially disaffected to prove the Dutch wrong on this score and sets about to provide arguments for supporting the king in the war against the Dutch. Stubbe argues his case on essentially three grounds. First, Cromwell himself had made war on the Dutch and for the same reasons as the king, namely, maritime trade and naval forces to maintain it.[12] Second, for Dissenters to support the Dutch republic (Stubbe completed the book before the De Witts were assassinated) against their own monarchy is for them seriously to misapprehend political reality, and that in two ways. First such misapprehension comes from a false attribution of guilt. If England under the restored king is not as strong as it might be, the king and court are not to blame, despite widespread Dissenting opinion to the contrary.

The seeming maladministration of the state, the decay of trade, the dispiritedness of the English, the arrogance of the Dutch, have really no other foundation . . . than ourselves: those failures and miscarriages which we charge upon the King, Council and Court, we are principally the occasion of, if not absolutely guilty.[13]

Stubbe goes on to explain why the nation and not the court is responsible:

We decline our duties; we break ourselves into schisms; we retain and multiply implacable animosities amongst ourselves; we defame our superiors, censure and derogate from every action of theirs; we by unnecessary and unseasonable contests retard the proceedings of Parliament, and exasperate the two Houses, and each Member thereof, so that they fall into factions and parties: we in the City and Country do repine, complain and rage till the whole voisinage prove malcontent.[14]

There is a second misapprehension. The aim of those Dissenters who support the Dutch against their own king would be ultimately to weaken the English government and then, presumably with Dutch help, to destroy the monarchy and set up a republic. Stubbe is at pains to show how vain such a project would be. According to Stubbe, it would be close to impossible to create a republic and make it work. He makes it clear that this is not merely his opinion but also that of former English dissidents who in the previous decade had actually collaborated with Jan de Witt until they became disillusioned by Dutch duplicity, whence they went over to their own king.[15] Of this group Stubbe writes:

experience had showed them how difficult a thing it was to overthrow an hereditary monarchy, and how impossible it was for a nation inured to monarchy, divided in interests, discriminated by degrees of honor, debauched in its manners, irreconcilable in its factions, to retain its liberty, though fortune upon any accident, or attempt, should dissolve its present monarchy: . . . nor could they upon the most diligent enquiries, propose to themselves any person in whose hands they could wish the conduct of affairs entrusted rather than those of His Majesty; of whose prudence, generosity and clemency they had seen so great and unexpected trials.[16]

Not only would these internal, domestic considerations tell against the success of a republican 'revolution';[17] certain external considerations would work in the same direction. The Dutch hated the English, especially the Dissenters, who would be the only ones to undertake such a risky project – they hated them because they represented the same interest that defeated the Netherlands in the first Anglo-Dutch War during the time of the Commonwealth in the early 1650s. So if a Dissenting republic were set up, even initially with Dutch aid, they would soon turn around and oppose it. 'All new governments,' moreover, 'are weak,' and this fact would be further incentive to the Dutch, and by itself sufficient incentive to the 'potent' French to endeavour 'to possess themselves of all, or some' of the fledgling English republic.[18]

There is little or no hope then for a lasting republican revolution, and would-be Dissenting insurrectionists should wake up, following the example of their more enlightened co-religionists, and rally round the king. The rewards will follow, as indeed they already have. Stubbe says that the king granted the Indulgence in part because of the behavior of some of the Dissenters themselves. The Dutch government under Jan de Witt had plotted with English dissidents to instigate civil war in England.[19] The Dutch strategy was 'the ruin' of the monarchy, 'a total alteration in the government,' and 'a final subjection' of England to Holland.[20] But those dissidents 'did not prove to be such absolute fanatics as the great minister of the States of Holland did imagine they would.'[21] Instead, they eventually renounced their republicanism, 'prepossessed their friends against the artifices of the Dutch, and fixed them unto the service of His Majesty and of their native country.'[22] The king was particularly impressed because these Dissenters, 'those generous fanatics,' as Stubbe describes them, went over to the monarchy, despite 'the rigor of the penal laws' and 'the ready assistance of John de Wit.' Charles II himself came to see that on the subject of the Dissenters he, like them on the subject of monarchy, had been misled. After the Restoration the orthodox clergy had 'boldly represented' the Dissenters as driven to rebellion by 'malice against the Church' and 'covetousness to regain the ecclesiastical and crown lands,' and it was patently not so.[23] The 'deportment' of the 'generous fanatics,' moreover, gave the lie to the church's argument, firmly entrenched in the public mind since Venner's rebellion in 1661, of a 'necessary connexion . . . betwixt schisme, heresie and rebellion' which underlay the policy of persecution.[24] When the king recognized that the clerical arguments no longer held, he was led to granting the Indulgence.[25]

Finally, in his appeal to Dissenters Stubbe answers the objection of those who ask why England has declared war in alliance with Catholic France on Protestant Holland. He draws a casuistical distinction between legitimate provocation to war and the possible consequences of it, saying that it is quite proper to take such actions in response to sufficient provocation by the Dutch, despite the fact that the war may lead to consequences harmful to Protestantism.[26] In the course of developing this argument he makes another significant distinction:

If we consult the law of nature, the respect we owe to our lives, liberties and estates requires . . . that we preserve ourselves, and if we cannot effect thus much by our domestic forces, we must recur to foreign assistance: the law of grace doth not destroy that of nature; hence it is that the obligation doth still remain, and that those alliances made by kings with infidels and heretics, when profitable or necessary, may not justly be blamed.[27]

Stubbe's new-found royalism is being pitched upon the same Hobbesian prudentialism that Glanvill had detected and attacked a year or so before.

Stubbe set himself, and was no doubt instructed, to appeal to the church as well as the Dissenters – and for good reason. The Declaration of Indulgence, licensing and tolerating Dissenting ministers and meetings as it did, flew in the face of the 'exclusive and intolerant church settlement' extracted after 1660 by church and parliament, especially the Commons, from a reluctant, tolerationist court, led by the king.[28] The Indulgence represented the king's reassertion of his prerogative against this settlement, and the reaction of the Anglican hierarchy was immediate and hostile. They regarded it as producing the worst crisis that the church faced since the Restoration.[29] If the Declaration was meant to pacify Dissenters during the prosecution of the war, as Arlington indicated was the case, it produced exactly the reverse effect on the orthodox clergy.[30]

So Stubbe had his work cut out for him. The general line of argument he adopted has been overlooked by all previous commentators. But this neglect should not reflect on the interest and importance of what he said. When taken together with his appeal to Dissenters, his attempt to justify the Declaration to the church sheds light on the nature of his recently acquired royalism and commitment to the court and throws new light on an old question, the meaning of the Indulgence itself, particularly to men like the first Earl of Shaftesbury (at the time of its proclamation still Lord Ashley), who took active part in devising it and later defended it wholeheartedly.[31] So Stubbe's argument at this point will repay close examination.

From the point of view of the Anglican clergy Stubbe's most telling argument may have been the economic one. Indulgence, he claimed, would increase trade and hence national wealth because it would keep English Dissenters from emigrating for reasons of conscience and equally because it would persuade Dissenters elsewhere to resettle in England in order to escape persecution.[32] Lying behind this argument was the assumption that Dissenters were heavily represented among merchants and shippers. It was a widely held view at the time. Others like Shaftesbury himself and Roger Coke, a member of the Green Ribbon Club during the Exclusion crisis, shared it and argued with Stubbe that because of the commercial importance of Dissent, toleration was all the more vital.[33] Stubbe went on, like Coke, to deploy this economic argument in such a way as to appeal to the orthodox clergy: upon trade hang land values, including the income of the church deriving from rents.[34] On this point Stubbe concluded: 'It is now no less requisite unto the clergy that the nation be puissant, populous and rich than it is unto the laity, and the common interest of all is that the monarchy be supported and rents duly paid: but these ends could not be accomplished without the Declaration.'[35]

Though this economic argument may have been particularly attractive to the clergy, Stubbe devoted far more space to other factors in his attempt to appeal to the established church. In particular he maintained at length that the Indulgence, far from undermining true Protestant Christianity, would provide the best possible foundation for it, better by far than persecution. The terms in which Stubbe argued his case on this score are especially revealing. He argued historically. Ever since the Reformation in England, Anglican apologists had justified the claim that their church was true and Apostolic by asserting that it was modelled upon purest

Christianity, the primitive church as it existed during the first four centuries of the Christian era. They then went on to contrast this primitive church, reborn in the English Reformation, to the Roman Catholic church, which departed from ancient purity beginning in the fifth century and thereafter grew more and more corrupt.[36] Stubbe adopted this standard Anglican historical perspective and turned it to his own account in arguing his case for the Indulgence.[37] His strategy was twofold.

First, he claimed that in granting the Indulgence, Charles II had matched the example set by emperor Constantine: once more the English church had lived up to the primitive practice of the first four centuries and proven itself to be truly Apostolic.[38] Like the great Constantine, Charles II had embarked upon a course of toleration, and Stubbe went on to list the specific parallels between the policies of the two rulers: '1. The general declaration for liberty of conscience. 2. The prohibition of private and clandestine conventicles. 3. The reservation of all public revenues and endowments unto the Catholics [the orthodox conformists]. 4. The declaration of his special favour unto, and designs of promoting of the orthodox Catholics [the Anglicans]'.[39]

Not only were the policies very similar but so was the principal motive for adopting them: a shrewd political calculation that the Dissenters (or heretics and schismatics as they were known in the ancient world) were too numerous and too strong to be persecuted.

It is one thing to encounter an heresy or schism in the beginning, and another when it has made a large progress. Then it may be suppressed easily, and the public receives little prejudice by the banishment or ruin of a few. But in the latter case. it is to be considered that the kingdom receives a great and irreparable damage in its strength, in its trade, in its unanimity, if multitudes come to be exiled or impoverished.[40]

This is economic argument again, which Stubbe said was telling for both Charles II and Constantine.[41] In England at least, an important political result would also follow from toleration: 'To conclude: the sectaries are irreconcileably divided one against the other: the penal laws unite their interest against the government: but indulgence continues them disjoined. Which is the most secure course?'[42] So the Apostolic practice of Charles II rested upon the (Hobbesian) political calculation that he shared with his ancient mentor, Constantine the Great! Stubbe, it seems, may have been up to his old tricks, saying unorthodox things in very orthodox guise, despite the fact that he was employed now as a servant of the court. As we shall see in a moment, there is more evidence to support this view.

Second, Stubbe claimed that in certain respects Charles's Indulgence surpassed Constantine's in wisdom and prudence.[43] Here Stubbe was at pains to show how the Indulgence protected the orthodox, while neverthe-less granting toleration to those who were not. It is on this score that

Charles improved upon Constantine. Thus Stubbe stressed those clauses in the Declaration itself which specified that the doctrine and revenue of the established church were not to be affected by the Indulgence, that all clerical offices must go to conformists, and that nonconformist ministers must be licensed to preach and their meetings must be open and not secret.[44]

According to Stubbe, Constantine's policy represented 'ancient prudence,' while Charles's represented 'modern prudence,' and the 'modern' at least revived and in some respects improved upon the 'ancient.' Here is another entirely neglected chapter in the debate between the ancients and moderns that went on so doggedly in seventeenth- and early eighteenth-century England.[45] What is especially interesting in Stubbe's handling of the theme is his vocabulary: ancient and modern prudence were the terms Harrington used to describe the two social and political systems in conflict, as he saw it, in his own day. According to Harrington, of course, modern prudence or hereditary, feudal monarchy was giving way, almost inevitably it seemed to him, to a new situation out of which would come a republic of citizen-soldiers, which would amount to a rebirth of ancient prudence.[46] Obviously Stubbe borrowed his vocabulary from Harrington but not his meaning. Stubbe used these Harringtonian terms to refer to religion rather than, as Harrington did, to politics, to the church, not the state. In Stubbe's usage, moreover, there were no republican associations attaching to 'ancient prudence,' as there were for Harrington. Both ancient and modern prudence, as far as Stubbe was concerned, referred to the religious policies of monarchs, not republics. The two kinds of prudence, furthermore, were not mutually incompatible, as they were for Harrington. Rather for Stubbe they amounted to much the same thing, the 'modern' being nothing more than a revival and refinement of the 'ancient.' The question then is why would Stubbe use the terms at all, why did he adopt a Harrington vocabulary for ends that were clearly not those of Harrington himself?

At this point one would do well to consider a phenomenon which Professor J. G. A. Pocock has discovered and described, the phenomenon of neo-Harringtonianism, coming into existence in the 1670s, the decade in which Stubbe wrote his defense of the Indulgence. In the late 1650s Harrington himself had advocated the creation of a republic through the revival of ancient prudence which would produce the necessary *political* balance between the Many and the Few to preserve the republican constitution and make it impossible for the Many to swamp the Few, which would lead to chaos or, alternatively, for the Few to lord it over the Many, which would see the restoration of monarchy. The king of course was restored, but when Shaftesbury and others organized a 'country' opposition in the 1670s, out of which would later emerge the Whig party, they (and presumably Shaftesbury in particular) adapted the Harringtonian vocabulary to fit the new situation of monarchical restoration. This revision is what Professor Pocock has labelled neo-Harringtonianism.[47] The object was no longer the creation of a republic but the reform of monarchy to prevent the growth of popery and arbitrary government. The means to this end would no longer be the maintenance of a simple two-way Harringtonian balance between the Few and the Many but a three-way balance between the One (the king), the Few (the House of Lords) and the Many (the House of Commons). The Lords would play an especially crucial role, preserving the balance between the king and the Commons by preventing the corruption of the Commons by royal patronage.[48] Playing this role, the Lords would be the representatives and purveyors of ancient prudence, preventing the court, the representative of modern prudence, from destroying the constitution and establishing monarchical absolutism.

We are now better placed to examine Stubbe's usage of the Harringtonian vocabulary of balance and corruption, ancient and modern prudence, and the curious deviousness of his argument. Professor Pocock traces the earliest revival and adaptation of Harringtonian language in the Restoration to the anonymous tract entitled *A Letter from a Person of Quality to His Friend in the Country*, and attributed to Shaftesbury. The tract was published in the heat of the debate over the Test Act of 1675, two years after Shaftesbury had left the court to lead the 'country' opposition. Stubbe's *Further Justification of the Present War with the Netherlands* (1673) suggests that there was an earlier revision of Harringtonian language and analysis, associated with the court, while Shaftesbury was a leading minister, which was thus probably also associated with him. Shaftesbury was closely identified with the Indulgence, which Stubbe was defending in his book. Stubbe stressed the economic argument for toleration, an argument which Shaftesbury had already used and made much of. Stubbe, moreover, followed Shaftesbury into opposition politics in late 1673 and became a pamphleteer in Shaftesbury's cause. There are indications too in these later pamphlets that he accepted Shaftesbury's 'neo-Harringtonian' view of a balanced constitution. So Stubbe's use in 1673 of Harringtonian language strongly suggests that there was already a revival of Harringtonian ideas at court and associated with Shaftesbury, two years before the 'country' neo-Harringtonianism appeared which Professor Pocock has explored.

The link between Shaftesbury and Stubbe, moreover, is stronger than this. Before the Indulgence was declared, John Locke, Shaftesbury's physician and confidant, supplied him with legal arguments supporting the royal supremacy in religious matters and by implication giving the king power to grant a toleration on his own authority.[49] After the Indulgence was proclaimed, Stubbe also drew up papers supporting the king's power in this matter.[50] More to the point, in *A Letter to a Person of Quality*, published in 1675, after Shaftesbury had gone into opposition, he maintained, assuming that he is the author, that the king possessed the power, deriving from his ecclesiastical supremacy, to proclaim an indulgence.[51] Indeed, he argued that the Indulgence had been, and presumably still would be, desirable in both church and state.[52] Shaftesbury argued that, on the other hand, the Test Act was an attempt on the part of bishops and churchmen to destroy the balance in church and state and to bring in 'perfect tyranny.'[53] It would require the Lords and the Commons to swear 'not to endeavour at any time the alteration of the government either in church or state.'[54] This would destroy the balance in two ways. First, such an oath would in effect overthrow the royal supremacy in church affairs. The bishops 'design to have the government of the church sworn to as unalterable, and so tacitly owned to be of divine right, . . . though inconsistent with the Oath of Supremacy.'[55] Second, the oath would reduce parliaments to doing nothing more than 'giving money.' This would be particularly unfortunate: 'For what was the business of parliaments but the alteration . . . of the government, either in church or state?'[56] This destruction of parliamentary independence was also part of the bishops' plan: 'Then in requital to the Crown, they declare the government absolute and arbitrary, and allow monarchy as well as episcopacy to be *jure divino*, and not be bounded or limited by human laws.'[57] According to Shaftesbury, in 1675, the role of the church, and especially the bishops, was as crucial to maintaining the constitutional balance as were the parts played by the king, Lords and Commons. The Test promoted by bishops and churchmen would destroy this balance, while Shaftesbury suggested that the royal Indulgence would still preserve it.

It would seem then that Harrington's vocabulary was being applied to understanding and criticizing relations between church and state as well as to interpreting relations among king, the Lords and the Commons, and that crucial to this application of Harrington's language to interpreting the religious situation was the royal Indulgence.[58] Here is the ideological link between Stubbe's defense of the Indulgence for a court in which Shaftesbury played a leading role and Shaftesbury's condemnation of the Test two year later for a 'country' opposition (which Stubbe had joined), of which he had become the leader.

This analysis is confirmed by other evidence. In 1672, Stubbe turned from his defense of the war to write and publish anonymously a short, satirical tract entitled *Rosemary & Bayes*, answering both Samuel Parker's *Discourse of Ecclesiastical Polity* (1670) and *The Rehearsal Transpros'd* (1672), which was of course Marvell's skillful reply to Parker. What makes Stubbe's tract especially interesting is that once more he analyzed the question of the religious settlement, the issue exercising both Parker and Marvell,[59] in terms which represented a drastic revision of Harringtonianism. Both men were wrong, Stubbe said, because both calumniated and would punish those clergy whom they saw as the enemy – for Parker this meant the Dissenters; for Marvell, the Anglicans. According to Stubbe, such hostile sentiments, spread abroad and drummed into the heads of the people, would undermine government.

It is most evident that the civil peace (if not our common salvation) doth depend upon a reverence unto the clergy: and they are in times of peace the great support of government: whilst their dictates are regarded awfully, the people are tractable, and the prince may with ease manage them: but when they become contemptible and are inodiated, then standing armies, arbitrary power, and such like contrivances must secure the peace and monarchy.[60]

Here again the clergy were crucial to maintaining a delicate constitutional balance – this time between king and subjects. Should the clergy be incapacitated by their critics from playing their role, the result would be those tyrannical 'contrivances' which both the Harringtonian and neo-Harringtonian analysis predicted would appear whenever the balance failed.[61] For Stubbe there was also a solution which recalled and revised Harrington: rather than the partisan ecclesiastical politics of Marvell, Parker and their ilk, which would destroy popular respect for the clergy and popular faith in priestcraft and thence the civil peace, 'it is more safe and consonant to old prudence to exact that the priests of all religions should be equally reverenced than that none should be.'[62] Stubbe's 'old prudence' was a clear reference to Harrington's 'ancient prudence,' brought up to date in its Restoration form. Stubbe thus turned his satire of Marvell and Parker into another defense of Charles II's Indulgence based upon a revision of Harrington: 'the priests of all religions should be equally reverenced.' Harrington of course would have shuddered at the thought, given his commitment to a priestless religion, the worship of the republic. Was *Rosemary & Bayes* also court-sponsored, like Stubbe's justifications of the war? If not, it was certainly consistent with their argument.

In the satire, moreover, Stubbe pushed his case further, perhaps because the satirical form lent a certain degree of safe license to the author. He rested his unwonted defense of the clergy upon entirely secular grounds: 'the civil peace (if not our common salvation) doth depend upon a reverence' of them.[63] Civil peace, not spiritual salvation, was the issue. The latter was almost beside the point and certainly subordinate to the former. Here was Harrington's civil religion, a worship of the republic, drastically revised. No wonder Stubbe chose to publish his satire anonymously! The departure from Harrington, despite the Harringtonian language, was of course immense. Not only was the civil religion now the religion of monarchy, worship being directed to serving the civil peace under a king rather than a republic or republican ideas. But, equally dramatic, the religious policy was designed to promote reverence for the clergy so as to keep the people quiet and make it easy for the king to manage them.[64] This was so far a departure from Harrington as to constitute a subversion. Here Stubbe was closer to Machiavelli's *Prince* than to Harrington's *Oceana*. He pointed out that Parker's *Discourse* was widely attacked as following Hobbes's *Leviathan*.[65] The same charge might be made against Stubbe's satire on Parker: the exploitation of religious feelings for political ends could be drawn from Hobbes as well as Machiavelli. Indeed Stubbe's civil religion could be interpreted as another example of that blend of Hobbes and Harrington so characteristic of his thinking before 1660. Despite the Hobbesian and Machiavellian understanding of the manipulative political uses of religion to produce among the people 'a reverence unto the clergy,' so central to Stubbe's new civil religion, this religion was designed not to erect tyranny but to prevent it,[66] and this is what makes Stubbe's thinking unmistakably an important early Restoration revision, drastic though it is, of Harrington.[67]

In this respect Stubbe may have been engaged in *Rosemary & Bayes* in a kind of Harringtonian dialogue with Marvell's *Rehearsal Transpros'd*. According to Christopher Hill, Marvell in that work adopted the Harringtonian view that change is inevitable and suggested that such change would lead to the destruction of monarchy in favor of republican government.[68] But Stubbe's point was that either tyranny or anarchy was the more likely consequence of the course Marvell was pursuing, which would make the eventual establishment of some acceptable form of constitution even less likely. For Stubbe the prior settlement of religion on proper (civil) foundations would increase the chances for the right sort of constitutional change.

Nor was this civil religion all that Stubbe's ancient prudence dictated. Stubbe, as we have seen, was as concerned to justify the trade war with Holland as he was the Indulgence, and so he also fitted the war into his scheme of Charles II's revival of ancient prudence. Was this an argument peculiarly designed to win over Dissenting Restoration Harringtonians to the war effort? I think very probably it was, though who these readers or followers of Harrington were after 1660 no one knows. The focus of his argument was that command of the sea, vague as this remained in Stubbe's treatment, was pivotal to England's prosperity and internal political stability, and so the defeat of a naval challenger like Holland was essential. He supported his argument by an appeal to past authority, recent and remote. In the recent past, the example of Elizabeth's policy was instructive. She made the navy powerful and used it to establish dominion of the sea. Her great teacher in this matter, and the architect of her naval policy, was John Dee, who showed her

that the only way for the Queen to be secure of her subjects at home and against her enemies abroad, without infusing any jealousies into the heads of her subjects, was to increase her fleets to such a constant strength that she might instill terror into her neighbors, . . . increase navigation and commerce (which would improve the riches of her cities and towns and raise the rents of land whereby her subjects would be better able to assist her), and augment the Crown revenue by customs and imposts.[69]

Dee's strategy was not his own, but, as Stubbe made clear, came from ancient authority, 'above all the advice and example of Pericles and the Athenians, and by the glory thereof he excited Her Majesty to fix upon the course of strengthening her navy royal.'[70] The fountainhead of ancient prudence, and the inspiration of Elizabethan practice, was Periclean Athens! Charles II's policy was informed then, rather surprisingly, by the wisdom of an ancient republic, as applied and handed down by an Elizabethan. No doubt Stubbe saw himself as following in Dee's footsteps, playing the role for Charles II that he had played for Elizabeth, instructing the monarch in the ways of ancient prudence.

Stubbe also disparaged wealth and luxury. Success came from poverty and distress, sacrifice and 'moral gallantry.'[71] There was more than a hint here of republican, Harringtonian virtue, now deployed in the service of monarchy. The tension between wealth and virtue became an important theme, as Professor Pocock shows, in neo-Harringtonian rhetoric, a rhetoric of which Stubbe now appears to be one of the leading precursors.[72]

In 1672 and 1673 Stubbe borrowed the Harringtonian language of ancient and modern prudence and gave it new meanings. In Stubbe's scheme ancient and modern prudence represented a spectrum. The first three centuries were witness to the purest times. Then came the age of Constantine which was less pure but still representative of ancient prudence.[73] Next came the most corrupt times, beginning with Justinian, when ancient prudence was abandoned in favor of 'uncouth and phantastical' doctrines,[74] And finally there was the revival, first under Elizabeth, then under Charles II, of ancient prudence in modern dress.[75] The modern prudence of Charles II was a mixture of Constantinian ancient prudence and the corruptions that set in with Justinian. The bishops considered as 'spiritual lords' and the Nicene Creed, which is 'about trifles,' were still here and indeed enforced. But an important step had been taken towards the revival of Constantine's prudence – namely, the Indulgence. The clear implication was that just as his prudence could be abandoned, so it could be, and was being, gradually restored. The circumstances of course had to be favorable, as they were favorable now, in 1673, for the Indulgence.

How would the Indulgence restore the prudence of Constantine? It extended toleration to Dissenting clergy, while doing nothing to jeopardize the power and authority of the Anglican clergy. It would thus reduce the pitch of religious rancor. Dissenters would express less animosity towards the orthodox clergy, and the orthodox less towards the Dissenting clergy. The result would be increasing respect and reverence among the people for the clergy – all clergy. This in turn would lead to civil peace, the only real foundation for effective government. Such a polity would avoid the extremes of anarchy and tyranny, both of which were the products of excessive religious passion publicly expressed. Anarchy comes with the division of the people into religious factions, the breakdown of society along sectarian lines. Tyranny might come in a desperate attempt to put an end to religious dissension. The cure would be at least as bad as the disease: constitutional power would be monopolized by the king and bishops, as Shaftesbury argued in 1675 against the Test Act. The only solution, according to Stubbe two years earlier, was the Indulgence, which would increase popular respect for the clergy, allow priestcraft to cast its spell over the people and thus restore the civil peace – exactly those goals that Constantine achieved by the same means. The extremes of anarchy and arbitrary government would be avoided at the price of enhancing popular superstition.

Here was the sum of Stubbe's deployment of Harrington's vocabulary. The clergy and popular superstition concerning them could be used as a makeweight against the extremes of tyranny and anarchy. The Indulgence, the ancient prudence of Constantine, could be introduced to modify the Restoration settlement, the modern prudence of king and bishops, and improve upon it. The language was Harringtonian, but the meaning represented a fundamental departure from Harrington for whom Constantine was not a representative of ancient prudence, which was strictly republican and not monarchical, and for whom there could never be any accommodation between ancient and modern prudence.

Stubbe's defense of the Indulgence, however, was not as uncompromised as we have made it out to be. A closer reading of the comparison Stubbe drew between the Indulgence and Constantinian Christianity reveals that he was not so much in favor of the position he was ostensibly defending as he appears to be, that there was in fact more going on in the text than meets any but the most watchful eye. As it turns out, Stubbe's argument can be subjected to the same analysis as his printed attacks on the Royal Society and, when this is done, made to yield a similar result, namely, that Stubbe was quite capable of masking his radical views in the cloak of orthodoxy.

First of all, when Stubbe initially considered ancient and modern prudence he said:

Hitherto the ancient politicks concur with the modern prudence of His Majesty; yet there is this advantage on the part of the Church of England above what the primitive Christians had, that the revenues of the conformists are better settled, and greater by far than the Nicene Fathers . . . could pretend unto. And the power and dignity which our bishops hold as spiritual lords (not to mention their influence upon the subordinate clergy) hath nothing parallel to it in the four first centuries . . .

The common schools and universities are not now . . . devoted to Gentilism, but managed by the church. The parliament (as of old the senate) doth not consist of paynims, or Arians, &c. Those which sway in our councils, and in the magistracy, are now no such kind of men as heretofore.[76]

This passage is replete with double meanings. The Church of England, which takes the first four centuries of Christianity 'for its pattern as to doctrine and discipline,'[77] nevertheless, possesses far greater 'revenues' than the primitive church and is governed by bishops whose status 'as spiritual lords . . . hath nothing parallel to it in the four first centuries.' The present church, moreover, is challenged neither by 'Gentilism' in the academy nor by 'paynims, or Arians' in parliament and 'the magistracy.' Stubbe of course in his contemporary clandestine *Account of the Rise and Progress of Mahometanism* was arguing that 'Gentilism' (or what he regarded as true Aristotelianism) and Arianism, far from posing any challenges to Apostolic Christianity, were more or less consonant with it. These advantageous 'conditions' in which the present church finds itself will allow it to escape any harm being done to it by the Indulgence. But the point is cryptically made: the present church, because of its wealth, the putative spiritual authority of its bishops, its monopoly of learning and the compliance of parliament and local magistrates, is at considerable variance with the first four centuries of Christian practice, the era of primitive purity. The implication is clear: the church, as it now is, is corrupt and its corruptions will probably allow it to withstand the effects of the Indulgence. The point as regards the bishops' power is made, again obliquely, when Stubbe insists only a few pages before that 'in the primitive ages' bishops were elected by the people of the diocese.[78] This of course would undercut the orthodox view that bishops were consecrated in a ceremony that perpetuated an Apostolic succession and conferred upon them a special spiritual authority, coming from God and setting them above other men.

There were, moreover, degrees of ancient prudence. Constantine's Council of Nicea produced a creed and embarked upon a policy of persecution to enforce it which violated the previous spirit of toleration that had grown up over generations among Arians, Trinitarians and others. The result was that the persecution conducted by the Trinitarians backfired. 'The Arians triumphed everywhere as victors, the whole world seemed to follow them, and the rest appeared to be justly exiled, and scorned, who had raised such divisions and animosities in the Church and State *about trifles*' (my italics).[79] So persecution and the enforcement of a uniform creed were alien to primitive Christianity, and the particular creed in question, the Nicene Creed, the basis of Anglican belief in Stubbe's own day, was 'about trifles.' Stubbe was sly here in his characteristic way: he insinuated heresy in a brief attack on comprehension schemes put forward as means to Christian unity.

So Constantine's reign, though representative of ancient prudence, was not so prudent as it might have been or as the earlier Apostolic church had been. Stubbe made this point, again very unobtrusively, at the outset of his comparison between Charles II's Indulgence and Constantinian Christianity: 'For three hundred years after our Saviour Christ, the Christian Religion was most pure, and indeed Golden – Constantine was a Prince of good zeal to our Religion . . . In those days, which were about four hundred years after our Saviour, the Church was much less corrupt, and more pure than now.'[80] In other words, the first three Christian centuries represented the purest, Golden Age of the faith. The next century, the reign of Constantine, saw a declension, though 'less corrupt, and more pure than now.' The prudence of Constantine was not so pure as the prudence of the Golden Age but purer than current practice. Here, it seems, modern prudence did not measure up to ancient, despite all that Stubbe said to the contrary.

On one level Stubbe defended the Indulgence by arguing that it represented a revival of the ancient prudence of Constantine. The result would be a religious settlement worthy of the duplicity of Machiavelli's prince. The king would decree toleration, while protecting the established church in the enjoyment of its wealth and power. Christians would worship openly and freely, each group in its own church or congregation and according to its own doctrines and rituals. The effect would be to reduce the heat of controversy and to increase popular veneration for priestcraft. Commitment to this policy on the part of its sponsors would rest not on sincere respect for the clerical profession but on the calculation that the fostering of such respect among the people was the path to public tranquillity and the prosperity of the kingdom. The ancient prudence of Constantine required the monarchy to maintain the appearance of piety for the sake of obtaining a favorable political result. This return to the religion of Constantine represented an improvement on modern prudence in religion. This latter, the Christianity that set in after Constantine, was a faith contrived by priests to shore up clerical power at the expense of civil authority. Constantine's prudence, on the other hand, dictated that the king declare a toleration not in order to enhance clerical authority but rather to achieve secular – economic and political – goals. Here then was the civil religion which Stubbe, borrowing the language of Harrington, advocated in print.

But there was another level of meaning to be read between the lines in Stubbe's defense of the royal Indulgence. Constantine's prudence still left much to be desired. It was a long way from representing a full recovery of ancient prudence, the Apostolic religion of the first three centuries during which the church did not acquire wealth but took care of the poor and needy, did not claim independent spiritual authority for a separate clergy but submitted to the authority of the civil sovereign and did not establish a narrow monopoly of learning but fostered freedom of inquiry. In both Stubbe's defense of the Indulgence and his attacks on the Royal Society this message was only obliquely stated. If it were not for his *Account of the Rise and Progress of Mahometanism* it would probably be missed altogether. This clandestine manuscript provides the key for decoding what is cryptic in Stubbe's published works dating from this period. A civil religion based on a recovery of Constantine's prudence was one thing. Quite another was the primitive Christianity appropriated by Mohammed which Stubbe explored in his manuscript and which represented a much more radical civil religion. In 'Mahometan Christianity' there was no separate clergy, no clerical wealth and no clerical monopoly of learning and power. Thus there was no need to resort to Machiavellian appearances and foster popular reverence for the clergy in order to obtain civil peace, as Constantine did. Instead, civil order came directly from priestless religion which eliminated wealth and poverty and produced a toughened, virtuous citizenry ready to accomplish difficult and useful tasks. There was still an element of Machiavellian policy, if not duplicity, about the religion: Islam was the product of Mohammed's shrewd borrowing; it was carefully constructed to fit circumstances and to achieve secular goals.

There was a relationship between Stubbe's clandestine *Account* and his pro-Indulgence tracts. It informed the cryptic message of those tracts just as it did his attacks on the Royal Society. The *Account* also set forth the radical ideals to which Stubbe still subscribed. It stated the case which could not be made in public or at least not in print.

The civil religion of Stubbe's *Account*, the religion of the first three centuries later appropriated by Mohammed, bears certain marked similarities to Harrington's civil religion, the religion of true republics, which had also been manifested in the churches of the Apostolic Christians. These churches represented, Harrington held, a latter-day return to the civil religion of ancient Israel, the first republic. They represented the religion of ancient prudence based on natural principles coming from God, the same principles that had informed the Hebrew republic, the original model for *Oceana*. Like the Jews before the decay of their republic, the primitive Christians were republicans, living in the urban republics to which autonomy had been granted within the Roman empire. They met in gathered congregations and modelled their government on that of the cities of which they were citizens. Thus they practiced toleration and chose by election their leaders and teachers who thus could not claim to have been chosen by Apostolic succession or to possess as a result of such succession any independent spiritual power. This Christianity for Harrington was the Christian form of the civic religion practiced in true republics of which Israel was the first, the worship of ancient prudence on which those republics rested.[81] The similarities between Stubbe's primitive Christians and Harrington's do not allow us, however, to argue that Stubbe's *Account* was Harringtonian or even that his published defense of the Indulgence was covertly Harringtonian. Where Harrington associated primitive Christianity exclusively with the free cities of the Roman empire, Stubbe's Apostolic Christianity got a second wind under Islam. It could be transplanted from its original setting in the cities of the empire to the deserts of Arabia in a way that Harrington's civic religion could not be. For him the religion was inseparable from the republic; for Stubbe it was exportable to Mohammed's prophetic monarchy. So Stubbe again borrowed the language of ancient prudence from Harrington but endowed it with a meaning that was not Harringtonian.

Thus, where Harrington's civic religion could not serve as a model for monarchs, Stubbe's *Account of the Rise and Progress of Mahometanism* could, and, despite the fact that it could not be published, was no doubt meant to do so. As we shall see in chapter 8, evidence suggests that it was circulating among radical Whigs during the Exclusion crisis. It is possible that Stubbe wrote it a decade earlier for the instruction and amusement of men at court, like himself, connected to Shaftesbury and that it continued to circulate among such men after Shaftesbury left the court and built a 'country' opposition. Its message was likely to be more palatable to a 'country' Whig than to a courtier during the 1680s.

If in his court propaganda Stubbe represented Charles II as Constantine *redivivus*, in *An Account* Mohammed became another, if more clandestine, model for the king's instruction. In both Stubbe seems to hold out hope that the royal policies, especially the religious policy, might become more and more enlightened and thus bring England progressively closer to ancient practice – first to the prudence of Constantine and finally to 'Mahometan Christianity', the lay religion of Greatrakes, Mohammed, Christ and the Apostles. All of Stubbe's Restoration writings, from *The Miraculous Conformist* on, have this in common – they hold up models of ancient practice wherewith to charm king and nation back, one step at a time, to primitive purity. The means is not chiliasm but history, historical process, instruction and example. And the goal, the Millennium if you like, is not a new heaven and earth, but a workaday world of Erastian rule, peace and prosperity – tolerant, secularizing, sober, industrious, perhaps polygamous and moderately levelling. In Stubbe's writings after 1660 we watch radical Protestant values being transformed into early Enlightenment ones.

There was one more link between Stubbe's court propaganda and his *Account of the Rise and Progress of Mahometanism*: in both he abandoned his earlier republicanism which probably lingered on at least until 1666, when there were still hints of it, as we have seen, in *The Miraculous Conformist*. Even in his subsequent attacks on the Royal Society in 1670 and 1671, he decried 'absolute' rule and seems to advocate something close to a mixed constitution in which legislative power, and hence sovereignty, was shared equally among king, the Lords and the Commons. This of course was a radical and extremely subversive view during the Restoration. In his court propaganda in 1672 and 1673 and in his *Account of the Rise and Progress of Mahometanism*, however, he treated absolute monarchy in very sympathetic terms. This similarity between the propaganda and the unpublished manuscript, incidentally, is more evidence that *An Account* was written just after the attacks on the Royal Society, when Stubbe had for the moment taken up a court pen. Mohammed was made out to be an enlightened despot, tolerant, efficient, charitable, socially and economically egalitarian, the inspired leader of a powerful and prosperous empire whose policies were to be admired and emulated. In the court propaganda absolute monarchy was vindicated from Dutch attempts to vilify Charles II by associating his policies with absolutism.[82] And in both the court propaganda and *An Account* Stubbe drew a sharp distinction between absolute rule and tyranny. Mohammed and Charles II, to the extent that he followed Constantine by tolerating Dissenters, and might in time follow Mohammed, were absolute rulers but they were not tyrants.[83] Andrew Marvell also interpreted the royal Indulgence as the act of an enlightened ruler, who therefore was not a tyrant.[84] To men like Stubbe and Marvell, who in many other matters disagreed, after the passage of the Conventicle Act (1670), which initiated the most severe persecutions yet seen under the Restoration, it was parliament that was cast in the role of tyrant, so that when the Indulgence came, the king appeared to be almost a deliverer. Stubbe said that, quite apart from Charles's own worthy inclinations, there were some specific political considerations that would dissuade him from attempting to establish a tyranny: 'if he have potent neighbours, or be involved in wars, . . . there is not any suggestion shall ever be powerful enough to convince me that he will pursue such projects.'[85] The same constraints that worked to check sedition on the part of dissidents would also check royal tyranny.

So for two years, in 1672 and 1673, Stubbe departed from the particular sorts of political radicalism he had held before, while hanging onto and deepening his radical religious and philosophical views: he had acquired a surprising new faith in monarchy. He is himself witness to the switch in his politics and loyalties. Writing in *A Justification of the Present War* (1672) of his earlier opposition to the Anglo-Dutch War and his pro-Dutch sympathies, he said: 'I was jealous of the growth of popery, and thought it to be the interest of this kingdom, not to weaken or destroy a Republick pretending to Protestancy . . . I brought with me all those surmises and misapprehensions which any . . . English malcontent could wish infused into me.'[86] He said that his recent about-face was due to the fact that he 'came to a better intelligence concerning affairs,' which of course sheds no light at all on what really happened to cause him to change his mind.[87] One suspects on the basis of the foregoing analysis that it was the possibilities for reform that the Indulgence held out.

In his attacks on the Royal Society Stubbe indicated that a republican revolution would not succeed, no matter how desirable in theory, because Englishmen, being selfish and 'debauched,' were not capable of making a republic work.[88] Monarchy, then, was the only alternative to chaos. This was an argument which, as Glanvill pointed out, by the standards of the day was not deemed adequate and proper grounds for loyalty to the king and which would have been looked upon as suspiciously Hobbesian, if not (as Glanvill also pointed out) crypto-republican.[89] Stubbe made much the same case for monarchy in his answer to Dutch propaganda and in his attempt to justify the war to English dissidents and republicans: 'how difficult a thing it was to overthrow an hereditary monarchy, and how impossible it was for a nation inured to monarchy, divided in interests, discriminated by degrees of honor, debauched in its manners, irreconcilable in its factions, to retain its liberty, though fortune upon any accident, or attempt, should dissolve its present monarchy.'[90] Monarchy was not in principle the best government. That honor was reserved to republics. In *An Account*, for instance, he wrote of republics 'dwindling' into monarchies.[91] And in both his attacks on the Royal Society and his court propaganda he indicated that republics were morally superior to monarchies by associating the former with public and private virtue and the latter with corruption and 'debauched' manners. Monarchy might not be the best form of government, but it commanded support because it worked in present circumstances; a republic would not.

This contingent royalism, however, begged an important question: what would Stubbe, the provisional supporter of monarchy, do if the monarch could no longer be trusted and, like the republic, embarked upon a course not of progressive enlightenment but the reverse, a path that led to tyranny? The question did not arise as long as Stubbe could be convinced that Charles II was a new Constantine and, at least potentially, a modern Mohammed. But what would happen when the new Constantine was exposed as a second Justinian or worse? As we shall see next, the course Stubbe then chose to pursue was opposition.

7

Court to country

. . . almost all sober men believe that the national clergy, besides all their other good qualities, have this too; that they cannot hope to make their hierarchy subsist long against the Scriptures, the hatred of mankind, and the interest of this people, but by introducing the Roman religion; and getting a foreign head and supporter, which shall from time to time brave and hector the king and parliament in their favour and behalf: which yet would be of little advantage to them, if we had as firm and wise a government as you have in Venice.

Henry Neville, *Plato Redivivus*

For a year and a half, from the spring of 1672 to the autumn of 1673, Stubbe was attached to the court. He wrote his two major propaganda pieces in 'the Paper Office at Whitehall,' and was paid £200 for the job.[1] But Stubbe's career as a court pamphleteer was short-lived. By October 1673 he was recognized as one of the leading propagandists for the 'country' opposition that was just then emerging.[2]

Churchmen had remained suspicious of Stubbe, while he wrote for the court. His vigorous defense of the Indulgence did nothing to win them over. During 1673 William Sancroft, Dean of St Paul's, received reports of Stubbe's activities, and in one of these he was clearly associated with the Erastian, tolerationist opinion at court, so despised by the clerical hierarchy. One of Sancroft's informants, the ultra-highchurchman George Seignior, reported in June that Stubbe was encouraged and protected by Arthur Annesley, Earl of Anglesey, the recently appointed Lord Privy-Seal, disliked by the clergy for his well-known Erastian tolerationism.[3] In particular Seignior speculated that Anglesey might intervene and get Stubbe's works past the official censor Roger L'Estrange in the same way that Anglesey had made it possible for the second edition of Marvell's *Rehearsal Transpros'd* to be published that very year.[4] If Seignior's report is any indication, Stubbe's court-sponsored arguments for the royal Indulgence seem to have left the clergy unpersuaded, and in the circumstances Stubbe must have appeared no less anticlerical in his role as court pen than he had to Glanvill and Beale.

In the course of the summer and early autumn Stubbe emerged as not only anticlerical but also critical of the court itself. From erstwhile defender, he quickly became open detractor. The outlines of this shift are traceable in a sequence of discernible steps, and his anti-court moves grow in boldness and cunning.

For a while, however, he was able to keep his criticism from materially affecting his position at court. As late as 19 October 1673, a warrant went out from Arlington declaring that Stubbe was to be granted 'the offices of Secretary of . . . Jamaica and Commissary Steward General of all such provisions as shall be sent for the use of our fleet or armies in the said island.' This office was to be taken up as soon as the incumbent, Richard Povey (who had held it for more than a decade), should vacate the post by either 'death . . . or forfeiture.'[5] The government, it seems, was sending Stubbe back to Jamaica, this time to an important, perhaps lucrative, administrative post.[6] Whether he had asked to go is unknown. As it turned out, only a few days after the warrant was issued Stubbe openly broke with the court, suggesting that he was not eager to be sent to Jamaica and that he had shifted his loyalty decisively from court to country. This sequence of events also suggests that the warrant was more an attempt by the court to retain Stubbe's loyalty than a reward for services already rendered.[7] In any case, there is evidence for a couple of steps leading up to the open break.

As early as 22 August 1673, Stubbe is reported spreading a rumor that Sir Robert Holmes had been murdered by highwaymen on his way from Bath to the Isle of Wight.[8] Holmes was the commander of the British ships that were ordered to attack the Dutch merchant fleet in March 1672 in contravention of the treaty between England and the Netherlands.[9] This attack began the third Anglo-Dutch War. In spreading the rumor (assuming the report is true) Stubbe probably meant Holmes's murder to be read as a sign from God, a providential punishment for a wicked deed, reflecting not only upon Holmes himself but the government that had given the orders – and all this from the man who only the year before had been busy writing the official justification for the war which Holmes's attack had initiated. Stubbe in his own sly way was already whistling a different tune.

The next month Stubbe revealed in a letter something of the motive for this change of heart. Still at court he writes to Anthony Grey, Earl of Kent on 28 September, relaying court gossip. The Stop of the Exchequer prevents the king's mistresses – Nell Gwynne and the Duchesses of Portsmouth and Cleveland (both papists) – from receiving large payments from the crown. But Portsmouth has received a pension from Louis XIV to make up her loss.[10] Stubbe also refers in distinctly uncomplimentary terms to the forthcoming marriage between James, Duke of York and the Roman Catholic Mary of Modena.[11] The marriage treaty had been concluded, and Mary was expecting to come to England in two months for the marriage to be consummated.[12] Stubbe had become anxious about the growing French Catholic influence at court. The Duchess of Portsmouth was a French Catholic supported by a royal pension to be paid for the time being by the

French king. And now Charles's successor was about to marry a Catholic princess, which made James's long-suspected conversion a virtual certainty and created the prospect of a Catholic dynasty.[13]

The fears these events raised drove Stubbe from his earlier attachment to the court and into the arms of the 'country' opposition. The first evidence of the nature of Stubbe's migration comes in this letter to Kent, who would later emerge as one of the leading Exclusionist peers and who must already have been in sympathy with the anti-court sentiments expressed in Stubbe's letter.[14] A copy of this letter also found its way into the papers of the first Earl of Shaftesbury, which further suggests the nature of Stubbe's new connections.[15] As early as June 1673 Shaftesbury had become 'the champion of Protestantism against James and Popery.'[16] Just as there is evidence linking Stubbe in his role as court propagandist to Shaftesbury in 1672, so there is evidence linking the two men in opposition. Stubbe, moreover, would have had his own reasons for his anti-court stance by late 1673. For him Catholicism was out of the question. The civil religion for which he had argued in his defense of the Indulgence would not stand a chance of surviving a Catholic succession. (What he would have made of James's own Declaration of Indulgence in 1687 we shall never know.) In Stubbe's mind the prospect of James on the throne must have represented a giant step back to Justinian rather than what Charles had boded promise of for a while, namely, progress towards Constantinian Christianity and beyond. Quite simply stated, Stubbe's support of the Indulgence was not pitched upon grounds that could accommodate or even contemplate a Catholic succession.

The next step in Stubbe's retreat from the court was the most decisive. Two events converged to make it also the most dramatic: the meeting of parliament on 20 October 1673 and the wedding of James II. It was a critical moment for the cause of Protestant monarchy. Charles's health was rumored to be poor. Mary of Modena was known to be both 'a stiff Roman Catholic' and a French protégée.[17] A marriage by proxy had already been celebrated and when parliament met, Mary was about to cross the Channel to consummate the match.[18] Parliament met on the 20th and was that day prorogued until the 27th – but not before the House of Commons, probably with Shaftesbury's connivance, voted an address petitioning Charles to forbid the consummation of James's marriage and insisting that he marry a Protestant.[19] Between the 20th and the 27th, Stubbe anonymously published a broadside, entitled *The Paris Gazette*, whose arguments exactly mirrored the intent of the Commons' address to the king.[20] This is more evidence for the connection between Stubbe and Shaftesbury, indeed in this case for their intimate collaboration, if Shaftesbury was responsible, as it is thought, for managing to delay the prorogation in order to get the address from the Commons.[21] Stubbe 'with great confidence and impudence' distributed his broadside among 'several parliament men.'[22] News of its publication was forwarded to Sancroft on the 27th by one of his informants, John Tillison, Clerk of the Works at St Paul's.[23]

Hastily thrown together, Stubbe's *Gazette* provides a number of historical precedents for breaking James's marriage contract. The cases Stubbe adduces all make the point that marriages made by proxy and unconsummated can and should be annulled when they run counter to the welfare of the realm, that in such situations the common good takes precedence over the sanctity of contracts, even those made between princes. In fact in his longest argument in *The Paris Gazette* Stubbe concludes that a king is less bound by his word than by the wishes of his people, as represented by 'nobles' and 'parliaments': 'the most obligatory and powerful toys [sic: ties?] upon princes, are those whereby they stand engaged to their people, whereunto for him to adhere, 'twas true honour and conscience.'[24]

This is an extraordinary statement for its time. It represents an attack on what was Restoration orthodoxy, namely, divine-right monarchy and a revival in rudimentary form of the then very seditious argument that the basis of government lies in a contract between king and people, represented by nobles and parliaments. Stubbe is not, however, antimonarchical, as he was before 1660, although his royalism is now distinctly tempered by an engagement or contract between king and people, the terms of which are mediated by nobles and parliaments. Assuming Stubbe is still thinking within a revised Harringtonian framework, it is these nobles and parliaments that are now seen as preserving the vital constitutional balance, and this kind of balance links him more closely to the neo-Harringtonianism of Shaftesbury and the early Whigs.[25] The point is that he anticipates them.

Despite Stubbe's continued adherence to a form of royalism, *The Paris Gazette* is a long way from his temporary advocacy of absolute (but not divine-right) monarchy in his justification of the Indulgence. But of course that advocacy was made in very different circumstances and seemed warranted by prospects for reform in 1672. His about-face in *The Paris Gazette* less than a year later is one measure of how quickly and thoroughly those hopes had been dashed by the sudden, new prospects for Catholic monarchy. Here is an early, clear case of how the resurgence of the Catholic threat during the Restoration could radicalize, or in Stubbe's case re-radicalize, political thought *and* action.

Stubbe must have known how dangerous it was to publish *The Paris Gazette*. Even though it was anonymous, the news quickly leaked out: Tillison identified its authorship in his report to Sancroft on 27 November, and added, 'ye Dr is not to be found; belike taken to his heels.'[26] Whether this was so or not, a warrant went out for his arrest on 30 October 'for seditious discourses and printing and publishing unlicensed papers,'[27] a clear reference to *The Paris Gazette*, if not others, and on 2 November, Stubbe writes to Sir John Malet, MP for Minehead in Somerset,[28] complaining of his arrest on an order signed by his old patron at court, Arlington, 'no cause being expressed.'[29] The 'cause' of course was obvious, and the fact that Stubbe wrote to Malet further implicates him in the politics of the 'country' opposition at the time, as Malet in 1673 was one of the most vigorous and extreme advocates in the Commons of the Test Act and the addresses against a Catholic marriage.[30] It was in that year that he, like Stubbe, moved into opposition.[31] Later Malet became an Exclusionist Whig and member of the Green Ribbon Club.[32] Also like Stubbe, he was an Erastian anticlerical tolerationist.[33] The evidence points then to an alliance between Stubbe and parliamentary radicals by October 1673, if not earlier.

What happened next is unclear. According to Wood, Stubbe 'was hurried in the dark from one prison to another, threatened with hanging, and . . . put to a great deal of charge.'[34] It is possible that Shaftesbury himself used his influence to gain Stubbe's release, given their apparently close connection at the time. In any case, Stubbe was freed, and later that same month published yet another, though again cryptic, attack on the court.[35]

This came in the form of a translation of a work by Jacques Godefroy, entitled *The History of the United Provinces of Achaia*. Stubbe says that he has prepared the translation for the 'delight and benefit' of the reader, and immediately, given what we know of the translator, our suspicions are aroused – with good reason.[36] Stubbe manages to convey his subversive message in two ways.

First he claims that the constitution of Achaia is the model 'from whence the Dutch framed their commonwealth.'[37] He proceeds to heap praise on the Achaian constitution for its 'singular justice and probity, the which procured them an universal reverence and made others desirous to contract amity with a people famed for all those virtues which beget esteem, but not terror, in their neighbors.'[38] The point is taken. The United Provinces, to the extent that Achaia is their model, represent a superior form of government, particularly by comparison to France, which could scarcely be said 'to beget esteem, but not terror,' in its neighbors. The more basic point is equally well taken. The United Provinces, like Achaia, are a republic: thus republics are represented as morally superior to monarchies, like those of France and (by implication) Britain. This was an assumption lying behind much of Stubbe's earlier thinking during the Restoration, but never since 1660 so clearly, if still obliquely, put forward. Again we see that Stubbe has reversed himself within the year – from a defense of British monarchy against the Dutch republic, a contingent royalism of sorts, to a coy assertion of the superiority of republics over monarchies.

There is another, more specific, way in which Stubbe's translation, superficially so innocuous, is subversive. He spells out the fundamental laws of the Achaians, 'esteemed to be very prudential,'[39] and it is obvious that this is a thinly veiled attempt to show how the English suffer by the comparison. Stubbe points to three Achaian laws against which to measure current English constitutional practice. First, 'no assembly should continue above three days, but the States of Achaia should come to their final resolution within that time,' a clear attack on the king's power to prorogue parliament.[40] Stubbe may have had the prorogation on 20 October specifically in mind. Second,

they did think it fundamental to their preservation that all things should be managed by joint consent, and no room be left for separate counsels: that all the cities should have the same alliances and move by the same maxims. So tender were they of this law that they expressly provided for it in their treaties with the Romans, cautioning that the Romans should not make any addresses to any of their cities privately, but to the public.[41]

This is a clear reference to secret negotiations. How much Stubbe knew about the secret Treaty of Dover is unknown. He may have known a great deal by late 1673, in view of his connections at court and now increasingly, it seems, with Shaftesbury. In any case he knew enough to attack the practice, covering himself by speaking in terms of the separate city-states of Achaia, by which he refers, it seems, to the separate estates of England, the king, the Lords and the Commons. So when he says 'that all things should be managed by joint consent,' he may be referring to the subversive theory of mixed monarchy, just as he had in his attacks on the Royal Society. The third law of the Achaians that bears reference to English practice is 'that none should receive any gifts or pensions from any foreign prince' because 'if this precedent were admitted of, the liberty of the republic would be exposed to sale.'[42] This again suggests that Stubbe knew the terms of the Treaty of Dover. In any case he had been dismayed by the pension that the Duchess of Portsmouth received from Louis XIV and no doubt knew of other examples.

All of this was too much for Stubbe's sense of constitutional balance. It was obvious that such balance could not be achieved, as he had once thought, by a civil religion instigated and nurtured by a royal Indulgence, when the king himself might be a papist, or at least a crypto-papist, and in the pay of the most powerful foreign prince, who was also Catholic. The only alternative was the attempt to achieve balance by parliamentary means – hence the position to which he had come by late October 1673, the position lying behind *The Paris Gazette* and his artful rendering of Godefroy's *The History of the United Provinces of Achaia* into English.

Just to drive the point home, having finished with the example of Achaia, Stubbe tells the story of the conquest of ancient Rhodes by the Romans – another cautionary tale to be kept in mind by the English in their dealings with France. The island maritime power of Rhodes (meant to be England) allied with Rome (France) against Asia Minor (the Netherlands) because the latter threatened Rhodian 'dominion of the sea.' The ensuing war made the Romans powerful enough, especially with the aid of Rhodian sea power, eventually to turn against their ally and to defeat Rhodes itself.[43] The result for the Rhodians was disastrous: 'They were reduced to the narrow confines of their own island, and their trade so impoverished that their naval strength and power declined therewith, and the Romans managed the dominion of the sea, according to the laws of Rhodes.'[44] From being the official propagandist of the alliance with France against Holland, Stubbe now warns against the French alliance. Whereas he had once argued that this alliance would increase prosperity and internal stability, he now sees it as potentially destructive of both. In sum: his view now is that just as there must be a new domestic balance, maintained by nobles and parliaments, there must also be a new external balance, maintained by disengagement with France, which would in turn no doubt redound to greater constitutional balance at home.

The evidence for Stubbe's life from November 1673 and the publication of *Achaia* to his death in July 1676 is very patchy. He wrote a series of letters in the early summer of 1674 to his patron the Earl of Kent, in which he recorded court life and court gossip. (Was he still at court or is his court news secondhand?) The letters are addressed from Westminster and Bath, between which he seems to have moved, perhaps as a physician.[45] Since the late 1660s Stubbe had maintained a fashionable medical practice, as his residence in Bath during the summer season indicates, a habit that continued to the last year of his life. One of his most important patrons was Edward, Viscount Conway, whom he served as physician, and this would also continue to his death.[46] But, as the letters to Kent in 1673–4 reveal, that family's patronage had also become important to him. He was their physician.[47] But to the Earl he was more than that, as he seems to have been expected to supply his patron with detailed news of the court.[48]

These reports, judging from the surviving correspondence, are of a certain sort. They consist mainly of gossip focussing on the libertine sex lives and riotous living of Charles, his intimates and his mistresses. Thus Stubbe writes at length about the king's venereal disease, about the marriages arranged for the royal bastards, the embarrassment these caused the queen and the expense connected with them, and about the papist Duchess of Portsmouth disporting herself in the waters at Bath.[49] The accounts, as Stubbe tells them, are mordant and were obviously meant to amuse. The wit is laced with sarcasm and moral reproach. Stubbe's intention was to alarm and condemn as well as to entertain. One example will suffice. From Bath he writes:

The Duchess of Portsmouth being recovered from the clap . . . hath bathed a week and drank them a week and after a week more she departs. She hath the king's music to play at meals and in the Bath, with her are the Lady Marshal, and Essex Griffith, also Rochester and some such like. But none of the Country visit her, though she invited my Lord Brooke and others to cards. She dines and sups in state, and all people are admitted to see her, as were she Queen. Every other day the king sends a page with an express to her . . . She is frolicsome in the Bath. Shows her feet and legs above water, and threw up her gentlewoman's as high to divert my Lord Rochester: they sport in the Bath and throw flowers at each other and do many things which in courtiers are acts of freedom, but the Country miscall them for impudence.[50]

Clearly Stubbe was on the side of 'the Country.' Nor was the issue mixed bathing in the nude, as this had gone on in Bath from at least the mid-fifteenth century right up through the seventeenth.[51] Stubbe's portrait is comic, but the seriousness of the issue comes through: the Protestant succession is at stake.

This indeed is the underlying theme of the letters to Kent: while the king fiddles, the country languishes without a proper heir. Worse still, not only is the king preoccupied by his pleasures, but James seems acceptable to him: 'The Duke of York here rules all (as if the king had transferred in a manner all unto him).'[52] No wonder there were men in the Commons in 1675 willing to legalize polygamy in order to get a Protestant succesor![53] (In the end the kingdom took the less drastic course and staged a revolution.) The letters are full of indignation at James's anti-Dutch diplomacy[54] and at papist sentiment among courtiers and the royal whores: 'Cleveland declares she will go to France . . . and thence to Rome to see the Jubilee next year, in which the Pope will restore her to innocence and youth.'[55] Greatrakes maybe, but never the pope! Stubbe remains opposed to the court, and the succession is the key issue fuelling his, and no doubt his new patron's, opposition.

Almost nothing is known about the last two years of Stubbe's life.[56] (Had he grown afraid?) He maintained his practice in Bath to the end, as it is there in 1676 during the season that he died. Bath must have had many attractions for him. It was just then becoming fashionable, in part because the king and Queen Catherine of Braganza had gone there in 1663 and the king's mistresses had paid the notorious visit, observed by Stubbe, in 1674.[57] Besides the well-born and prosperous, the spa attracted the sick from all social classes and those who came to prey upon them.[58] Rich and poor used the same baths.[59] There was very little segregation according to status, the only difference being that the prosperous were accompanied by 'guides' into the baths.[60] It must have been one of the few places in England where high and low met in such intimate proximity. Nor were the poor entirely left to their own devices. There was a hospital reserved for the treatment of the indigent, the Hospital for Strangers or Bellot's Hospital, founded earlier in the century and named after its donor Thomas Bellot.[61] It was maintained and paid for by donations and administered by physicians appointed by the mayor of Bath.[62] Its resources, however, were few. It accommodated 'twelve men only, and that but for three months in the year.'[63] Women were excluded from Bellot's Hospital because 'the founder of it . . . had no kindness for the infirm of that sex.'[64] The custom was also for spectators at the baths to give money to the poor.[65] After the Restoration there was unrest among the poor who came to Bath, which erupted into frequent public 'clamours' during the mid-1670s, and attempts were made to provide 'support of the many poor that came hither for relief' by assessing all bathers who could pay, 'every man or woman . . . from a Duke to a Yeoman.'[66]

Stubbe was no doubt a party to these attempts. He was well known, respected and quoted approvingly for his medical views by some leading Bath physicians, including Thomas Guidott, the principal advocate of regularized municipal poor relief.[67] Stubbe in turn owned copies of Guidott's books, describing the spa and its healing powers.[68] Like Guidott, Stubbe was immensely sympathetic to the medical plight of the poor, recommending free medicine 'where there is occasion,'[69] and urging his fellow medics shortly before he died to 'study all ways possible to find out and appoint medicines of cheap rate, and effectual; for money is scarce, and country people poor.'[70] It was said of him, moreover, that 'he was not a person greedy of gain'[71] and that 'he scorned money and riches, and the adorers of them.'[72] All of this recalls his views in *An Account of the Rise and Progress of Mahometanism*, where he espoused institutionalized charity and moderate economic levelling to eliminate the extremes of wealth and poverty.

Death came suddenly. On the night of 12 July 1676, he was called from a social engagement in Bath to attend a patient in Bristol. On the way his horse stumbled, he fell and was drowned 'in a shallow river . . . two miles distant from Bath.'[73] His death created something of a stir. Marvell noted in a letter on the 17th: 'Dr Stubbe physician atheist found dead I meane drowned betwixt Bath & Bristol. 23 guinnies and 3 broad pieces in his pockett suppost drunk. *es magne Deus.*'[74] Putting the matter more colorfully, Anthony Wood has Stubbe 'going a by-way at 10 of the clock in the night . . . (his head being then intoxicated with bibbing, but more with talking, and snuffing of powder).'[75] Stubbe's old adversary Glanvill 'preached his funeral sermon, but said no great matter of him,' and he was 'buried in the great church at Bath dedicated to S. Peter and S. Paul.'[76]

Lord Conway described Stubbe's estate as consisting principally of his books, 'thought to be worth £800' and 'three horses, one of which his mother gave the messenger who acquainted her with his death.' Conway also indicated that Stubbe had a child, though there is no record that he ever married.[77] His estate was forfeited to the crown[78] – because, so rumor had it, he was a bastard and died intestate.[79] In any case his papers were 'locked up at Warwick,'[80] and a warrant went out that because:

there are several [papers] containing matters dangerous to both Church and State . . . , they shall not be unsealed but in the presence of some person appointed by the

Bishop of London, who is to inspect the same and seal up such of them as he shall find to contain any dangerous matter, to be disposed of as the king shall direct.[81]

I have not been able to trace these papers; one can only hope that they will eventually turn up, assuming they still exist, as they might be of immense scholarly value.

During the next few years Stubbe's library was catalogued and sold.[82] On 28 April 1678, the virtuoso Robert Hooke 'chose at Martins several of Stubbe's books,' probably referring to books from Stubbe's library.[83] 'Martins' probably refers to the shop of John Martin the London bookseller, who was publisher to the Royal Society and died in 1680.[84] Hooke seems to have known him and dealt with him on other occasions.[85] On 25 June 1680, Hooke saw 'the remainder of H. Stubbe Library' at Ragley, Lord Conway's house in Warwickshire, and remarked that these books were 'to be yet sold.'[86] A sale of the books of one Henry Stubbe by public auction took place on 29 November 1680,[87] but, oddly enough, this Stubbe is another Henry, a nonconformist minister.[88] Hooke's comments suggest that Conway was responsible for disposing of the entire collection, first giving some to Martin to sell and a couple of years later auctioning or otherwise selling the rest.[89] Did he also dispose of the papers? On 17 December 1678, Hooke 'borrowed of Martin, Mahomet's book.'[90] Was this the Martin to whom part of Stubbe's library had been consigned for sale by the previous April? And was 'Mahomet's book' Stubbe's manuscript *Account of the Rise and Progress of Mahometanism?* Of the curious life of that manuscript after its author's death more will be said in the next chapter.

In 1676 John Aubrey became interested in Stubbe's life and drew up a horoscope of his nativity which, he claimed, prefigured his death by drowning.[91] That autumn Aubrey wrote to his old friend Thomas Mariett for information relating to Stubbe.[92] Two replies from Mariett survive. In one he says of Stubbe: 'He is by many lamented and by some as holding a rod over the Royal Society,' suggesting that he and his most publicized cause enjoyed something of a popular following to the end.[93] In Mariett's other reply to Aubrey he remarks of Stubbe: 'as plain as you now see drowning in his nativity most people thought him more like to be hanged,'[94] a possible reference to the fact that he had been threatened with hanging, it seems, for publishing *The Paris Gazette*[95] and a response entirely in line with the interpretation set forth in this book. Mariett, moreover, being a JP in Warwickshire, Stubbe's own county, was in a position to know.[96] Could Stubbe's death have been the result of something more than an accident?

8

Civil religion and radical politics: Stubbe to Toland

Stubbe was dead, but his influence continued through the remainder of the Restoration and after the Revolution of 1688–9, until at least 1720. This chapter seeks to trace the course of that influence. In the process it will be possible to show the connection between Stubbe, the early English deism of Charles Blount and the civil religion or 'Mahometan Christianity' of John Toland, and hence to chart the intellectual links between the radical Protestantism and subversive naturalism represented by Stubbe and the deism and vitalistic materialism or pantheism (to use Toland's own word) of the early Enlightenment. This is nothing less than to connect through Stubbe the radicalism of the mid-century English revolution with the radicalism of the early eighteenth century. The principal medium of this connection, it will be seen, was Stubbe's manuscript *An Account of the Rise and Progress of Mahometanism*, which circulated underground between the 1670s and 1720.

Stubbe and the radical Whigs, 1678–82

After his death Stubbe was not forgotten. Hooke, the perpetual man about town, discussed him with his acquaintances in 1678 and 1679.[1] And to keep the discussion alive, a book was published in 1678, claiming to be by him. *A Caveat for the Protestant Clergy. Or a True Account of the English Clergy upon the Restitution of Popery in the Days of Queen Mary*, judged by its title, might easily have issued from Stubbe's pen. The title-page announces this to be the second edition, perhaps to convince the reader of Stubbe's authorship (the first presumably having been published during the author's lifetime), but no first edition has turned up.[2] Whether the work is by him or not, those who printed it under his name must have assumed that by doing so they would attract sales – witness, along with Hooke's interest, to his continuing posthumous reputation. The publishers also knew to associate him with the appropriate cause. *A Caveat* is another exercise in antipopery, which was reaching a white heat in 1678, the first year of the furor raised by the imaginary Popish Plot and the ensuing Exclusion crisis.[3] As the title suggests, *A Caveat* is a warning to the clergy that popery threatens 'their wives and livings,' just as it did in the days of Queen Mary. But the warning does not stop there: 'Perhaps you will say that such a revolution would endanger the laity also, and bring the crown of His Majesty into question, whether it be feudatory, or no.' These threats to the laity are then spelled out: ''tis true indeed, that the papists do now entitle some of their clergy to our old abbeys and monasteries . . . 'Tis most true that the pope doth reckon upon our kingdom as held in fee of the papacy.'[4] The two great shibboleths of the Whig standard raised during the Exclusion crisis – Property and the Protestant Succession – are thus woven into the fabric of Stubbe's (if it is his) tract. Clearly, his was a name still to conjure with in the cause of antipopery two years after his death, and the Exclusionists were making the most of it.

Posthumously, moreover, he seems to have been almost as closely linked with radical Whigs and freethinkers in Shaftesbury's entourage as he was with the Earl himself in the autumn of 1673.

Charles Blount, one of the most active of the radicals during the Exclusion crisis and a prominent member of the Green Ribbon Club,[5] had read and copied at least portions of Stubbe's *Account of the Rise and Progress of Mahometanism* by 1678. In that year he wrote a letter to Hobbes and another to John Wilmot, Earl of Rochester, himself a notorious libertine and freethinker,[6] which consisted mainly of extracts from Stubbe's manuscript. As was Blount's habit, he did not acknowledge his source and passed off what he had copied out of Stubbe as his own.[7] Stubbe's views accorded well with Blount's. There is a close similarity between the deism of Blount, derived partly from Cherbury, and Stubbe's 'Mahometan Christianity.' Blount was deeply influenced by Hobbes just as Stubbe had been.[8] Blount and Stubbe also shared a very similar view of nature in which, conflating God and nature, the power of both was seen to be infinite and coextensive, and it could thus be claimed that miracles were the result of natural processes.[9] The two men, moreover, were both secular historicists. This factor was one which particularly attracted Blount to Stubbe's manuscript, as the section he quoted from it in his letter to Rochester made the point that historical change comes not through supernatural agencies but from human action and that these actions are motivated not by piety but by self-love. Following Hobbes and Stubbe, he quite banished spiritual factors from history. Thus he prefaced his extended quotation from Stubbe's manuscript in his letter to Rochester with these remarks:

My Lord,

I humbly ask your Lordship's pardon for this presumption; but when I had last the honour of waiting upon you, your Lordship's candour gave me the freedom of venting my own thoughts; and then, as the subject of our discourse was about the great changes and revolutions that from time to time had happened in the universe, so I made bold to assert that in all mutations, as well ecclesiastical as civil, I would engage to make appear to your Lordship that a temporal interest was the great machine upon which all human actions moved; and that the common and general pretence of piety and religion, was but like grace before a meal: accordingly, I have presumed to trouble your Lordship with these ensuing remarques, to justify the same assertion.[10]

Here was Blount's radical Whig view of history which fed his intense anticlericalism, his Hobbesian Erastianism and his Exclusionist politics, and the 'justification' of his position was provided by a long quotation from Stubbe's manuscript two years after its author's death. Clearly that manuscript had passed clandestinely to Blount and was providing some of the fuel for his emerging Whig radicalism. For obvious reasons Blount chose not to publish the letter under his name until after the Revolution of 1688–9, and even then it was extremely risky to say such things in print.[11]

Nor was Blount the only Whig freethinker whose views resonated with those of Stubbe. In 1680 Albertus Warren published *An Apology for the Discovery of Humane Reason, Written by Mr. Clifford, Esq.* Martin Clifford's *A Treatise of Humane Reason* was first published anonymously in 1674, and its deistical argument that the truths of religion must be founded upon human reason produced a considerable reaction.[12] Warren wrote his *Apology* for Clifford's *Treatise* more than two years before it was published, probably in 1677,[13] at 'Clifford's request (who died soon after).'[14] Clifford had been Arlington's secretary in 1668,[15] and Shaftesbury had been Clifford's patron in the 1670s,[16] so he and Stubbe may have known each other. Warren dedicated his *Apology* to Shaftesbury, suggesting that he was his patron too.[17] It is likely that Blount and Warren knew and collaborated with each other as fellow members of Shaftesbury's stable of writers and journalists during the Exclusion crisis. In 1693, Blount published *The Oracles of Reason*, in which he printed, besides the letters to Hobbes and Rochester that prove Stubbe's influence on Blount, a letter addressed to him and signed 'Your friend without reserve, A.W.,' probably Albertus Warren.[18] The letter by A.W. is entitled 'Of Natural Religion, As Opposed to Divine Revelation,' and conforms to Warren's mildly deistical, published views.[19]

Warren's *Apology* itself provides further evidence for the connection between Stubbe's ideas as contained in his clandestine manuscript and elsewhere. Warren's book reflects Stubbe's position principally in two ways. First, Warren was what might be called a Hobbesian tolerationist in the same sense in which Stubbe was and always had been even before 1660. Like Stubbe, Warren borrowed Hobbes's devastating critique of the spiritual authority of the clergy and likewise Hobbes's conclusion, drawn from this critique, that the civil sovereign should exercise a monopoly of authority in religious matters.[20] Like Stubbe, too, Warren held that such civil authority should be used to grant and nurture toleration among Protestants.[21] Quite clearly Hobbes was being deployed during the Restoration by radical

Protestant or freethinking Whigs, like Warren and Blount (another Hobbesian tolerationist), not only to vaunt the authority of the state in religious matters over the continuing claims of the clergy, but also to promote a policy of Erastian toleration, a position which Hobbes himself had never taken, so far as I know, with any degree of definiteness. One wonders what Hobbes made of this use of his ideas by Warren, Blount, Clifford and others.[22] Of course Stubbe had followed this course before the Restoration, and it constituted one of the principal links between his pre-1660 and post-1660 thinking. Warren, too, had been a radical Independent and republican in the 1650s.[23] In 1680, he alluded to the key text in *Leviathan* giving support to Erastian toleration, when he wrote: 'T[homas] H[obbes] says, Paul or Cephus, or Apollo may be followed . . . according to a man's liking, so it be done without contention . . . See the Leviathan ch. 47.'[24]

There was a second, equally interesting way in which Warren's *Apology* linked up ideologically with Stubbe's ideas. As well as being Hobbesian tolerationists, they were both advocates of civil religion and to one degree or another looked back to Harrington. Warren's debt was greater than Stubbe's, and this was due no doubt to the fact that, as Professor Pocock has shown, events from 1675 on acted as a major catalyst in the rethinking and reworking of Harrington.[25] Warren based his understanding of the religious and political crisis upon a Harringtonian analysis of the historical situation and came up with a solution in the form of a neo-Harringtonian civic religion.

Harrington himself had argued that under the first two Tudors royal policy had resulted in a transfer of wealth which produced a political imbalance leading to the Civil War, the victory of parliament and the makings of a new balance. The next step would be the revival of ancient prudence which would take proper account of and institutionalize this new balance of wealth and power so that a permanent, stable republic would be forthcoming.[26] Warren appropriated this analysis and applied it to the situation in 1680. The transfers of property and power under the Tudors and during the Civil Wars benefited the staunchly Protestant 'trading men,' and those in London in particular, to such an extent that they now hold the balance of power. The conclusion follows – not Harrington's agrarian and republican solution, and not the neo-Harringtonian agrarian and aristocratic one delineated by Pocock, but a neo-Harringtonian commercial and Whiggish one. The king must listen to the trading men of London, now 'the body of the nation, in whose riches His Majesty's strength consists.'[27] This means specifically that in the face of the popish threat Charles II must pursue an Erastian policy, outlawing popery, tolerating Dissenters and exercising civil control over the clergy, which is exactly the policy the trading men in London represent. If the king disregards the mercantile 'body of the nation,' and continues to permit Dissenters to be persecuted, this will 'hinder trade,' produce imbalance and instability, and leave England vulnerable to her enemies.[28] The introduction of civil control and toleration, on the other hand, will have the reverse effect, rendering the monarchy 'more secure at home, and more formidable abroad,' because it will take into account and conform to the actual balance of wealth and power within England, just as Stubbe had maintained in 1672.[29]

Hobbesian Erastianism and Harringtonian analysis again converge, just as they had in Stubbe's works in 1659 and 1672. Warren's book turns out on close inspection to be not only an *Apology* for Martin Clifford but also a deftly constructed political pamphlet arguing the Whig case, on Hobbesian and neo-Harringtonian grounds, for Erastian tolerationism in the heat of the crisis over Exclusion. In this respect Warren's tract is an update on the argument Stubbe had devised eight years before to justify the Indulgence.

There is then an ideological continuity between Stubbe, the sometime court pen, sometime 'country' spokesman, and the radical Whigs of the Exclusion crisis – so profound in fact that one wishes he had lived to take part in the campaign organized by the Green Ribbon Club, for one knows that he would have been there, alongside Blount and the others, at its active center.[30] Indeed the evidence – Stubbe's all but certain collaboration with Shaftesbury in the autumn of 1673, the publication of *A Caveat for the Protestant Clergy* under his name in 1678, the clandestine circulation of Stubbe's manuscript, and the writings of Blount and Warren – all points to more than an ideological affinity and influence but a continuity of actual political organization emanating from and revolving around the First Earl himself.

The paganizing potential in toleration at the king's command

The Exclusion crisis produced more than an anti-Catholic mass hysteria and the first experiments in party politics.[31] It also saw a new explosion of radical religious opinion of the sort that its orthodox critics condemned as, in a word, atheistical, but which was in fact not so simple and single-minded. Critics of such subversive opinion would have included Blount and Hobbes in their blanket condemnation of atheists and atheism, and, as we have seen, neither was an atheist, technically speaking. In fact it was such subversive religious views as Blount and Hobbes represented that seem to have enjoyed greater currency during the Exclusion crisis, partly as a result of the temporary lapsing of the Licensing Act from May 1679, which made it much easier to get such ideas into print, and partly in reaction to the religious excesses unleashed by the so-called Popish Plot.

Whatever the sources of these ideas Stubbe's name and views continued to be associated with them, so that, for example, in a letter to Boyle in July 1682, John Beale, Stubbe's old enemy out in Somerset, lumped together

'Hobbians and Stubbians, atheists, scoffers, blasphemers,'[32] and Boyle for his part undertook to answer in print the views of Blount, Stubbe and their ilk. In the circumstances surrounding Boyle's decision to publish *A Free Enquiry into the Vulgarly Received Notion of Nature* we can see the sort of threat that the religious and philosophical views earlier held by Stubbe still posed to the orthodox during the 1680s. We can also see more particularly, in the context of publication, how and why Boyle set out to answer such views. In order to put the matter in proper perspective we must, in the course of our account, review some of the evidence presented in chapter 3. We shall then be able to explore an entirely new, and particularly curious, episode in the posthumous career of Stubbe's ideas, for we shall see that under James II they came for a time to be associated in the minds of Boyle and his powerful fellow churchmen with the growth of popery, the very thing Stubbe himself had always opposed.

Boyle tells us that much of *A Free Enquiry* was written in 1665 or 1666[33] to satisfy a friend, probably Henry Oldenburg. The manuscript, however, went unprinted and was left in disarray. Years later at the request of 'some philosophical heads' not otherwise identified, Boyle resurrected it, put it into new order and prepared it for publication.[34] The preface is dated 29 September 1682. But for some unknown reason publication was delayed, and it did not find its way into print until early 1686. The question to be treated here is not why publication was delayed, since no evidence is yet forthcoming which sheds light on that, but rather why it was published when it was. To answer that, however, we should examine its contents and why Boyle wrote it in the first place some two decades before he finally saw it in print, because we shall see that in 1686 the issues with which it deals were not only still matters of lively public debate but had gained an even greater urgency and intensity.

Boyle tells us in his preface that he wrote his *Free Enquiry* in order 'to keep the glory of the divine author of things from being usurped or intrenched upon by his creatures.'[35] As it turns out, he is trying to protect religion from two threats at once, the atheists and the Roman Catholics, both of whom (strange bedfellows though they make) find support in 'the vulgarly received notion of nature.' The Roman Catholic writers whom he has in mind would explain the natural order in terms of the operation *in* nature of some unseen spiritual agency (rather than *on* nature from outside, as Boyle thought) and so come dangerously close to confusing Creator and creature, to worshipping nature, the sin of idolatry.[36] Of the other enemy, the atheists, Boyle says:

there is lately sprung up a sect of men, as well professing Christianity, as pretending to philosophy, who (if I be not mis-informed of their doctrine) do very much symbolize with the antient Heathens, and talk much indeed of God, but mean such a one, as is not really distinct from the animated and intelligent universe; but is, on that account, very differing from the true God, that we Christians believe and worship.[37]

These men are not atheistic materialists. They believe in God and a divine order, but their God does not exist outside of and above nature, and this divine order is immanent in nature. They are atheists, in other words, not because they deny God's existence but simply because they are not theists, though because they worship a God immanent in nature they might also be called deists of sorts. Their idolatry is obvious because they explicitly confound God and nature, whereas the idolatry of Catholic natural religion is merely implicit. Both Catholic and atheist are guilty of the same irreligion springing from the same source, the vulgarly received notion of nature. Boyle writes his *Free Enquiry* to expose this common error and to rectify it by offering a new philosophical foundation for Christianity, his corpuscular philosophy, in place of the old.[38] This new foundation would promote a proper understanding of the relationship between God, man and the cosmic order, where the Scholastic continued to work in the opposite direction to subvert true religion.[39]

The task must have seemed urgent to him in 1665 and 1666 when he wrote the book. The Catholic threat continued to preoccupy him and his friends in the Royal Society throughout the Restoration. The apologists for the early Royal Society formulated a natural religion that was consciously anti-Catholic. The philosophy of the Royal Society, according to their official mouthpiece Thomas Sprat, was experimental rather than dogmatic; their business sober observation rather than logical deduction from Scholastic assumptions. The same philosophy applied to Protestantism would lead to the discovery of religious truth, and the English church would thus flourish. In contrast the Catholic church would stagnate because its corresponding philosophical foundation in Scholastic dogma inhibited the search for further truth, religious or otherwise, in favor of submission to papal authority and ecclesiastical tradition.[40] Boyle's *Free Enquiry* should be read as a contribution to this assault on Catholicism conducted by Fellows of the Royal Society. The very phrase, 'a free enquiry' in the title of Boyle's book gives it away. It is to be a Protestant inquiry productive of more truth in contrast to Catholic reliance on ancient and defective dogma. Boyle hints at this point in his preface as well as in the title itself. Where Sprat and others preached that the aims and methods of the Royal Society advanced the cause of Anglicanism, Boyle in *A Free Enquiry* was performing a related service by establishing the connection between the cosmic system, as he and other leading Fellows understood it, and true religion.

This was to take aim against Catholicism; but there was also another target, the atheists, or as Boyle describes them, the 'sect of men, as well professing Christianity, as pretending to philosophy, who' make no distinction between God and 'the animated and intelligent universe.' Boyle does not shed any more light on whom he had in mind. Indeed we cannot say for sure whether his references to this atheistical 'sect' were contained in the original manuscript of *A Free Enquiry* written in 1665 and 1666 or were added 'many years later' when he revised it for publication. It is highly plausible, however, that these references were included in the original because, during the very period in which *A Free Enquiry* was written, Boyle was in dialogue with Stubbe concerning ideas remarkably similar to the ones that are associated with the 'sect' referred to in the *Enquiry* itself.[41]

Daniel Coxe, a close friend of Boyle's, wrote to him in March 1666, accusing Stubbe and his followers of denying the existence of a deity separate from and transcendent over nature. Coxe also claimed that Stubbe denied the immortality of human souls.[42] Stubbe himself wrote a letter addressed to Boyle, dated 18 February 1666 and published early that year, in which he argued that spiritual power did not belong to a transcendent God but was immanent in nature itself. Because man was a part of nature he could manifest this power in acts of miraculous healing. In this respect the miracles of Christ and the Apostles recorded in the New Testament were no different from what other men could and have performed.[43] The spiritual power to work miracles came from nature and not from a supernatural divinity. To this extent the Bible was not a unique supernatural revelation but merely an historical account of what a few men among many others had managed to perform merely by relying on the spiritual forces inherent in natural processes. Finally, according to Glanvill, Stubbe claimed sometime before 1671 'That the Arguments to prove a Deity, drawn from that Wisdom, Beauty, Order, and Usefulness that is in the Frame of the Creation, signifie nothing, because We cannot tell what Is Wisdom, Beauty, or Order.'[44]

Here was a comprehensive attack on traditional Christianity and in particular on Boyle's, and the Royal Society's, natural religion. For Stubbe nature is laced with spiritual forces, and these natural forces are divine. Nor does he stop at espousing the mortalistic heresy. His view of nature allows him also to attack other foundations of Christian doctrine – the Biblical miracles, the supernatural divinity of Christ, the supernatural origin of the Bible and the argument from design. Boyle did not allow Stubbe's views to go unanswered. Boyle wrote a private reply in early March to Stubbe's printed letter to him of the month before. He takes Stubbe to task for attempting to give a natural explanation for the Biblical miracles. The upshot of his remarks is that Stubbe's explanation and others like them do not work because they presuppose the operation in nature of rational, spiritual principles, or as Boyle says, 'the animated and intelligent universe.'[45] True religion is spared the depredations of the atheistical

Stubbe because Boyle's mechanical explanations preserve the correct distinction between God and nature while Stubbe's do not. This is also the burden of *A Free Enquiry*, written during the same period as Boyle's exchange with Stubbe. Boyle has harnessed the corpuscular philosophy to religion in part to save it from the likes of Stubbe.[46]

In writing the *Enquiry* Boyle employed his natural philosophy to defeat the threats posed to true religion by the virtual idolatry implicit in the Scholastic natural religion of the Catholics and the flagrant idolatry of the atheists. Both would debase Christianity into one form or another of pagan naturalism, if not stopped by a correct understanding of the relationship between God and nature, creator and creation, which Boyle's philosophy alone could supply. We are now in a position to see why his *Enquiry* was finally published when it was in early 1686. The issues that had shaped its arguments two decades earlier were still alive and even burned with a new glow; the ideological heat of the moment at last coaxed the manuscript into print.

By 1686 Stubbe had been dead ten years, but his ideas did not die with him. On the contrary, his works continued to be purchased and discussed in the 1670s and 1680s.[47] To the same period we can trace the emergence of English deism as a sustained, if tortuous, current in English thought, and in the development of this new intellectual strain Stubbe's ideas played a role. The close similarity between what Stubbe preached in the 1660s and deism as it evolved in the next two decades is clear. Much of the evidence for the deism of the 1670s and 1680s comes from the published tracts of Charles Blount.[48] His deism was more formulary than Stubbe's, harking back as it did, to Edward Lord Herbert of Cherbury's natural religion.[49] Man is endowed with five innate ideas which are the sum of true religion.[50] But Blount's objective and that of his fellow deists was the same as Stubbe's, to replace revealed religion by rational civil religion, and early deism would thus be open to Boyle's charge of pagan naturalism no less than Stubbe had been. In particular Stubbe, Blount and other early English deists shared the view that God's power and the laws or processes of nature are coextensive.[51] Nothing, therefore, can happen outside of the natural order.[52] Even transactions between God and man take place in the arena of nature. Hence miracles, for example, are acts of nature rather than supernatural interventions,[53] and revealed religion is effectively overthrown in favor of the religion of nature. So if Boyle had Stubbe in mind when he wrote his *Enquiry*, he was probably thinking of Stubbe's deistical successors when he prepared the manuscript for publication in 1682 and finally sent it to press four years later. If anything, deism was more entrenched and widespread when Boyle published his book than it had been when he wrote it. But this was not the only motive that induced him to see it into print. The growth of deism should be seen in combination with certain other factors.

Boyle's *Enquiry*, we recall, was aimed against deist and Catholic alike, and its arguments against the latter had assumed at least as great an urgency by 1686 as its anti-deistical ones. From as early as 1683 it was obvious that recent attempts to exclude Charles's Catholic brother from the throne had failed and that, given Charles's failing health, James would soon be king. Already in 1684 the Catholics were beginning to breathe easier and to make serious attempts to spread their faith.[54] The pace of these efforts quickened after James's accession in February 1685.[55]

Both leading and lesser known Anglican polemicists lost no time in mobilizing their talents to combat this ever more menacing disease. From 1684 onward the staunchly anti-Catholic clergy produced a flood of tracts and sermons retailing the doctrinal errors of popery. Their main charge was that Roman doctrine tended toward idolatry. This was not a new claim; there is an Anglican literature dating back to the sixteenth century arguing the case. But the earlier Restoration tracts do not compare in quantity with the numbers produced between 1684 and the Revolution of 1688–9.[56]

From the Anglican point of view Catholic doctrine as formulated at Trent is implicitly if not explicitly idolatrous. Transubstantiation, invocation of the saints, Roman Mariology – all come in for the same attack: the worship which should be reserved for God is let out upon creaturely things – the mother of God, other departed men and women and, worst of all, wafers and cups of wine.[57] Not only do the Catholic clergy encourage the worship of these creatures, but they can even be called upon for spiritual aid and protection. Indeed, among Catholic believers each saint has his proper sphere of territory to look after, so that according to Samuel Johnson, the most notorious of the Anglican Catholic baiters, Roman doctrine has left to God 'neither heaven, nor Earth, nor Water, nor Country, nor City, Peace nor War, to rule and govern, neither Men, nor Beasts, nor their Diseases to Cure.'[58] By the anti-Catholic propagandist, Roman doctrine was depicted as being tantamount to paganism. David Abercromby, a former Jesuit who joined the Anglican pamphlet battalions, said of the Romanists, 'They adore God in Pictures and Images, as he was adored by the Heathens in the Sun, Moon, and other less noble creatures.'[59] The title of Samuel Johnson's most famous contribution to the literature, *Julian the Apostate*, published in 1682, was intended to point to the danger presented to Protestant Christianity in James's succession by comparing it to that of the paganizing late Roman emperor.

Boyle, who after all was a leading lay spokesman for the church, took a lively interest in this campaign. He was especially concerned about the new efforts to spread popery. His old friend Thomas Barlow, now Bishop of Lincoln, informed him that in a church in his diocese

some few of the parishioners (upon pretence of beautifying the church) washed out all the sentences of scripture formerly writ upon the walls; then they set up in their places the images of . . . apostles . . . and . . . patriarchs. The picture of St. Peter they placed above the ten commandments, and that of Paul above the king's arms, and they picture Moses (after the ridiculous popish way) with horns.[60]

Boyle and Barlow agreed that these Romanizing corruptions, undertaken in his diocese and elsewhere, must be stopped. Of this particular instance Boyle wrote to Barlow, 'it seems a thing well becoming your station and your wonted zeal for the purity of religion, to endeavour the early closing of a gap, that, left open, will probably be more and more widened, and prove an inlet to innovations dangerous to the church of England, and consequently to the protestant cause.'[61] Boyle also approved Barlow's contributions to the literature that made Roman doctrine out to be a form of pagan idolatry.[62] In 1687 Boyle published his own contribution entitled *Reasons Why a Protestant Should Not Turn Papist* and there praised the work of his good friend John Tillotson, Dean of Canterbury, which also argued the Catholic tendency towards paganism.[63]

The point is that there is a connection between this literature of controversy and Boyle's *Enquiry*. Just as Boyle's Anglican associates were exposing the idolatrous consequences of Catholic theology he was pointing out the paganizing tendency in Catholic, Scholastic philosophy. The philosophy, Boyle suggests, supports the objectionable theological doctrines. There is in the *Enquiry* an oblique attack on the Scholastic explanation of the miracle of transubstantiation. This is slipped in while Boyle is discussing whether the Schoolmen mean to represent nature as a spiritual or physical phenomenon.[64] The *Enquiry* is published in 1686 in the thick of the Anglican response to the re-Catholicizing efforts of the new king and his co-religionists. The book is Boyle's major contribution, though not his only one, to this response.

Plans for translating it into Latin had been made at least as early as the beginning of 1686, and the translation was advertised to appear that year.[65] In fact the Latin edition was not published until 1687. The translator was the former Jesuit David Abercromby, who had become Boyle's protégé sometime during the 1680s and in the course of the decade wrote several polemical tracts of his own, including one attacking Catholic doctrine for its implicit paganism.[66] Before the *Enquiry* appeared, he and Boyle had discussed the subject of the book, and Abercromby had been converted by Boyle to his view of 'vulgar Opinions' about nature.[67] So the translation was the work of a disciple who was also a fellow apostle in the anti-Catholic Anglican cause. This evidence further suggests that Boyle's intention in publishing the *Enquiry* was to make his own timely contribution to the assault on popish paganism.

The explanation of Boyle's intention, however, is not quite so simple. His book attacks deists as well as Catholics, and it may have been published in early 1686 because at exactly that time the Catholic threat seemed to be threaded in with the deistical one so as to present a particularly alarming dual challenge to Boyle's powerful Anglican friends and associates.

From early 1685 the new king worked without success to get from parliament a religious settlement that would remove legal restrictions on Catholics and Catholic worship. By November he had given up. Parliament was prorogued until February and in early 1686 prorogued again. In the winter of 1685–6 many believed that James would grant a general toleration to Catholics and Dissenters alike, that in other words, having failed to gain the support of parliament, he would act on his own authority to establish Catholic toleration and at the same time extend the privilege to Dissenters not because he loved them – the reverse in fact was nearer the truth – but to build political support.[68]

James's actions were not by themselves responsible for the rumor of a general toleration authorized by the crown. In 1685 the Duke of Buckingham, the powerful courtier, and William Penn, the Quaker leader and the king's confidant, had written tracts arguing the cause of general toleration. In their arguments and what was made of them at the time we can see the possible connection between the leading religious issues of 1685–6 and the publication of Boyle's *Enquiry* that winter.

Buckingham argued for toleration because persecution, he said, was itself irreligious and unchristian.[69] But his view of religion, from which this conclusion sprang, was not orthodox, to say the least. He concluded, to be sure, that of all religions Christianity 'is probably the best.'[70] But this was only a probability. More dangerous still were his thoughts on the subject of what probably constituted the best religion among Christians. It would rest entirely upon 'reason,' by which he meant 'that part of us which is nearest a-kin to the nature of God,'[71] and he therefore said, 'I am forced to lay aside all arguments which have any dependence upon the authority of scripture.'[72] His religion rejected Scriptural authority and magnified human reason to fill its place. He also wrote, 'That being . . . I call God, and those who out of a foolish aversion they have for the name of God will call it nature, do not in any kind differ.'[73] Buckingham may not have understood the implications of this remark, though I find it difficult to think that he did not, but his opponents in the exchange that ensued were quick to point them out.

They accused him of deistical tendencies, and it is true that apart from the evidence I have already adduced to support this accusation, there is a close parallel between Buckingham's brief for a reasonable religion and Blount's and Cherbury's five common notions or principles of natural religion.[74] Buckingham was also accused of espousing a doctrine of reasonableness as the test of religious truth that would permit the practice of any form of pagan idolatry and even the commission of crime on the grounds of conscience.[75] Finally, some feared his views gave encouragement to seditious conspiracy by either republicans or Catholics or both.[76]

These suspicions were heightened when, shortly after Buckingham's book appeared, Penn produced a series of defenses of it. He argued for a general toleration on the grounds, among others, that 'the Protestants and Papists, all . . . agree as to the substance of Christianity'[77] at a time when, as we have seen, Anglicans went to enormous lengths to point out the differences between themselves and their enemies, particularly the Catholics. For such reasons Penn was long suspected by some[78] of being a crypto-Catholic and by others of inclining towards deistical views.[79] In fact at least one person thought Buckingham's ideas came from Penn.[80]

The fear of a general toleration rekindled a suspicion that was at least as old as the mid-century revolution, namely, that a subversive alliance had been forged between Catholics and sectaries.[81] This suspicion was being entertained in 1685–6 by none other than Boyle's close Anglican associates Evelyn and Tillotson, the latter even venturing to suggest that Penn was in league with the Jesuits, if not one himself.[82]

It is in this context that Boyle's *Enquiry* was published, and it is this context that throws light on why it was published and what it was intended to mean and to do. We know already that Boyle was aiming his work against popery. We now see that he may also have been addressing himself to the threat of the deists. In the winter of 1685–6 both threats were alive and particularly urgent given the imminent possibility of a grant of general toleration by the king. There is no direct evidence that Boyle, like others at the time, feared a joint conspiracy of Catholics and sectaries. But in the *Enquiry* he did assimilate the paganizing naturalism of the one enemy to that of the others; Catholics and deists posed a single threat based on their common allegiance to the vulgarly received notion of nature. It is thus arguable that he may have shared the fears of his friends Tillotson and Evelyn that (to quote the latter) the pope might send 'an hundred priests into . . . England, who were to conforme themselves to all Sectaries, and Conditions for the more easily dispersing their doctrine among us.'[83] Certainly a general toleration would help the popish legions 'conforme themselves to . . . Conditions' so as to accomplish their mission. Likewise, deistical ideas, current among sectaries and based on assumptions about nature similar to those of the papists, would allow the latter 'to conforme themselves to . . . Sectaries' in order to intrude Catholicism into England. Popery might be grafted onto deism via a shared paganizing naturalism, and the result would spell the ruin of religion in England. In previous years Boyle in one role or another – as President of the New England Company, member of the Council for Foreign Plantations, and Director of the East India Company – had worried about the Jesuits' capacity for assimilating pagan notions to their Catholic creed as a means of converting the peoples of India and British America.[84] The same syncretizing capacity might now be demonstrated to work closer to home in England itself.

Nor was this the only danger Boyle saw. Catholics might use a common notion of nature to convert sectaries. But sectaries of the freethinking variety might turn around and use this common notion to subvert revealed religion. Here we are on firmer ground in the evidence furnished by the *Enquiry*.

The Catholic natural religion of the Schoolmen supposed that nature, active and intelligent, always does that which is best. Certain heretical thinkers, whom Boyle did not identify but whose views correspond to those of the deists, used this doctrine to attack the ideal of divine providence by claiming that if nature, guided by providence, always acts for the best, how is it possible to explain 'plagues, earthquakes, inundations, and the like destructive calamities?'[85] On this question deistical assumptions about nature departed from Catholic ones. Both postulated a vital, rational principle operating in nature. But the deistical critics of revealed religion turned this shared postulate against the pious view it was meant to support, namely, that a supernatural God operates in and through nature providentially and by design.[86] In attacking Christian providentialism these critics were challenging the argument from design in favor of their own religion of nature. Not only were Scholastic notions paganizing in and of themselves; when used to support Christian natural religion they opened the door to the deistical attack on the doctrine of providence, whether Catholic or Protestant, and the further subversion of Christianity. The vulgarly received notion of nature applied to explaining providence might backfire and drive Christians into the arms of deists.[87]

There was another associated peril implicit in the attack on the notion of a designed universe. For Boyle and the Royal Society it was this notion that authorized the pursuit of experimental natural philosophy: God had designed a universe that men could and were expected to learn to read, and the more industriously they went about the performance of this obligation to study nature, the more they would fulfill God's two purposes in creating the universe, namely, his own glorification and the satisfaction of human needs and desires, the profit and benefit of man.[88] This was 'the usefulness of experimental natural philosophy,' the title of one of Boyle's major works on the subject and the underlying theme of all of his essays on natural religion, and this 'usefulness' was now being threatened by paganizing critics of a Christian providentialism based on traditional Scholastic design arguments.

To blunt the force of their attack, Boyle substituted in place of the Scholastic dictum that nature always acts for the best his own providentialist argument based on the corpuscular philosophy. This substitution allowed him thus to say of God's providence:

He is not over-ruled, as men are fain to say of erring nature, by the head-strong motions of . . . matter, but sometimes purposely over-rules the regular ones [motions of matter], to execute his justice; and therefore plagues, earthquakes, inundations, and the like destructive calamities, though they are sometimes irregularities in nature, yet for that very reason they are designed by providence, which intends, by them, to deprive wicked men of that life, or of those blessings of life, whereof their sins have rendered them unworthy.[89]

According to Boyle (*pace* the Scholastics), it is not nature but God who acts for the best. Boyle thus explained the 'irregularities in nature' and explained away the threat to Christian providentialism implicit in the Scholastic idea of nature, seized upon and exploited by the deists.

Boyle's *Enquiry*, when finally published, performed a number of timely ideological chores for the Anglican establishment whose views it represented. It sought to undermine fundamental Catholic doctrines like transubstantiation and the mediation of the saints by showing that these rested on specious arguments drawn from Scholastic natural philosophy and led to idolatrous consequences. Bishop Gilbert Burnet included Boyle's arguments in his authoritative *Exposition of the Thirty-Nine Articles of the Church of England*, which was carefully read, corrected and approved by Tillotson and Edward Stillingfleet, and this gave them a permanent place in official Anglican theology.[90] By mechanizing or despiritualizing nature, Boyle also took the bite out of the argument that it was impious to study nature in order to benefit man or to establish, as Boyle said, 'the empire of man over the inferior creatures of God.'[91] As for the deists, he answered their equally specious paganizing natural religion, based like that of the Catholics on the outmoded vulgarly received notion of nature. And from both deists and papists he saved the doctrine of God's providence properly conceived. This was a particularly important victory over the deists because their view, based on Scholastic assumptions, undermined the argument from design common to both Catholic and Protestant orthodoxies. In place of the old design argument, now rendered suspect by the deists' use (or abuse) of it to subvert true religion, Boyle substituted his view. He asserted the necessary existence of a supernatural Creator and guaranteed both his perfection and his providential care, thereby legitimating 'the usefulness of experimental natural philosophy' and the anti-Catholic, anti-freethinking order built partly upon it.

Boyle died in 1691. But his will provided for the famous Lectureship which carried forward the apologetical task he had begun. In the meantime the Revolution of 1688–9 had overcome the Catholic threat. But paganizing freethinkers were if anything more active than before, and against this threat the Boyle Lectures took up where the *Enquiry* had left off.[92]

Stubbe to Toland: 'Mahometan Christianity' revived

The Revolution of 1688–9 eliminated the Catholic threat at least as an immediate peril, but it did not silence the freethinkers. From their point of view the Revolution Settlement did not go far enough, despite the Toleration Act, towards promoting liberty of conscience and reducing the authority of the clergy and the established church. In 1693 Blount at last published a collection of short treatises, including the two letters plagiarizing Stubbe's *Account of the Rise and Progress of Mahometanism*, which had previously circulated only in manuscript.[93] Fragments of Stubbe's most explicit statement of his subversive religion had finally got into print, even though falsely attributed to Blount. This was a foretaste of things to come. With the lapsing of the Licensing Act in 1695, the radical Whigs were free to publish their anticlerical attacks and heretical ideas in uncensored form, and they did so as never before. The next twenty-five years saw an explosion of heterodoxy exceeded only by that which occurred during the 1640s and 1650s.

The man who contributed more perhaps than anyone else to this radical religious current was John Toland. His career has been studied elsewhere.[94] We are interested here only in showing that his religious views echo ideas that Stubbe had articulated a generation before and in particular that when in 1718 at least one Anglican churchman answered Toland he had Stubbe's 'Mahometan Christianity' in mind as well. Here is an explicit link between the two heresiarchs, a link that seems to have existed for the most part underground in the continued clandestine circulation of Stubbe's manuscript *Account of the Rise and Progress of Mahometanism* some fifty years after it had been written.

Toland first made his religious views available in print by writing *Christianity Not Mysterious*, published in 1696. Here he put forward the subversive idea that mysteries in religion should be treated in the same way that natural philosophers were accustomed to treating mysteries in nature, that is, as things 'absolutely unintelligible,' and hence not to be taken seriously. The effect of this radical surgery would be to reduce the articles of Christian belief to only those truths which 'can be made as clear and intelligible as natural things which come within our knowledge and comprehension.'[95] The book produced a sensation and became something of a bestseller, especially in Ireland where it was sent in 1697.[96] The conservative and clerical reaction was swift and harsh. The Irish parliament ordered the book to be burned and Toland arrested and prosecuted for publishing it. This action made the book even more scarce and sought after.[97] The book burning was duly conducted on 11 September 1697, but Toland, to escape arrest and prosecution, 'very wisely took his way back to England.'[98]

Toland was widely attacked for heresy, Socinianism, deism and worse. The next year, for instance, Robert South dedicated his *Twelve Sermons upon Several Subjects and Occasions* to Narcissus Marsh, Archbishop of Dublin and Primate of Ireland, and in 'The Epistle Dedicatory,' dated 30 April 1698, wrote, referring to Toland and his infamous book:

when a certain Mahometan Christian (no new thing of late), notorious for his blasphemous denial of the mysteries of our religion, and his insufferable virulence against the whole Christian priesthood, thought to have found shelter amongst you [in Ireland], the Parliament . . . sent him packing, and without the help of a faggot soon made the kingdom too hot for him,[99]

The dedication went on to attack Socinianism, and one of the *Twelve Sermons* upheld the Christian mysteries against the Socinians.[100] Thus early in his career Toland was accused of the very heresy with which Stubbe had been associated. Toland, like Stubbe, was being linked to the Arianism of Islam. Toland's accuser South was the Public Orator of the University of Oxford in the late 1660s, and at the very time that Stubbe was speaking out against the Royal Society in Somerset barns and alehouses, South attacked it in his oration at the dedication of the Sheldonian Theater, built by Christopher Wren, FRS.[101] South would have been in a position to know Stubbe's views and may have had him in mind when in his attack on Toland he referred parenthetically to earlier Mahometan Christians.[102] By the end of the century Socinians and Muslims had become linked in the public mind. There was a public meeting in London in 1682 between English Socinians and the Moroccan ambassador to England,[103] and the Boyle Lectures, which had gone on once a month for eight months a year since 1692 (excepting 1693), had been set up 'for proving the Christian religion against the notorious infidels, viz. atheists, theists, pagans, Jews and Mahometans.'[104]

Stubbe and Toland shared more than an association with 'Mahometan Christianity.' Toland's polemical attacks on the established church and his conception of how religion should be settled in England have much in common with what Stubbe thought and argued. In particular Toland, throughout his career, championed a view of the church which was very reminiscent of Stubbe and very different from the church erected by the Revolution settlement. To begin with, Toland argued for what he called 'entire liberty of conscience' which would have extended the same civil and religious liberties to all Protestants, Dissenters and conformists alike.[105] Thus he sought to tear down those laws which penalized the nonconformists. His argument was pitched on the same grounds that Stubbe had used to argue for the Indulgence:

Entire liberty of conscience is not only the most equitable in itself . . . ; the most expedient in politics, as it furnishes the king with more hearts, and the nation with more hands: but tis also the most certain way of preserving the Church of England not only safe, but even flourishing in all its dignities and emoluments.[106]

Despite this profession of his desire to see the established church in a 'flourishing' condition, the clergy were alarmed by his proposals for reform, and with good reason. Toland was intensely anticlerical. In *The Primitive Constitution of the Christian Church*, written in 1704 or 1705,[107] but published posthumously in 1726, he set forth his conception of what the church should be. In the ideal church, modelled on 'the primitive constitution,' there would be no separate priesthood removed from the laity by the false ritual of ordination. Instead of the division between priests and laymen, there would simply be 'the people and their teachers,' and the teachers should be chosen by the people, not by bishops or fellow priests, according to corrupt current practice. As Toland said, 'I affirm then that any society of Christians may out of their own number, or any other body of people, pitch upon willing persons, with the necessary qualifications to be their overseers.'[108] He was vague regarding 'the necessary qualifications,' but made it perfectly clear that these teachers, again contrary to current practice, would be 'deposed for just causes, as being ignorant, debauched or an enemy of the government.'[109] Here was a full-scale assault on both established and dissenting churches, based as they were on the division between laity and clergy and the spiritual and disciplinary power of the latter over the former. In place of this, Toland would have substituted a civic religion – without priests but with teachers whom the people appointed and, if need be, deposed at will. This was Toland's conception of what he called 'a national religion,'[110] and much of the inspiration for it came from Harrington, 'to whom,' Toland said, 'every man is obliged who writes on this subject.'[111] This is very reminiscent of Stubbe's Independency before the Restoration and after 1660 his conception of civil religion, an Erastian church that would be national and nonsectarian. Milton in his last published work in 1673 also argued for a union of Protestants, a national church, based upon mutual toleration and a common offensive against popery.[112] Toland cited this tract by Milton as supporting his own cause.[113] Toland also followed Milton when he argued that a separate priesthood should be abandoned in favor of mere teachers made responsible to the people.

One other thread linking Stubbe to Toland was the latter's repeated argument that learning in the schools and universities was 'popishly affected' by the claptrap of sacerdotal and Trinitarian doctrine. Stubbe claimed that the noble ancients were being displaced by the corrupt and popish moderns, while Toland said, quoting from Harrington's *The Prerogative of Popular Government*, that ancient learning was being corrupted:

since the heads and fellows of colleges are become the only Greeks and Romans, the Greeks and Romans are become servilely addicted, of narrow principles . . . Pedants they may be . . . in the University, but I see no necessity, why they must . . . be disloyal or superstitious . . .; for as it is to educate youth in principles contrary to these . . . , no less than to accomplish them in all useful learning and knowledge that the universities are set apart.[114]

Useful learning was not enough unless combined with ancient wisdom.[115] The wisdom he referred to, in contrast to the 'superstitious' version of the ancients put forward by the 'pedants,' was that which taught true civil religion, 'entire liberty of conscience' in 'a national religion' based upon 'the primitive constitution of the Christian church.' This was so close to the concealed message of Stubbe's attacks on the Royal Society that one hopes for a study that would show the continuity of argument, leading from Stubbe to Toland and beyond, around this very issue.

Toland, like Stubbe, held a vitalistic conception of nature, and just as Stubbe opposed his radical Galenism to the natural philosophy of Boyle and the Royal Society, so Toland deployed his pantheistic materialism against Newton and the Newtonians.[116] Stubbe, for his part, was particularly concerned that the new philosophy was being used to uphold belief in a separate transcendent spiritual order which provided the ideological foundation of clerical dominion. Two decades later, the earliest Newtonians, latitudinarian Anglicans to a man, were making the same use of their master's teachings.[117] To the extent that Newtonianism had been accepted into the university curriculum by the first or second decade of the eighteenth century, Toland would have been concerned for the same reason that Stubbe had been, namely, that science was being used to prop up superstition and hence priestly power.

What made Toland especially dangerous and a particular target for clerical attacks was not merely his polemical ability or the outrageousness of his vision but also the fact that he was far from being alone in the causes he espoused. The revolution had lifted the strict censorship that Stubbe had faced, and the radical Whiggery represented by men like Toland could gather political momentum as never before. Thus Toland could be counted upon to put the radical Whig view each time the religious settlement was severely tested during the second decade of the eighteenth century – first in the reaction to Dr Henry Sacheverell, then in the protracted Bangorian controversy and finally in the attempt to remove the restrictions upon the rights of nonconformists.[118] Here we are interested in Toland's contribution to the polemics surrounding the latter two, the storm over the Bishop of Bangor's pronouncements and the attempt to extend the toleration, because it is here that we see most clearly and convincingly the connection between Toland and Stubbe.

In March 1717, Benjamin Hoadley, Bishop of Bangor, preached a sermon before the king in which he divested the clergy of all spiritual authority by claiming that Christ was the sole law-giver to his subjects and that as a result the laws of Christ were not subject to interpretation by any mundane authority including the clergy.[119] The next year the Whigs in parliament, led by James, first Earl of Stanhope and Robert Viscount Molesworth, fought to repeal legislation against Dissenters.[120] Toland had already written on behalf of this latter cause,[121] probably at the request of Molesworth, who was his patron.[122] Equally, Toland was associated by his enemies with Hoadley's views, and there were obvious similarities between them.[123] In 1718, the very year in which both the Bangorian controversy and the parliamentary debate over toleration reached their height, Toland published *Nazarenus: Or Jewish, Gentile and Mahometan Christianity*, a historical and polemical work which he intended as a contribution to the argument for toleration.[124] It was probably addressed to Molesworth.[125]

Like Stubbe, he borrowed from Selden the notion of the precepts of Noah, the fundamental natural law observed first by Old Testament Jews and then by the first Christians, Nazarenes as Toland called them, who were also Jews.[126] These Nazarenes were Arians and the Noahic precepts prescribed that they tolerate all Gentile Christians who held divergent views.[127] Toland insisted that this was the sort of Christianity enjoined by the Scriptures, which were in this regard in complete accord with the law of nature.[128] Going further, he wrote: 'the one main design of Christianity was to improve and perfect the knowledge of the law of nature . . . Now, all this is very intelligible, easy, and consistent, according to the Nazarene System: . . . and I foresee that many . . . will say that I advance a new Christianity, though I think it undoubtedly to be the old one.'[129] The upshot of Toland's historical argument concerning the primitive church was to banish special supernatural revelation from Christianity and to reduce true religion to the observance of merely natural law. Though he claimed that the Scriptures deliver the truths of natural law, it was not Scripture that he cited in spelling out his case. Rather he quoted the pagan Cicero at length to make the point that the whole purpose of religion was to teach 'the Noahic precepts: . . . since sound reason or the light of common sense is the catholic and eternal rule, without which mankind could not subsist in peace or happiness one hour. It is the fundamental bond of all society, where there is or there is not revealed religion.'[130] By deploying Selden's Hebrew studies, Toland succeeded in paganizing Christianity, and in terms very similar to Stubbe's, who half a century earlier achieved the almost identical result, also with Selden's help.

Like Stubbe, Toland argued that this first Christianity of Jesus and his immediate followers survived in pockets in the late Roman empire and was eventually appropriated by Mohammed to become the basis of Islam.[131] This 'Nazarenism' was the closest thing to Toland's own beliefs: 'I have less exception to the name of Nazaren than to any other.'[132] Likewise, this Scriptural (and natural) Christianity supplied the example for a new religious settlement in England. In a remark recalling Harrington he wrote: '*No innovation* is the word, when the question is all the while about reducing things to the *Old Foundation*.'[133]

Toland's work also recalls Stubbe's views. Toland's argument at many points – the account of the first Christianity and its subsequent corruption,[134] the argument from the congruence of natural law and the Scriptures,[135] the disparagement of Paul's additions and the nexus established between Christianity and Islam – are quite close to Stubbe's *Account of the Rise and Progress of Mahometanism*. That work was still in manuscript, and the manuscript was still in circulation. It had been copied in 1705 by Charles Hornby, a book collector and Tory pamphleteer.[136] It was next mentioned by Thomas Mangey, chaplain to the Bishop of London, in 1718 in his answer to Toland's *Nazarenus*, published that year.[137] In a section of Mangey's book devoted to an attack on Toland's 'Mahometan Christianity' he said of the Muslims and their defenders in contemporary England:

There have been likewise some amongst our selves that out of ignorance or ill will to their own religion, have professed to think better of them than they deserve. A physician of some note a few years ago wrote, as it is said, a thorough defence of their sentiments, a manuscript copy of which I have seen, and it is surprising that among the many unbelieving books that have been lately published, this should escape.[138]

Whether Toland knew and used Stubbe's manuscript is not certain.[139] But Mangey was associating Toland with Stubbe's views, and Mangey's surprise that the work had been left unpublished suggests that it was circulating among those men, like Toland, who would have had reason to publish it. In any case, Mangey saw fit to go on to answer both Toland and Stubbe, which further indicates that the manuscript was circulating and was seen, like Toland's work, to be a part of the current radical polemic requiring an effective reply.[140] There is then a direct link between Stubbe and the radical Whig views represented by Toland during the first decades of the Enlightenment in England.

Toland represented essentially the same challenge to the religious settlement as Stubbe had. They shared a materialistic conception of nature: Stubbe was a radical Galenist and Hobbesian secular historicist, Toland a pantheist, a word of his own invention.[141] Such views challenged the pieties of latitudinarian natural religion and the natural philosophy of the Royal Society. Stubbe had been answered by Boyle and Glanvill *inter alia*, and Toland by the first generation of Newtonian churchmen. This has been established by Professor M. C. Jacob and me in previous work.[142] What has not been clearly seen before is what I have established here.

There was a close link between Stubbe's civil religion and Toland's. In both Christianity could and should be divested of its adventitious mysteries – 'unintelligible jargon,' as Toland said [143] – and made to yield a Scriptural minimum in harmony with natural law, which could then serve as the basis of 'a natural religion,' tolerant, reasonable and dedicated to civil ends rather than priestly ones – the advancement of learning, national power and prosperity.[144] An essentially pagan or at least paganizing vitalistic or pantheistic conception of nature outlawed from the universe all notions of a separate spiritual order presided over by a separate priesthood or clergy. What was prescribed, instead, was a religion enjoining toleration, in which people would be instructed in the wisdom of the ancients for the pursuit of moral and political goals in this life. Much of the inspiration for this was Harringtonian, and Stubbe must be credited with reviving civil religion, couched in Harringtonian language, during the Restoration. Nor did his ideas die with him. They continued to circulate both before and after the revolution to the fright and distress of churchmen and survived long enough for them to be directly associated in the eyes of the church with the challenge of Toland's 'Mahometan Christianity' and the struggle in the early Enlightenment for 'entire liberty of conscience' and equality under the law. Stubbe, I think, would not have taken any of this very much amiss, if at all. Finally, it is the *corpus* of Stubbe's works, so long neglected or misinterpreted, that constitutes the missing link between the civil religion of the 1650s and the revival of this tradition at the beginning of the eighteenth century. Stubbe's works, carefully reinterpreted, provide an essential key to unlocking the connection between the radical Protestantism of the mid-seventeenth century and the paganism of the early Enlightenment.

Epilogue: the paganizing thread

The peregrination of Stubbe's manuscript in the eighteenth century did not end quite with Toland. Charles Hornby had possessed two copies since 1705, and when after his death his library was sold, they were sold with it.[1] These two manuscripts turned up next, with one other copy, in 1817 in the sale catalogue of the great eighteenth-century library belonging success-ively to Thomas Hollis, Thomas Brand Hollis and John Disney – all episcopal Unitarians.[2] It is highly possible that Thomas Hollis, the first of those men and the one most responsible for building the collection, had purchased the Stubbe manuscripts offered in the sale of Hornby's library in 1739 or shortly after, as the manuscripts would have appealed to Hollis's reading and collecting tastes. Like Stubbe, he was interested in the question of historical change and sought the reasons for it.[3] He was not only a Unitarian but a champion of anticlericalism and republicanism and an avid collector of books on both themes.[4] He sent books by Charles Blount, along with many others, to Harvard College, presented a copy of Gerrard Winstanley's *Law of Freedom* (1652) to Henry Fielding,[5] and with Disney took a serious interest in the mortalism of Richard Overton, the radical pamphleteer who flourished during the 1640s.[6] Hollis spent his life collecting and distributing books of the sort he thought would foster liberty.[7] The two subsequent owners of his library were scarcely less interested in promoting rational Protestantism, republicanism and civil liberty.[8] Disney was 'in the van-guard of the Unitarian movement' from the 1760s onwards.[9] All three men saw England by mid-century as beset by those forces making for luxury, corruption and tyranny. They responded by advocating austerity, public virtue and liberty, and in this struggle their book collection was their principal weapon.[10] Their library is a testament to that, as it was filled with the works that constituted the mainstream of the English, Scottish and continental republican tradition from the *Vindiciae Contra Tyrannos* and the works of John Ponet and George Buchanan to those of the commonwealth-men of their own day.[11] Their collection included the Vanian Army tracts of Henry Stubbe.[12] In a variety of ways his manuscript *Account of the Rise and Progress of Mahometanism* would have been attractive to these three collectors and custodians of the greatest library of libertarian works in eighteenth-century England. Their possession of three copies of Stubbe's manuscript should be seen as a political act – and so his influence lived on exactly where one would expect it to.

Our attention, however, has been concentrated on that influence in the period running from Harrington to Toland. Before I made this study, there were two Stubbes – the young, radical don and the older Scholastic reactionary. The explanation for the switch was simple: Stubbe was an unprincipled turncoat who always sided with the winning party. But I had found some evidence that created doubts – the vitalistic materialism or radical Galenism that lay at the root of his contribution to the controversy percolating around Greatrakes's brief career as a healer, and that curious *Account of the Rise and Progress of Mahometanism* that, based as it was on a kind of Hobbesian historicism, defied being labelled simply reactionary. So I re-read the evidence, as much of it at least as I could find, and came up with the interpretation offered here.

There is a continuity between Stubbe the young Turk during the late 1650s and Stubbe the supposed conservative royalist and churchman after 1660. It is a question of reading the evidence the right way. On the surface Stubbe's writings between 1660 and late 1673 appear as so many defenses of traditional loyalties and institutions. But as I have shown, there is another, deeper level of meaning in these works which, when exposed, reveals Stubbe as a radical critic of the Restoration settlement. He was not free to express his real views openly, and so resorted to subterfuge and contrived a new rhetoric of double meaning. Sometimes the concealed message is almost transparent, as in *The Miraculous Conformist* (1666), even though a correct reading of this tract had to wait until now. In other works the cryptic message is much more opaque – in, for example, the attacks on the Royal Society (1670-1) and the defenses of the Indulgence (1672). But even here a careful reading or decoding strips away the masks and lays bare the double meaning.

Historians of the new philosophy and the Royal Society have mis-interpreted Stubbe's attacks, whereas his contemporaries did not. Glanvill, More, Boyle, Beale and Evelyn, and no doubt others as well, were not taken in by the camouflage, as the historians have been, perhaps in part because they have wished to believe, more than is good for ferreting out historical truth, that the confrontation between Stubbe and the Society was simply a conflict between darkness and light, progress and error, Scholastic humanism and modern science. This study attempts to correct that bias by reading the texts, insofar as possible, through the eyes of Stubbe's contemporaries. If this effort has done nothing else, at least it has shown that the debate over the Royal Society was far richer, more complicated and intriguing than has been thought.

In particular it has shown that during the Restoration there were two views of the relationship between science, on the one hand, and religion and society, on the other. There was the official view, institutionalized in the Royal Society and propagated by men like Sprat and Glanvill, a view which linked science to a version of orthodox Protestantism and which interpreted the scientific enterprise as providing an antidote to the excess of revolution. According to this view, the mission of the Royal Society was to pour oil on the troubled waters of Restoration political and religious life churned up by the mid-century crisis. The result of this effort, it was hoped, would be stability, prosperity and the defeat of Protestant radicalism in favor of latitudinarian Anglicanism. In contrast there was Stubbe's view which exposed and attacked the alliance being forged between the philosophy of the Royal Society and the magisterial Reformation. Not only was Stubbe sharply critical of what he saw; he also offered an alternative – a paganizing naturalism and secular historicism which fundamentally challenged any form of orthodox Protestantism and which put in its place a civic religion which harked back to Selden, Harrington and Hobbes and looked forward to the Enlightenment.

This reinterpretation of Stubbe's polemical career also takes account for the first time of his contribution to the cause of the country opposition during the autumn of 1673. It is doubtful whether the older interpretation could stand up under the weight of the evidence of Stubbe's activities as a polemicist for the country party. One reason why that interpretation stood at all was its neglect of the whole of Stubbe's career in favor of the single episode of his challenge to the Royal Society. To be consistent, those interpreters would have to say of his involvement in country polemics that he did so for reasons of expediency, just as they say he had done by attacking the Royal Society. But it is difficult to believe – indeed it is quite impossible – that it was more expedient to become a country pamphleteer in late 1673 than to remain where he already was, namely, attached to the court.

What we now have then is one Stubbe where there used to be two; one Stubbe traced through the twists and turns of his career and found to be not the unprincipled hack that the older interpretation would have us believe, but a man who, in coming to terms with the Restoration, relinquished what he saw as his earlier, naive belief in people's ability, moral as well as political, to bring the good old cause into being and salvaged what he still thought possible to achieve. From outspoken, even flamboyant, radical, he became cautious and cryptic – but only somewhat less radical in the message he preached by new surreptitious means. It is true that he became a court pamphleteer for a time, but even here he intruded his anticlericalism and civil religion into his books and based his defense of the war and the Indulgence upon a revised understanding of Harrington which was anything but traditionally royalist and which at least to some extent reflected Shaftesbury's thinking at the time. The introduction of a revised Harringtonian analysis into his court propaganda may have escaped the censor's pen because it was taken for granted that anything so official in its sponsorship would be acceptable in its content and argument. The authorities should have known their man better than that. Alternatively, the works may not have been read by the government carefully enough, thus anticipating the mistakes of recent historians.

Not only do we now have one Stubbe instead of two. But this reinterpretation of his career has shown something of the utmost importance for the history of radical ideology, namely the survival throughout the Restoration of a Hobbesist and Harringtonian critique of established institutions, the monarchy and especially the church, the clerical Reformation and the new philosophy represented by the Royal Society. This survival provides a vital link between one revolution in the 1640s and 1650s and another in 1688–9, between the civil religions of Harrington and Hobbes and those of Blount, Molesworth and Toland. Here is an important strand connecting radical Protestantism to the early Enlightenment, and Stubbe plays a major, if not even essential, role in the story.

In particular we can now say that many issues were the same for Stubbe and Toland – to reduce, if not eliminate, the power of the clergy; to put in place of a clerically dominated Christianity a civil religion whose purposes would be secular, moral and political, to build a nation of virtuous patriots and soldiers rather than Christian believers obedient to clerical authority; and to sever science and learning from conventional Protestantism and attach them to the purposes of civil religion, the secular state and the people. Not only were these issues the same for both men, but Stubbe's influence was still felt in Toland's lifetime and denounced in the same breath with Toland himself by at least one official detractor, the Bishop of London's chaplain. Thus in the eyes of the clerical enemy the association of Stubbe with Toland was close, the link between them direct.

Stubbe's ideas represent a minority report in the Restoration, but no less important for that, as the reaction on the part of Boyle, Glanvill and More – all leading minds – makes clear. His views, once disclosed, make him one of the most interesting and original thinkers of his age; anything but a Scholastic throwback, he was an acutely perceptive critic of the Royal Society and its version of the new philosophy, a radical humanist preaching a unique and important message – both for his time and ours – concerning the purpose to be served by knowledge and science.

Postscript (July 1982)

Since this book was completed, and while the type was being set, a paper by Nicholas H. Steneck has appeared which attacks my interpretation of the controversy surrounding Valentine Greatrakes and in particular Stubbe's and Robert Boyle's involvement in it.[13] Steneck bases his attack on the work I published relating to the controversy before I wrote this book. But since my interpretation, elaborated in chapters 3 and 8 of this book, remains in essentials unchanged, Steneck's own views are as much at odds with the interpretation set out here as they are with my earlier work.

The disagreements between Steneck and me are fundamental. Contrary to what I have argued, Steneck claims 1) that no significant ideological difference between Boyle and Stubbe is manifested in their disagreement regarding Greatrakes's putative healing powers; 2) that Stubbe's position in the controversy can be assimilated to Greatrakes's own explanation of his cures which was significantly different from Boyle's; 3) that Boyle's *Free Enquiry* was not meant in any important sense to answer Stubbe or views like Stubbe's; and 4) that, instead, it should be read *inter alia* as an attack on the Cambridge Platonists, and More and Glanvill in particular, who should not therefore be seen as being 'of one mind with Boyle in the Greatrakes affair.' Regarding each of these claims I have taken an opposing view. Steneck, moreover, is making two larger claims. He concludes that his challenge to my interpretation of the debate over Greatrakes's cures undermines 1) my view that the development of Boyle's thought can be understood as a response in part to the ideological challenges thrown up by the English Revolution, conceived of as a crisis stretching from the 1640s to the 1680s and beyond[14] and 2) the interpretation worked out by Margaret Jacob and me which maintains that the scientific revolution in seventeenth-century England must be understood as in part a liberal Anglican response to the contemporary social and political crisis.[15] I shall reply to all of Steneck's claims large and small. First I shall answer his four attacks on my interpretation of the Greatrakes episode, and in the process point out where he has misread me and where he has misread the evidence. Second I shall take up his claim that his attack has dealt a serious blow, perhaps even a deathblow, both to my interpretation of Boyle and the interpretation (worked out by Margaret Jacob and me) of 'the Anglican origins of modern science.'

Steneck's first challenge to my view of the Greatrakes affair is to claim that Boyle and Stubbe's different interpretations of Greatrakes's cures did not involve any significant ideological conflict. To support his case against me Steneck maintains that Stubbe had given up his radicalism at the Restoration and adduces evidence of Boyle's respect for Stubbe's scholarship and of the previous intellectual exchange between the two men.[16] As to the first claim, I have shown in chapters 3 through 7 of this book that Stubbe modified his radical opinions after 1660; he did not abandon them. There is, moreover, a continuity between his views, particularly his religious, philosophical and ecclesiological ones, before and after 1660, despite appearances and what Stubbe seemed to say to the contrary. Steneck seems to be taken in by Stubbe's duplicity; Boyle and others were not. The fact that Boyle was one of Stubbe's patrons at the time did not make it impossible for the two men to disagree in ideological terms; indeed I have indicated that Boyle may have patronized Stubbe in part because of their ideological differences and that Stubbe for his part may have addressed *The Miraculous Conformist* to Boyle in an effort to turn the purpose of that patronage upon itself and expose its limits.[17] What I miss in Steneck's account at this point and others is any sense of people acting out of shrewd, even devious, calculation rather than for apparent or stated motives. In Steneck's version Boyle and Stubbe, not to say the others, are what they seem to be and say what they mean, no more and no less. This point of view strikes me as being historically insensitive, in view of the post-revolutionary context in which there was so much for everyone to hide and so much more, given the censorship and repression, that could only be insinuated. This context and its impact on discourse are missing in Steneck's treatment.

Having claimed that Boyle and Stubbe were in no apparent ideological conflict, how does Steneck try to explain away Boyle's answer, written posthaste, to *The Miraculous Conformist*? He conjectures that the urgency of Boyle's reply 'could well have been motivated by a desire not to alienate friends, rather than a desire to counter subversives.'[18] The particular 'friend' Steneck has in mind was Daniel Coxe, who wrote to Boyle four days before he answered Stubbe's letter to him. Coxe's letter claimed that *The Miraculous Conformist*, which he had heard was in the works, was intended to show that Greatrakes's cures were no different from those that Christ had performed, that the cures of both were 'the result' of a merely human 'Constitution,' in order to disprove (or at least cast serious doubts on) the divinity of Christ and so 'enervate the very basis of Christianity.'[19] Coxe went on, Steneck says, to issue to Boyle an 'ominous warning' that if he did not answer Stubbe's interpretation of Greatrakes's healing powers, the pious would turn against him. Steneck concludes: 'It is little wonder that Boyle, faced with such dire consequences advanced from quarters that he seems to have respected, put pen to paper as soon as Stubbe's work arrived.'[20]

Steneck's view on this score raises more questions than it pretends to solve. Why did Boyle not wish to alienate Coxe and the pious? Presumably he did not wish to, because by Steneck's own account he 'seems to have respected' them. More to the point, why did Boyle respect them? Presumably he did so because he shared their views and their piety. Certainly Coxe thought he did. If so, it follows in all probability that he also shared their reading of Stubbe's heretical message. Finally, in that case Coxe's warning was not so 'ominous' as Steneck would have us believe, nor would the consequences that Coxe foresaw of Boyle's refusal to reply to Stubbe be as 'dire' as Steneck imagines. Coxe was not ominously warning Boyle of dire personal consequences; he was rather dramatizing the seriousness of the problem. He was not threatening but coaxing him to reply.

If Boyle 'respected' Coxe and the pious party and shared their piety and thus their opinion of Stubbe's deviant and subversive interpretation of Greatrakes's cures, one would expect Boyle to indicate his agreement with them and his disagreement with Stubbe in his reply to the latter. On this issue Steneck is extremely confused and on certain essential points quite simply wrong. He assures us that 'Stubbe had not equated Greatrakes's cures directly with the miracles of Christ and the apostles,'[21] when it is clear that this is exactly what he did or came as close to doing as he could in print in 1666 without risking prosecution. He wrote: 'If he [Greatrakes] doth the things that never man did, except Christ and the Apostles &c. judge what we are to think.'[22] This view was very much at the root of Stubbe's heresy: Greatrakes, Stubbe implied, can do by natural means, his 'temperament,' 'complexion' or what Coxe called his 'Constitution,' what Christ and the Apostles did, thereby implying that the New Testament miracles were also the results of natural processes and that Christ was not divine but entirely human. Coxe pointed all of this out to Boyle, and again Steneck misinterprets what it is that Coxe told him.[23] Boyle for his part agreed that Stubbe seemed 'to make a parity' between Greatrakes's cures and the New Testament miracles.[24]

On the basis of his mistaken readings in this matter Steneck goes on to claim that all that Boyle thought Stubbe was doing was something far less subversive (if subversive at all) than what he was in fact doing. According to Steneck, all that Boyle thought that Stubbe was doing was 'mixing . . . the supernatural or miraculous with the natural,' which 'tended to degrade truly supernatural events, such as the true miracles of Christ and the apostles.'[25] This is quite mistaken. Stubbe was not 'mixing;' he was conflating the miraculous and the natural and by implication eliminating the supernatural. Miracles are being absorbed into the natural order, and by implication there is no supernatural order. No wonder Coxe thought that Stubbe was not only challenging Christ's divinity and the validity of the New Testament as divine revelation, both of which hung on the authenticity (as supernatural performances) of the New Testament miracles. Coxe thought that Stubbe, in attacking the uniqueness of these miracles as he did, was also undermining the immortality of the soul, the doctrine of future rewards and punishments and belief in a providential God.[26] Not only did Coxe interpret Stubbe's views in this way; he also informed Boyle of their implications. Boyle's answer to Stubbe, Steneck's misreading notwithstanding, clearly shows that he thought at the very least that Stubbe could be read as conflating the miraculous and the natural and was thereby jeopardizing what was fundamental to orthodox Christian belief, namely, the existence of a transcendent supernatural order.[27]

Failing to understand that this was Stubbe's position, and that Boyle saw that this was Stubbe's position, Steneck can conclude that Boyle 'did not accuse Stubbe of continuing to hold to a radical ideology.'[28] It is true that Boyle did not directly accuse Stubbe and offered him a way out by saying that the implications of what he was saying may have been the result of the speed with which he wrote rather than of any deliberate intent. This was characteristic of the way Boyle dealt with his opponents. Rather than pushing them to the wall, he tried to bring them around to his view by gentle persuasion.[29] This was the tactic Boyle adopted in his dispute with Stubbe, but it was only a rhetorical device. Again Steneck is misled by the way the argument was conducted; he mistakes caginess for meaning, stratagems for substance. In short Boyle's polemical tactics should not disguise, as for Steneck they do, the fact that he clearly understood the subversive implications, spelled out by Coxe, of what Stubbe was saying and that in his reply to him attempted to counter his opinions.

Here then is further evidence that Boyle's reply was motivated by ideological considerations, the 'desire to counter subversives' which Steneck disallows, and not merely 'by a desire not to alienate friends,' as Steneck would have it. Nor is it reasonable to think otherwise and deny the ideological factor. Steneck has isolated Boyle's exchange with Stubbe from his earlier polemical involvements. But I have shown in detail that from the late 1640s on Boyle was engaged in dialogue with groups and individuals who maintained ideological positions opposed to his, and in the process constructed a natural philosophical design to meet the ideological challenges posed by these various polemical encounters.[30] Nor did he cease to engage in such dialogue after the Restoration. At the very moment of the Greatrakes business Boyle was sponsoring what he and his circle hoped would be a definitive answer to the freethinkers who denied that the New Testament was divinely inspired.[31] Such a view was very close to what Coxe took to be the intent and Boyle regarded as at least the implications of Stubbe's interpretation of Greatrakes's strokings. During this period (or if Steneck is right, shortly before), moreover, Boyle was at work on an important treatise entitled *A Free Enquiry into the Vulgarly Received Notion of Nature*, in which he attacked views very much like Stubbe's which conflated the natural and the divine.[32] He also saw that *The Miraculous Conformist* could be read as supporting such a conflation and wrote to Stubbe that 'some readers' might 'take a rise from your epistle to maintain it.'[33] No wonder then that Boyle reacted with such urgency to Stubbe's letter. It must have represented to him a larger current challenge that was very much on his mind. But of course before this can be seen one must rescue the debate between Boyle and Stubbe over Greatrakes from the isolation to which Steneck consigns it. One must also see the debate as a confrontation between two different and antagonistic conceptions of the relationship between nature and the divine, a confrontation loaded with ideological significance in post-revolutionary Restoration England, and this is something Steneck completely fails to do.

There is one further measure of his failure in this respect. I have argued that Boyle and Greatrakes took the same view of the latter's cures and one opposed to Stubbe's.[34] Steneck, on the other hand, argues that 'on the key issue of the source and operation of his power Greatrakes was more in agreement with Stubbe than with Boyle.'[35] One of us is plainly wrong. Steneck bases his conclusion on two claims both of which, I think, are mistaken. First he maintains that Boyle 'was convinced' that the cures could be explained entirely by reference to natural processes. Boyle's position, according to Steneck, was characterized by the view that 'miracles are events in nature that by definition cannot be explained using natural mechanisms.'[36] Greatrakes's cures were therefore not miraculous because Boyle thought they could be explained by such natural mechanisms. Second Steneck holds that Stubbe and Greatrakes both interpreted the cures to be genuine 'Protestant miracles,' gifts of God that worked 'by natural means.'[37] For Stubbe and Greatrakes then both natural and supernatural forces were involved; for Boyle only natural ones were.

Let us examine each of Steneck's two claims in turn. First, did Boyle think that Greatrakes's cures could be entirely explained in natural terms? To support this view Steneck points to the following statement by Boyle: 'I hold it not unlawful to endeavour to give a physical account of his cures.'[38] But this scarcely amounts to insisting that they can be entirely explained without reference to supernatural causation. Nor, contrary to Steneck, did Boyle ever take this view. Even Steneck has to admit, thereby contradicting himself, that Boyle held out the possibility that the cures were miraculous.[39] So it seems that Boyle could not make up his mind as to whether there was 'anything in them of a supernatural gift' or whether they should be understood in completely natural terms. His position, however, was more refined than that, a refinement which Steneck misses. The evidence indicates that Boyle tended towards the view that the cures, though explicable in natural terms, did indeed have something 'in them of a supernatural gift.' He says, for instance, that 'I am not yet fully convinced that there is . . . anything that is purely supernatural' in the cures, 'and therefore till the contrary doth appear, I hold it not unlawful to endeavour to give a physical account' of them.[40] This is a long way from Steneck's view that 'Boyle was convinced . . . that, unless contrary evidence should appear, "a physical account of his [Greatrakes's] cures" could be given.'[41] Steneck, first by not taking into account that Boyle said he was 'not yet fully convinced' (which suggests that he was close to being convinced) of the supernatural origin of the cures and second by substituting 'unless contrary evidence should appear' for Boyle's own much more positive 'till the contrary doth appear,' has managed to create the mistaken impression that Boyle denied that supernatural causation was involved in Greatrakes's cures. It is partly on this basis that Steneck can make a false distinction between Boyle's explanation of the cures, on the one hand, and Stubbe and Greatrakes's on the other.

So Boyle thought that more likely than not there was supernatural agency involved in Greatrakes's cures. He also thought that the cures could be explained in physical terms. There was yet a third feature of Boyle's view of the cures, and this he was absolutely insistent upon: 'if they have anything in them of a supernatural gift, it is . . . far short of the gifts of . . . Christ and his apostles.'[42] The cures may be supernatural in origin but not in the same degree as the New Testament miracles, which, he says, 'I am far from believing that any mechanical or physical hypothesis will make out.'[43] Boyle is thus making a careful distinction, which Steneck fails to see, between Greatrakes's cures and those of Christ and the Apostles. The New Testament miracles are supernatural in origin, and Greatrakes's cures also probably are. But his are not miraculous in the same degree as the Biblical ones, and the difference in degree is expressed in the fact that whereas Greatrakes's cures are susceptible of being explained by 'mechanical or physical hypothesis,' the New Testament miracles are not.

Having explained Boyle's view, and shown where it departs from Steneck's distorted characterization, we must in the second place consider Stubbe's and Greatrakes's interpretations of the cures, concerning which Steneck is also wrong. Greatrakes sees his cures as resulting from a combination of natural and supernatural agencies, as Steneck correctly sees: 'I suppose,' Greatrakes says, 'no man will question but that an ordinary gift may be exercised by natural means, or that God may confer in an extraordinary manner such a temper of body upon a person as may, by a natural efficacy produce these effects.'[44] But Steneck soon goes wrong because he claims that Greatrakes's explanation amounts to the same thing as Stubbe's, who says 'that God had bestowed upon Mr Greatrakes a peculiar temperament or composed his body of some particular ferments.'[45] True, Stubbe's words of explanation are superficially similar to Greatrakes's, but if read closely even the words they use, are seen to diverge sharply. According to Greatrakes, God has given him 'an extraordinary gift' to be 'exercised by natural means;' God has conferred 'in an extraordinary manner such a temper of body.' Significantly, in Stubbe's account the phrases 'extraordinary gift' and 'extraordinary manner' do not appear. They are absent because Stubbe's meaning departs drastically from Greatrakes's. On the basis of his own account Stubbe suggests two things. First it is nature in the form of Greatrakes's 'peculiar temperament' that cures and not a supernatural God.[46] True, God has bestowed his temperament, but in no extraordinary sense. God has bestowed it, according to Stubbe, only in the sense that Greatrakes was born with it and not in the sense of instilling or activating it at some point after birth, as Greatrakes maintained. In using the phrase 'peculiar temperament,' Stubbe is merely adopting the Galenical terminology that describes each person's natural endowments. Second, and following from this, Stubbe, as we have seen, is implying that miracles are nothing more than acts of nature, whether performed by Greatrakes or by the dramatis personae of the New Testament. Here again Stubbe is conflating the natural and miraculous and thereby casting doubt on the existence of a separate supernatural order. Greatrakes never drew either of these two conclusions from his explanation of the cures. To quite the contrary, those cures were 'extraordinary gifts of God,' though 'exercised by natural means,' and as such they were not meant to challenge the miracles recorded in the New Testament.[47] In fact Greatrakes's latitudinarian supporters were quick to underscore his doctrinal orthodoxy and Christian uprightness, a response very different from their suspicious reactions to Stubbe.[48]

We are now in a position to overturn Steneck's mistaken claim that 'on the key issue of the source of operation of his power Greatrakes was more in agreement with Stubbe than with Boyle.' To the contrary, my original assessment which Steneck seeks to undermine still stands. Boyle and Greatrakes were in essential agreement and opposed to Stubbe. The cures could be explained by reference to a mixture, very imperfectly understood, of natural and supernatural agents. For Boyle it could be no other way because only the miracles of Christ and the Apostles enjoyed the distinction of being understood exclusively in terms of supernatural agencies. Lesser gifts of God, like Greatrakes's strokings, though still 'extraordinary,' worked 'by natural means.' Boyle and Greatrakes preserved the fundamental Christian distinction between the natural and supernatural, the divine and created orders, by explaining the cures as they did. Stubbe's views, on the other hand, were heterodox because his at least implicitly naturalistic account of Greatrakes's miracles, conflated the natural and the miraculous, the divine and the human, and by implication cast doubt on the very existence of the supernatural.

Steneck, I think, shows correctly that Boyle's *Free Enquiry* was written less than a year before *The Miraculous Conformist*.[49] But I do not accept his conclusion that Boyle could not have known of Stubbe's opinions before his letter to Boyle and that, therefore, *A Free Enquiry* did not address itself to Stubbe's own views. In order to assert these conclusions Steneck must maintain that 'there is no evidence of Stubbe preaching radical ideas after the Restoration . . . or of Stubbe publicizing the view of nature rejected in the *Free Inquiry*.'[50] On the contrary, *The Miraculous Conformist* offers at least by implication an extremely radical view of nature, according to which nature and the divine are conflated and the existence of a separate supernatural order is denied, and this idea of nature comports with the view attacked in *A Free Enquiry*.[51] Stubbe's subversive view of the relation of God to nature, moreover, was known even before *The Miraculous Conformist* was published, as Coxe's letter to Boyle indicates. If Coxe and others, 'who have reason to pretend to understand Dr. Stubbe's designs,' could know his views, then so could Boyle, something all the more likely because of the decade-long association between Boyle and Stubbe.[52] With regard to *A Free Enquiry*, there is one other point of contention between Steneck and me. According to him, I claim that the work 'was largely motivated by antiradical sentiments.'[53] This is vastly to overstate my case. My aims were more modest and defensible. They were first to show that the *Enquiry* was written *in part* in response to views like Stubbe's and second to suggest that it was published in 1686 because its message resonated with the ideological issues of the moment, a subject explored in chapter 8 of this book.[54]

The last specific challenge that Steneck hurls at my interpretation of the Greatrakes sensation and Boyle's role in it concerns the Cambridge Platonists and in particular Henry More, who was perhaps the most important one of them. I have argued, as Steneck observes, that this circle of thinkers was 'of one mind with Boyle in the Greatrakes affair.'[55] Steneck argues that, on the contrary, More and others in his circle developed an 'animistic view of nature' that 'closely mirrors the erroneous vision of nature Boyle so severely criticized in the *Free Inquiry*.' 'More,' Steneck goes on to say, 'could be described, in other words, as a thoroughgoing naturist,' which is of course the position I attribute to Stubbe and not to More and the Platonists.[56] Some time ago Robert Greene pointed out that, as Steneck sees, Boyle and More disagreed. More allowed for spiritual operations in nature which Boyle thought unwarranted because they could not be confirmed by experimental means and because indeed experiments often demonstrated the reverse of the explanations More offered.[57] It is also true that, as Steneck sees, Boyle's *Free Enquiry* attacked animistic views of nature similar to those of the Cambridge Platonists.[58] But none of this justifies the conclusion Steneck draws that More, Glanvill and others were in anything but complete agreement with Boyle concerning the heretical construction that Stubbe put on Greatrakes's cures.

Steneck goes wrong on this point because he gets the Platonists' views wrong and confuses their idea of nature with the one I have attributed to Stubbe. The two conceptions, his and theirs, could not have been further apart. They were devoted to a natural philosophy grounded in a sharp distinction between matter and spirit, according to which natural processes could be explained by resort to spiritual forces at work in nature whose ultimate source was a supernatural God. They saw their task to lie in preserving the Christian providentialist view of the relation between Creator and creation in face of various contemporary threats, among them Hobbes, Spinoza, Descartes and their followers like Stubbe, whom Glanvill quite correctly regarded as a Hobbesist of sorts.[59] Stubbe for his part, as we have seen, at least insinuated that the distinction between God and nature did not exist, that there was no separate spiritual order and that all causation, even putative divine causation, could be explained in terms of natural processes. Stubbe was a vitalistic materialist or paganizing naturalist. It was he who was 'a thoroughgoing naturist' and not Henry More, as Steneck claims. In fact, so far from being naturists, the Cambridge Platonists took precisely the opposite view in order to defeat opinions like Stubbe's which Steneck erroneously ascribes to them. Boyle and More had their differences, as Robert Greene has shown. But those differences did not extend to Stubbe's interpretation of Greatrakes's cures. Thus Steneck is also wrong when he says: 'the only near unanimity that existed [among More, Glanvill and Boyle] was the belief that the cures were real. Beyond that consensus broke down.'[60] There was also consensus that Stubbe's explanation jeopardized Christian providentialism; on this point these three clearly stood together.[61]

I have now answered Steneck's specific charges made against my arguments published before the appearance of this book. Steneck's alternative readings of the evidence have not persuaded me to change my mind about any of the essential points of disagreement between us. If anything, I have come away from answering his counterclaims confirmed in my original estimates because I have been able to show that my own views conform more closely to the evidence than do his. In my opinion his views have been shown to represent a distinct step backwards from the understanding of the Greatrakes episode achieved thus far.

Nor can the general conclusion he draws be sustained. His attack on my interpretation of the Greatrakes incident does not endanger the standing of either my account of the development of Boyle's thought in terms of the ideological challenges to which he responded or the account Margaret Jacob and I have rendered of 'the Anglican origins of modern science.' That Steneck thinks that the case he makes does in fact undermine our work springs more perhaps from his misunderstanding of the sort of history that I (and we) have been writing than it does from his misreading of the evidence, as serious as that is. Concluding his case against me, he writes: 'Debate did take place in the wake of the Greatrakes affair, but that debate seems more to reflect conflicting natural philosophies than it does conflicting political ideologies.'[62] Here and elsewhere Steneck betrays a fundamental difference between our approaches to the subject. I have argued in my work 1) that there was a territory in the debates between natural philosophers in revolutionary and post-revolutionary England in which conflicts between ideas of nature reflected ideological differences, and 2) that these conflicts, at once philosophical and ideological, created a tension and a dialectic which contributed to the origins of modern science. I do not claim that this approach offers the possibility of a total explanation, as Steneck suggests that I do. But it does offer a way to greater understanding without which our treatment of the scientific revolution would be much the poorer. Steneck claims that I (and we) have attempted to reduce 'historical change to a few simplistic . . . categorizations' which 'break down when applied to historical reality' because they do not take account of 'the richness of the record that underlies them.'[63] Steneck has not neglected the richness of the record, but he has, I submit, seriously misread and misrepresented it because he has systematically denied that the Greatrakes debate resonated with some of the most profound ideological issues that divided men in late seventeenth-century England. And, what is worse, he would, if he had his way, impoverish our attempts at explanation as a result.

Notes

The following abbreviations are used in the notes.

Add.	Additional
AO	Anthony Wood, *Athenae Oxonienses*, 4 vols. (London, 1817)
BL	The British Library
Bodl.	The Bodleian Library, Oxford
Censure	Henry Stubbe, *A Censure upon Certain Passages Contained in the History of the Royal Society*, 2nd edn (Oxford, 1671).
CHO	A. Rupert Hall and Marie Boas Hall (eds.), *The Correspondence of Henry Oldenburg* (Madison, Wisconsin, 1965–)
Commonwealthman	Caroline Robbins, *The Eighteenth-Century Commonwealthman* (New York, 1968)
Conway	Marjorie H. Nicolson (ed.), *The Conway Letters* (New Haven, Conn., 1930)
CR	Henry Stubbe, *Campanella Revived* (London, 1670)
CSP	*Calendar of State Papers*
CSPD	*Calendar of State Papers, Domestic*
DNB	*The Dictionary of National Biography*, ed. Sir Leslie Stephen and Sir Sidney Lee
Evelyn, *Diary*	E. S. de Beer (ed.), *The Diary of John Evelyn* (Oxford, 1959)
Evelyn MSS.	Christ Church Library, Oxford, Evelyn MSS.
HMC	Historical Manuscripts Commission
HMCR	*Historical Manuscripts Commission Report*
Hooke, *Diary*	Henry W. Robinson and Walter Adams (eds.), *The Diary of Robert Hooke, 1672–1680* (London, 1935)
HRS	Thomas Sprat, *The History of the Royal Society of London* (London, 1667)
Jacob, *Boyle*	J. R. Jacob, *Robert Boyle and the English Revolution* (New York, 1977)
Legends	Henry Stubbe, *Legends No Histories* (London, 1670)
Leviathan	Thomas Hobbes, *Leviathan*, ed. C. B. Macpherson (Harmondsworth, UK, 1968)
MC	Henry Stubbe, *The Miraculous Conformist* (Oxford, 1666)
Newtonians	Margaret C. Jacob, *The Newtonians and the English Revolution, 1689–1720* (Ithaca, NY, 1976)
Pepys, *Diary*	Robert Latham and William Matthews (eds.), *The Diary of Samuel Pepys* (Berkeley, 1970–)

175

Praefatory	Joseph Glanvill, *A Praefatory Answer to Mr. Henry Stubbe* (London, 1671)
PRO	The Public Record Office
PUR	Henry Stubbe, *The Plus Ultra Reduced to a Non Plus* (London, 1670)
PWJH	J. G. A. Pocock (ed.), *The Political Works of James Harrington* (Cambridge, 1977)
Reply	[Henry Stubbe], *A Reply to a Letter of Dr. Henry More* (Oxford, 1671)
RO	Record Office
RPM	[Henry Stubbe], *An Account of the Rise and Progress of Mahometanism with the Life of Mahomet*, ed. Hafiz Mahmud Khan Shairani (London, 1911)
RS	The Royal Society of London
WRB	Thomas Birch (ed.), *The Works of the Honourable Robert Boyle*, 6 vols (London, 1772)

Introduction

1 Perez Zagorin, *A History of Political Thought in the English Revolution* (London, 1954), pp. 159–63.

2 See especially Herschel Baker. *The Wars of Truth* (Cambridge. Mass., 1947). pp. 362–6; Richard Foster Jones, *Ancients and Moderns*, 2nd edn (St Louis, Mo., 1961), pp. 244–62; and R. H. Syfret, 'Some Early Critics of the Royal Society,' *Notes and Records of the Royal Society of London*, 8 (Oct. 1950), pp. 20–9. Also see Charles Webster, *The Great Instauration: Science, Medicine and Reform, 1626–1660* (London, 1975), pp. 172–8. Webster departs from Baker, Jones and Syfret by claiming that Stubbe was at once radical and conservative. His treatment has the merit of examining Stubbe's idea of science before 1660, but stops at the Restoration. I cannot agree, however, with Webster's conclusion that Stubbe's intention was 'to frighten his audience into renewing their faith in Anglican and scholastic values' (ibid., p. 177). That is again to put too conservative a stamp on his opinions. One scholar has anticipated the interpretation offered here in a treatment of one of Stubbe's more obscure works, *The Indian Nectar* (1662). See C. E. Main, 'Henry Stubbe and the First English Book on Chocolate,' *Journal of the Rutgers University Library*, 23 (June 1960), p. 47, where Stubbe is described as 'a writer . . . whose spirit is as anti-clerical, rationalistic, and utilitarian as any the so-called Age of Enlightenment produced.' But Main's fragmentary insight has remained ignored and un-developed. For Stubbe as an enlightened medical thinker: Marjorie Hope Nicolson, *Pepys' Diary and the New Science* (Charlottesville, Va., 1965), pp. 166–7; and Lester S. King, *The Road to Medical Enlightenment 1650–1695* (London and New York, 1970), pp. 167–72. Both Nicolson and King accept the interpretation of Stubbe worked out by Jones and Baker, while, nevertheless, pointing out that certain of his medical views were more enlightened than those of his opponents in the Royal Society. Michael Hunter goes too far, however, in rejecting the interpretation offered by Baker and Jones, by claiming

that Stubbe was 'not really an "ancient"' and was not concerned with the debate between ancients and moderns: Michael Hunter, *Science and Society in Restoration England* (Cambridge, 1981), p. 150. For the essential compatibility of science and humanism: Barbara Shapiro, 'History and Natural History in 16th and 17th Century England,' in Barbara Shapiro and Robert Frank, Jr, *English Scientific Virtuosi in the 16th and 17th Centuries* (Los Angeles, 1979). I would agree with Shapiro's thesis as applied to Stubbe: his science and his humanism were not in conflict, and his attacks on the Royal Society did not arise out of any such conflict. Rather they were the result of two conflicting views of the proper relationship between humanism and science, his and theirs, which in turn arose out of two fundamentally different religious and political ideologies. Into such matters Shapiro does not pry.

3 The most recent treatment of this process is: Hunter (see n. 2).

4 *RPM.*

5 For the church settlement see I. M. Green, *The Re-Establishment of the Church of England, 1660–1663* (Oxford, 1978).

6 Howard Nenner, *By Color of Law* (Chicago, 1977); Herbert John McLachlan, *Socinianism in Seventeenth-Century England* (Oxford, 1951), esp. p. 338; Christopher Hill, 'Milton and Marvell,' *Approaches to Marvell*, ed. C. A. Patrides (London, 1978), pp. 14–15; Christopher Hill, *Some Intellectual Consequences of the English Revolution* (Madison, Wisconsin, 1980), pp. 46–50.

7 Steven N. Zwicker, 'Language As Disguise: Politics and Poetry in the Later Seventeenth Century,' *Annals of Scholarship*, 1 (1980), pp. 47–67. For background: Leo Strauss, *Persecution and the Art of Writing* (Glencoe, Ill., 1952).

8 James R. Jacob and Margaret C. Jacob, 'The Anglican Origins of Modern Science: The Metaphysical Foundations of the Whig Constitution.' *ISIS.* 71 (June 1980), pp. 251–67.

9 J. R. Jacob, 'Restoration, Reformation and the Origins of the Royal Society.' *History of Science*, 13 (1975), pp. 155–76.

10 *Newtonians*, ch. 6; and Erwin N. Hiebert, 'The Integration of Revealed Religion and Scientific Materialism in the Thought of Joseph Priestley.' *Joseph Priestley Scientist, Theologian, and Metaphysician*, ed. Lester Kieft and Bennett R. Willeford, Jr (Lewisburg, Pa., Bucknell UP, 1980), pp. 27–61.

11 Christopher Hill, 'The Norman Yoke,' in *Puritanism and Revolution* (New York, 1964), pp. 50–122.

12 *PWJH*, pp. 47–60.

13 J. G. A. Pocock, 'Machiavelli, Harrington and English Political Ideologies in the Eighteenth Century,' in *Politics, Language and Time* (New York, 1971), pp. 104–47.

14 Maurice Ashley, *John Wildman Plotter and Postmaster* (London, 1947); *Commonwealthman*; George L. Mosse, 'Puritan Radicalism and the Enlightenment,' *Church History*, 29 (1960), pp. 424–39; R. L. Emerson, 'Heresy, the Social Order and English Deism,' *Church History*, 37 (1968), pp. 389–403; Christopher Hill, *The World Turned Upside Down*, 2nd edn (New York, 1972), p. 410; Christopher Hill, *Milton and the English Revolution* (London, 1977), p. 335; J. G. A. Pocock, *The Machiavellian Moment* (Princeton, NJ, 1975), pt 3: J. G. A.

Pocock, 'Post-Puritan England and the Problem of the Enlightenment,' *Culture and Politics from Puritanism to the Enlightenment,* ed. Perez Zagorin (Berkeley and Los Angeles, 1980), pp. 91–112; and Philip Jenkins, '"The Old Leaven": The Welsh Roundheads after 1660,' *Historical Journal,* 24 (1981), pp. 807–23.

15 Jacob and Jacob (see n. 8).

16 P. M. Rattansi, 'Paracelsus and the Puritan Revolution,' *Ambix,* 11 (1964), pp. 24–32; Jacob, *Boyle; Newtonians;* Hill, *The World Turned Upside Down* (see n. 14), ch, 14.

1. Hobbesian Independent

1 C. L. S. Linnell, 'Daniel Scargill: "A Penitent Hobbist",' *Church Quarterly Review,* 156 (1955), pp. 256–65; and J. L. Axtell, 'The Mechanics of Opposition: Restoration Cambridge v. Daniel Scargill,' *Bulletin of the Institute of Historical Research,* 38 (1965), pp. 102–11.

2 *AO,* iii, p. 1067.

3 Ibid.

4 Ibid.

5 Ibid., p. 1068.

6 Quentin Skinner, 'Conquest and Consent: Thomas Hobbes and the Engagement Controversy,' in *The Interregnum: The Quest for Settlement, 1646–1660,* ed. G. E. Aylmer (London, 1972), pp. 79–98.

7 Geoffrey Nuttall, *Visible Saints: The Congregational Way, 1640–1660* (Oxford, 1957), pp. 62–3.

8 Francis Thompson, 'Lettres de Stubbe à Hobbes,' *Archives de Philosophie,* 12 (1936), p. 100.

9 Thomas Hobbes, *Markes of the Absurd Geometry, Rural Language, Scottish Church-Politicks and Barbarismes of John Wallis* (London, 1657), pp. 20–31.

10 Ibid., p. 16; and BL Add. MS. 32553, fo. 33.

11 Hobbes (see n. 9), pp. 17–19; John Wallis, *Due Correction for Mr. Hobbes, or Schoole Discipline for Not Saying His Lessons Right, in Answer to His Six Lessons Directed to the Professors of Mathematicks, by the Professor of Geometry* (Oxford, 1656); and John Wallis, *Hobbiani Puncti Dispunctio* (Oxford, 1657).

12 *Leviathan,* pt 3, and pp. 241–5.

13 Ibid., pp. 629–30; and J. G. A. Pocock, 'Time, History and Eschatology in the Thought of Thomas Hobbes,' in *Politics, Language and Time* (New York, 1971), pp. 148–201.

14 *Leviathan.* p. 525.

15 Ibid., pp. 516, 525, 576.

16 Ibid., pp. 561–76.

17 Ibid., p. 706.

18 Ibid.

19 Ibid., p. 629.

20 Ibid., p. 630.

21 Ibid.

22 Hobbes (see n. 9), p. 19; idem, *Behemoth or the Long Parliament,* ed. Ferdinand

Tönnies, 2nd edn (London, 1969), pp. 2–4, 49–50, 56–7; and *Leviathan*. ch. 29.
23 Ibid., ch. 34.
24 Ibid., p. 688.
25 Ibid, pp. 93, 687.
26 Ibid., p. 689.
27 Ibid., pp. 383–5, 686–90.
28 Ibid., p. 691.
29 Ibid., pp. 691–2.
30 J. F. Scott, *The Mathematical Work of John Wallis* (London, 1938), pp. 170–1.
31 Jacob and Jacob (see Intro., n. 8), p. 257.
32 *PWJH*, pp. 83–4.
33 Ibid., pp. 84–7.
34 Ibid., p. 83.
35 Jacob, *Boyle*, ch. 3.
36 *The Prerogative of Popular Government*, in *PWJH*, p. 431.
37 Wm Craig Diamond, 'Natural Philosophy in Harrington's Political Thought,' *Journal of the History of Philosophy*, 16 (Oct. 1978), p. 388.
38 *Prerogative* (see n. 36), in *PWJH*, p. 431.
39 *PWJH*, pp. 85–6; and Diamond (see n. 37), p. 388.
40 *Prerogative* (see n. 36), in *PWJH*, pp. 430–1.
41 Jacob and Jacob (see Intro., n. 8), p. 257.
42 Seth Ward, in T. Hobbii, *Philosophiam Exercitatio Epistolica* (Oxford, 1656).
43 Jacob and Jacob (see Intro., n. 8), p. 257.
44 Jacob (see Intro., n. 9), pp. 155–71.
45 Bodl. MS. Aubrey 12, fo. 166, Hobbes to John Aubrey, 24 Feb. 1674.
46 For a contrary view that discounts ideological factors in the exclusion of Hobbes from membership of the Royal Society: Quentin Skinner, 'Thomas Hobbes and the Nature of the Early Royal Society,' *Historical Journal*, 12 (1969), pp. 217–39. For a recent answer to Skinner, emphasizing the ideological split: Michael Hunter, 'The Debate over Science,' *The Restored Monarchy 1660–1688*, ed. J. R. Jones (London, 1979), pp. 189–90.
47 BL Add. MS. 32553, fos. 17, 25, 27.
48 Quentin Skinner, 'The Ideological Context of Hobbes's Political Thought,' *Historical Journal*, 9 (1966), pp. 286–317.
49 The letters have been transcribed and annotated: Onofrio Nicastro, *Lettere di Henry Stubbe a Thomas Hobbes*, Università degli Studi, Facoltá di Lettere e Filosofia (Siena, 1973).
50 John Owen, *Of Schisme* (Oxford, 1657); and BL Add. MS. 32553, fo. 7.
51 *Leviathan*, p. 711.
52 Thompson (see n. 8), p. 102.
53 BL Add. MS. 32553, fos. 5, 7.
54 Ibid., fo. 5.
55 Ibid., fo. 7.
56 Ibid.
57 Ibid.
58 Ibid.

59 Ibid.

60 Ibid., fo. 9

61 Ibid., fos. 9–11.

62 Ibid., fo. 11.

63 Ibid., fos. 10–11.

64 Henry Stubbe, *Clamor, Rixa, Joci, Medacia, Furta, Cachini, or, a Severe Enquiry into the Late Oneirocritica Published by J. Wallis* (London, 1657).

65 Anon., *The Bodleian Library in the Seventeenth Century* (Bodleian Library, Oxford, 1951), pp. 17–18, 43–4.

66 BL Add. MS. 32553, fo. 12.

67 Ibid.

68 Hobbes (see n. 9), pp. 16–18.

69 Ibid., pp. 17–18

70 BL Add. MS. 32553, fo. 24.

71 Ibid., fos. 12, 14; Hobbes (see n. 9), pp. 20–31.

72 Wallis, *Hobbiani Puncti Dispunctio* (see n. 11), pp. 15, 30, 36; and BL Add. MS. 32553, fo. 30.

73 BL Add. MS. 32553, fo. 14.

74 Ibid., fo. 18.

75 Ibid.

76. Ibid., fo. 32.

77 Bodl. MS. Savile 104, fo. 1.

78 Stubbe (see n. 64), p. 1.

79 BL Add. MS. 32553, fo. 12v.

80 Jacob, *Boyle*, pp. 167–72, 174–6.

81 For Hobbes's view: *Leviathan*, p. 401; and Don Cameron Allen, *Doubt's Boundless Sea* (Baltimore, 1964), pp. vi–vii.

82 BL Add. MS. 32553, fos. 17, 25, 27.

83 Nicastro (see n. 49), pp. 67–8; Skinner (see n. 48), p. 294; and John Bowle, *Hobbes and His Critics* (London, 1951), pp. 25–6, 86–100.

84 BL Add. MS. 32553, fo. 18.

85 Hobbes (see n. 9), p. 19.

86 Ibid.

87 Ibid.

88 BL Add. MS. 32553, fo. 18.

89 Ibid., fo. 29.

90 Herbert Thorndike, *Theological Works V*, in *The Library of Anglo-Catholic Theology* (London, 1854), lxxix, pp. 31–3.

91 BL Add. MS. 32553, fos. 19, 22.

92 Ibid., fos, 22–3, 24.

93 Ibid., fo. 27.

94 Ibid., fo. 29.

95 Ibid., fo. 24.

96 *Leviathan*, p. 711.

97 Ibid., pp. 365–7, 370–2, 691–2.

2. Republican Independent

1 *PWJH*, pp. 103–4.
2 Ibid., pp. 47–8.
3 Ibid., p. 57.
4 Ibid., pp. 62–3.
5 Ibid., pp. 53, 64–8.
6 Ibid., pp. 69–70.
7 *Catalogue of the Pamphlets, Books, Newspapers, and Manuscripts . . . Collected by George Thomason, 1640–1661* (Nendeln, Liechtenstein, 1969), ii, p. 258.
8 Henry Stubbe, *An Essay in Defence of the Good Old Cause* (London, 1659), Preface.
9 *PWJH*, pp. 51–3, 65–8.
10 Stubbe (see n. 8), Preface.
11 Ibid.
12 Thomason's date is 26 Oct. 1659: *Catalogue* (see n. 7), ii, p. 262.
13 Christopher Hill, *The Century of Revolution 1603–1714* (Edinburgh, 1961), p. 142.
14 Henry Stubbe, *A Letter to an Officer of the Army* (London, 1659), p. 53.
15 Stubbe (see n. 8), Preface.
16 Ibid.
17 Stubbe (see n. 14), p. 52.
18 Hill (see n. 13), pp. 130–2.
19 Stubbe (see n. 14), p. 52.
20 Lois G. Schwoerer, *'No Standing Armies!' The Antiarmy Ideology in Seventeenth-Century England* (Baltimore, 1974), pp. 64–7, 69. For background: *PWJH*, pp. 43–50.
21 *PWJH*, pp. 58–61.
22 Stubbe (see n. 14), pp. 59–60.
23 Ibid., p. 61.
24 Ibid., pp. 61–2.
25 Ibid., p. 62.
26 *Valerius and Publicola* (London, 1659), in *PWJH*, p. 805.
27 Stubbe (see n. 14), p. 6.
28 Elizabeth Rawson, *The Spartan Tradition in European Thought* (Oxford, 1969), pp. 195–6.
29 *A Letter unto Mr Stubbe*, in *PWJH*, pp. 830–1.
30 Ibid., pp. 53–4.
31 Stubbe (see n. 8), 'Premonition to the Reader.'
32 Richard Schlatter (ed.), *Richard Baxter and Puritan Politics* (New Brunswick, NJ, 1957), pp. 45–60.
33 G. R. Abernathy, 'Richard Baxter and the Cromwellian Church,' *Huntington Library Quarterly*, 24 (1961), pp. 227–31. See also for background Norman Sykes, *Old Priest and New Presbyter* (Cambridge, 1956), pp. 134–5; and John F. Wilkinson, *1662 – and After: Three Centuries of English Nonconformity* (London, 1962).
34 Henry Stubbe, *Malice Rebuked* (London, 1659), p. 38.
35 Ibid., pp. 1–2.

36　Ibid., pp. 2–7.

37　Ibid., pp. 7–8.

38　Stubbe (see n. 8), pp. 26–8, 39–40.

39　William Haller, *Liberty and Reformation in the Puritan Revolution* (New York, 1955), pp. 230–1.

40　Hill, *Milton* (see Intro., n. 14), p. 151.

41　Haller (see n. 39), p. 234.

42　John Selden, *Table Talk*, ed. Sir Frederick Pollock (London, 1927), pp. 69–70.

43　Andrew Clark (ed.), *The Life and Times of Anthony Wood*. 5 vols. (Oxford, 1891–1900), i, p. 282.

44　Stubbe (see n. 8), p. 104.

45　Ibid.

46　Ibid.

47　Ibid., pp. 26–7.

48　Ibid., p. 28; see *Leviathan*, p. 711.

49　Stubbe (see n. 8), pp. 105–7, 110–12, 115.

50　Ibid., p. 2.

51　Ibid., pp. 26–7.

52　Ibid.

53　Ibid., pp. 26–7, 39–40.

54　S. B. Liljegren, *Harrington and the Jews* (London, 1932), claims that Selden was Harrington's chief source for rabbinical commentary on the Talmud; and *PWJH*, pp. 45, 49, 55.

55　*PWJH*, pp. 69–70, 72–4.

56　Ibid., pp. 76–99.

57　*Leviathan*, pp. 561–76; and Pocock (see ch. 1, n. 13), pp. 148–201.

58　*PWJH*, pp. 72, 78–87, 91–6.

59　*Leviathan*, p, 185.

60　*AO*, iii, pp. 1073–6.

61　*Leviathan*, p. 525.

62　Hobbes (see ch. 1, n. 9), pp. 17–19.

63　[Henry Stubbe], *A Light Shining out of Darkness* (London, 1659), pp. 1–19.

64　Ibid., pp. 19–26.

65　Ibid., pp. 6–26, esp. 16.

66　Ibid., p. 15.

67　Ibid., pp. 174–5.

68　Christopher Hill, *The Religion of Gerrard Winstanley*, Supplement 5, *Past and Present* (1978), p. 54.

69　Ibid., pp. 50–1.

70　Stubbe (see n. 14), p. 61.

71　[Stubbe] (see n. 63), pp. 82–92.

72　Ibid., pp. 82–5.

73　Ibid., pp. 82–3.

74　Ibid.

75　*Leviathan*, pt 3, esp. chs. 42 and 43.

76　Ibid., p. 615.

77　[Stubbe](see n. 63), p. 91.

78 Ibid., pp. 98–9.
79 S. I. Mintz, *The Hunting of Leviathan* (Cambridge, 1962), pp. 50–2.

3. Surreptitious naturalism: the invention of a new rhetoric

 1 Stubbe (see ch. 2, n. 14).
 2 Wilbur C. Abbott, 'English Conspiracy and Dissent, 1660–1674,' *American Historical Review*, 14 (1909), p. 505; Hill (see ch. 2, n. 13), pp. 249–50; and Frederick Seaton Siebert, *Freedom of the Press in England 1476–1776* (Urbana, Ill., 1952), chs. 12–14.
 3 *AO*, iii, p. 1069.
 4 Ibid., p. 1068.
 5 Ibid., p. 1069.
 6 R. G. Frank, Jr, *Harvey and the Oxford Physiologists* (Berkeley, Los Angeles and London, 1980), pp. 123, 172.
 7 Ibid., pp. 51, 237.
 8 Ibid., p. 126.
 9 Jacob, *Boyle*, ch. 3.
10 Green (see Intro., n. 5), pp. 21–3.
11 *AO*, iii, p. 1069.
12 Ibid.
13 Stephen Saunders Webb, *The Governors-General* (Chapel Hill, NC, 1979), pp. 218–25.
14 Joannes Casa, *The Arts of Grandeur and Submission* (London, 1665). 'The Dedication.'
15 Ibid.
16 Henry Stubbe, *The Indian Nectar* (London, 1662), Preface.
17 Ibid., 'The Epistle Dedicatory.'
18 Ibid., Preface and pp. 178–80; on Willis and Stubbe: Frank (see n. 6), pp. 237, 345; on Lord Windsor: Frank Cundall, *The Governors of Jamaica in the Seventeenth Century* (London, 1936), p. 14; and Webb (see n. 13), pp. 212–18. See also Main (see Intro., n. 2), p. 45.
19 Jacob, *Boyle*, pp. 144–59.
20 Henry Stubbe, *An Epistolary Discourse Concerning Phlebotomy* (London, 1671), 'The Epistle Dedicatory.'
21 Stubbe (see n. 16), Preface, pp. 69, 98, 99, 178–9.
22 Ibid., pp. 125–7, 129–32, 141.
23 Ibid., p. 128
24 Bernal Díaz, *The Conquest of New Spain*, trans. J. M. Cohen (Harmondsworth, UK, 1963), p. 226.
25 Main (see Intro., n. 2), pp. 43, 44.
26 Stubbe (see n. 16), p. 141.
27 Ibid., pp. 130–1.
28 Ibid., Preface and p. 137.
29 Ibid.
30 Ibid., pp. 142–3.
31 Ibid., p. 137.

32 Ibid., p. 142.
33 Ibid., Preface.
34 Ibid.
35 Ibid.
36 Ibid.
37 Hill, *The World Turned Upside Down* (see Intro., n. 14), ch. 7 and pp. 267, 275.
38 Stubbe (see n. 16), Preface.
39 Maurice Ashley, *The Stuarts in Love* (London, 1963), chs. 11–12.
40 R. E. W. Maddison, *The Life of the Honourable Robert Boyle, FRS* (London, 1969), pp. 86–7.
41 For Stubbe and Barlow; ch. 1; for Boyle and Barlow; Jacob, *Boyle*, p. 130.
42 Jacob, *Boyle*, pp. 136–8; and BL Add, MS. 32553, fo. 24.
43 Jacob, *Boyle*, ch. 4.
44 Ibid., pp. 133–44.
45 Ibid., ch. 3.
46 Ibid.
47 *AO*, iii, p. 1071.
48 *CSP, Colonial Series, America and the West Indies, 1661–1668*, p. 76.
49 Frank (see n. 6), p. 237.
50 Jacob, *Boyle*, pp. 164–5.
51 Marc Bloch, *The Royal Touch*, trans. J. E. Anderson (London, 1973), pp. 208–13. For background: Gerard Reedy, SJ, 'Mystical Politics: The Imagery of Charles II's Coronation,' *Studies in Change and Revolution*, ed. Paul Korshin (London, 1972), pp. 19–42; and Carolyn A. Edie, 'The Popular Idea of Monarchy on the Eve of the Stuart Restoration.' *Huntington Library Quarterly*, 39 (1976), pp. 343–73.
52 BL Harley MS. 3785, fo. 111.
53 Edward M. Thompson (ed.), *Correspondence of the Family of Hatton*, Camden Society, n.s., xxii–xxiii (1878), i, p. 49.
54 *Conway*, p. 274.
55 Henry J. Cadbury (ed.), *George Fox's 'Book of Miracles'* (Cambridge, 1948), pp. 117, 133, 135; Valentine Greatrakes, *A Brief Account of Mr. Valentine Greatraks* (London, 1666), pp. 15–18.
56 [David Lloyd], *Wonders No Miracles* (London, 1666), p. 14.
57 Raymund Crawfurd, *The King's Evil* (Oxford, 1911), p. 112.
58 Pepys, *Diary*, vii, pp. 46–7.
59 [Lloyd] (see n. 56), pp. 11–12, 21, 33–5.
60 Anon., *A Representation of the State of Christianity in England, and of It's Decay and Danger from Sectaries aswel as Papists* (London, 1674); John Bedford, *London's Burning* (London, New York, Toronto, 1966), pp. 150–58, 173–4; Pepys, *Diary*, vii, p. 277; and David Ogg, *England in the Reign of Charles II* (Oxford, 1934), i, p. 307.
61 [Lloyd] (see n. 56), pp. 33–5.
62 *CSP, Ireland, 1666–69*, p. 474; and *CSPD, 1667*, p. 338.
63 *Conway*, p. 303.
64 *MC*, pp. 10–11, 14, 25.
65 Frank (see n. 6), pp. 165–9, 345; and R. H. Kargon, *Atomism in England from Hariot to Newton* (Oxford, 1966), ch. 9.

66 *MC*, p. 10.
67 Ibid., p. 11.
68 Ibid., p. 14.
69 Ibid., pp. 4–6, 27.
70 Ibid., p. 10.
71 RS, Boyle Letters, ii. fo. 65v.
72 Ibid.
73 Jacob, *Boyle*, pp. 113–14, 167–8; and Pocock (see ch. 1, n. 13), pp. 175–6.
74 Owsei Temkin, *Galenism: Rise and Decline of a Medical Philosophy* (Ithaca, NY, 1973), p. 82.
75 Herschel Baker, *The Dignity of Man* (Cambridge, Mass., 1947), pp. 275–8.
76 Ibid., pp. 279–80.
77 Temkin (see n. 74), p. 85.
78 Ibid., p. 84.
79 Ibid., p. 89.
80 George Thomason, Μισοχυμείας "Ελεγχος (London, 1671), p. 43; see also Robert Peirce, *Bath Memoirs* (Bristol, Bath and Devizes, 1697), p. 392; Tobias Venner, *The Baths of Bathe* (London, 1650), p. 360; and H. M. Margoliouth (ed.), *The Poems and Letters of Andrew Marvell*, 2nd edn (Oxford, 1952), ii, p. 325.
81 Temkin (see n. 74), p. 82.
82 Ibid., pp. 89, 91.
83 *MC*, pp. 10,11.
84 Frank (see n. 6), pp. 179, 248.
85 [Lloyd] (see n. 56), p. 26; and Falconer Madan, *Oxford Books* (Oxford, 1931), iii, p. 2758.
86 D. P. Walker, *Spiritual and Demonic Magic from Ficino to Campanella* (London, 1958), pp. 110–11.
87 Martin Pine, 'Pomponazzi and the Problem of "Double Truth",' *Journal of the History of Ideas*, 29 (1968), p. 171.
88 Petrus Pomponatius, *Opera: De Naturalium Effectum Admirandorum Causis, seu de Incantationibus Liber* (Basel, 1567), pp. 48, 78; and Peter Burke, *Culture and Society in Renaissance Italy 1420–1540* (London, 1972), p. 180. For the negative reaction to Pomponazzi's book: Giancarlo Zanier, *Ricerche sulla Diffusione e Fortuna del 'de Incantationibus' di Pomponazzi* (Florence, 1975).
89 BL Sloane MS. 35, fos. 17r, 20v.
90 Temkin (see n. 74), p. 170.
91 *MC*, p. 10.
92 Frances Yates, *Giordano Bruno and the Hermetic Tradition* (London, 1964), p. 159.
93 [Lloyd] (see n. 56), p. 45.
94 *Newtonians*, pp. 222, 226–34, 245–7.
95 *WRB*, i, p. lxxvi.
96 Ibid.
97 Ibid., p. lxxvii.
98 Ibid.
99 Ibid.
100 *MC*, pp. 4–6.
101 *WRB*, i, p. lxxvii.

102 Ibid., p. lxxviii.
103 Ibid.
104 Ibid.
105 Ibid., pp. lxxviii–lxxix.
106 Ibid., p. lxxx.
107 Ibid.
108 Ibid., p. lxxix.
109 Ibid., p. lxxxii, and v, p. 159.
110 Ibid., v, p. 183.
111 Ibid., i, p. lxxix.
112 Ibid., p. lxxxv.
113 Ibid.
114 Ibid., p. lxxvi.
115 *Conway*, p. 269.
116 Ibid., p. 273.
117 *MC*, p. 8; and *WRB*, i, p. lxxvi.
118 Jacob, *Boyle*, pp. 112–15; and J. R. Jacob, 'Boyle's Atomism and the Restoration
     Assault on Pagan Naturalism,' *Social Studies of Science*, 8 (1978), pp. 211–33.
119 For Willis's orthodoxy: Frank (see n. 6), pp. 179, 248–9.
120 *WRB*, i, p. lxxvi.
121 *MC*, p. 8.
122 *HRS*, pp. 342–5, 370–5, 400, 408, 426–9.
123 Ibid., pp. 65–76, 130–1.
124 Jacob, *Boyle*, p. 156.
125 *MC*, p. 8.
126 Jacob, 'Boyle's Atomism' (see n. 118), pp. 216–18.
127 *Leviathan*, p. 401.
128 Pocock, 'England and the Enlightenment' (see Intro., n. 14), pp. 101–2.
129 Temkin (see n. 74), p. 91.
130 Jacob, *Boyle*, pp. 173–5.
131 *MC*, p. 2.
132 *Leviathan*, pp. 562–3, 664–5.
133 *MC*, pp. 25–7.
134 See nn. 55–61.
135 [Lloyd] (see n. 56), pp. 13–14.
136 *AO*, iv, p. 352; and Madan (see n. 85), iii, p. 2758.
137 [Lloyd] (see n. 56), pp. 44–5.

4. *'Mahometan Christianity': Stubbe's secular historicism*

1 Stubbe (see ch. 3, n. 16), p. 181.
2 *RPM*, pp. vii–viii.
3 P. M. Holt, *A Seventeenth-Century Defender of Islam: Henry Stubbe and His Book
   (1632–76)*, Friends of Dr Williams's Library, 26th Lecture (London, 1972),
   p. 10.
4 Stubbe (see ch. 3, n. 20), p. 181.
5 Ibid., pp. 181–2.

6 *RPM*, pp. 1–3, 30–48, 56–7, 72, 75, 110, 139–40.
7 Ibid., pp. 158–9.
8 Ibid., pp. 96–7.
9 Ibid., pp. 145–6. Stubbe also makes a similar point in another work, *PUR*, pp. 15–16, published a year before his *Discourse Concerning Phlebotomy*.
10 For a useful start on answering this question: Holt (see n. 3), pp. 17–19, 26–9.
11 *RPM*, p. 39.
12 Ibid.; also Holt (see n. 3), p. 28.
13 Pocock (see ch. 1, n. 13), p. 195.
14 Arthur B. Ferguson, *Clio Unbound* (Durham, NC, 1979), chs. 5–6.
15 *RPM*, p. 6.
16 Ibid.
17 Ibid., p. 7.
18 Ibid., pp. 8–11.
19 Ibid., p. 11.
20 Ibid., p. 12.
21 Ibid., pp. 15–16.
22 Ibid., p. 18.
23 Ibid.
24 Ibid., p. 19.
25 Ibid., pp. 19–20.
26 Ibid., p. 24.
27 Ibid.
28 Ibid., p. 25.
29 Ibid., pp. 28–9.
30 Ibid., p. 97.
31 Ibid., pp. 28–30.
32 Ibid., pp. 56–7.
33 Ibid., p. 54.
34 Ibid., pp. 55–6.
35 Ibid., p. 56.
36 Ibid., p. 30.
37 Ibid., p. 31.
38 Ibid., p. 29.
39 Ibid., pp. 28, 29.
40 Ibid., p. 31.
41 Ibid., p. 33.
42 Ibid., p. 34.
43 Ibid., p. 35. Stubbe's opinion of Constantine's effect on Christianity is close to his view on the same subject in *A Light Shining out of Darkness*, pp. 174–5. It was a standard radical Protestant view (Hill, *Milton* (see Intro., n. 14), p. 84). For a contemporary conservative Protestant view: William M. Lamont, *Richard Baxter and the Millennium* (London, 1979). (After the Restoration, was Stubbe still in dialogue with Baxter?).
44 *RPM*, pp. 35–6.
45 Ibid., p. 38.
46 Ibid., pp. 42–4.

47 Ibid., pp. 46–7.
48 Ibid., p. 47.
49 Ibid., pp. 47–8.
50 Ibid., p. 57; and Holt (see n. 3), p. 29.
51 *RPM*, p. 72.
52 Ibid.
53 Ibid., pp. 145–6. See Sir Charles Wolseley, *The Reasonableness of Scripture Belief* (London, 1672), pp. 167–8, 172, where Islam is also traced to Arians and Jews. But for Wolseley such sources are not associated with purest Apostolic Christianity but represent imposture and corruption (ibid., pp. 167–8), thus reversing Stubbe's view. It is possible that Wolseley was answering Stubbe; certainly Wolseley was engaged in polemic against advocates of rational (Arian) Christianity, whose creed was close to Stubbe's 'Mahometan Christianity': Philip Harth, *Contexts of Dryden's Thought* (Chicago, 1968), pp. 112–15, 117–22, 124–7.
54 *Leviathan*, ch. 31: 'Of the Kingdome of God by Nature.'
55 *RPM*, p. 109.
56 Ibid., p. 165.
57 Ibid., p. 166.
58 Ibid.
59 Ibid.
60 *Leviathan*, pp. 401–3.
61 Ibid., p. 402.
62 Ibid., p. 404.
63 Ibid., p. 406.
64 Ibid., p. 399.
65 Ibid., pp. 522–4.
66 *MC*, pp. 10–11, 14, 25.
67 *Leviathan*, p. 401.
68 Quoted in Harth (see n. 53), p. 85.
69 Charles Blount, *Religio Laici* (London, 1683), pp. 56–70.
70 *RPM*, p. 178. Francis Osborne also praised the government of Muslim Turkey for the same reason and traced the invention of such a civil religion to Moses, who united 'the sacred rites and civil sanctions into one body, making the law of the land a piece of God's law, and the justice of the magistrate, religion': *Political Reflections upon the Government of the Turks* (London, 1656), p. 111. Stubbe knew Osborne's book: BL Sloane MS. 35.
71 *RPM*, p. 168.
72 Ibid.
73 Ibid., pp. 95, 104–8. Osborne (see n. 70), pp. 24–7, also praises Muslim abstinence as a means of keeping military discipline. Another work, a copy of which was in Stubbe's library (BL Sloane MS. 35, fo. 19a), makes the same point: Henry Blount, *A Voyage into the Levant* (London, 1636), pp. 82–3. (Henry Blount was Charles Blount's father.)
74 *Leviathan*, pp. 160–1.
75 *RPM*, p. 105.
76 Ibid., pp. 104–5.

77 Ibid., pp. 109–11, 187.
78 Ibid., p. 104.
79 Ibid., p. 169.
80 Ibid., p. 170.
81 Ibid., p. 175.
82 Ibid.
83 Ibid., p. 174.
84 Ibid., pp. 173–4.
85 Ibid., pp. 89, 180–3, 188.
86 Ibid., p. 88.
87 Ibid., p. 183.
88 Ibid., pp. 187–8.
89 Ibid., pp. 112–13.
90 See Paul Rycaut, *The Present State of the Ottoman Empire* (London, 1668), 'The Epistle to the Reader,' a work in Stubbe's Library (BL Sloane MS. 35, fo. 2b), which compares Turkish 'servitude' unfavorably to British 'freedom' under Charles II.
91 *RPM*, pp. 93–4.
92 Ibid., p. 90.
93 Ibid., p. 128.
94 See ch. 2.
95 [Stubbe] (see ch. 2, n. 63), pp. 112–14, 124–5.
96 *Praefatory*, pp. 48–9.
97 PRO, SP 29/319/220.
98 *CSPD, July–Sept., 1683*, pp. 351–2; Pepys, *Diary*, vii, p. 326; Bodl. MS. Sancroft 135, fos. 218–9; P. M. Holt, 'Arabic Studies in Seventeenth-Century England with Special Reference to the Life and Work of Edward Pococke,' Oxford University, BLitt thesis; Esmond S. de Beer, 'King Charles II's Own Fashion: An Episode in Anglo-French Relations 1666–1670,' *Journal of the Warburg Institute*, 2 (1938–9), pp. 105–15.
99 BL Add. MS. 23215.

5. *Aristotle on the ale-benches*

1 Baker (see Intro., n. 2), p. 365; and Jones (see Intro., n. 2), p. 262. For a discerning critique of this view and of Jones in particular: Hans Baron, 'The *Querelle* of the Ancients and the Moderns as a Problem for Renaissance Scholarship,' *Journal of the History of Ideas*, 20 (1959), pp. 3–22, esp. pp. 4–5.
2 Harcourt Brown, *Scientific Organization in Seventeenth-Century France (1620–1680)* (Baltimore, 1934), pp. 256–7; and *Reply*, p. 59.
3 *AO*, iv, pp. 122–4.
4 Joseph Glanvill, *The Vanity of Dogmatizing* (London, 1661), revised as *Scepsis Scientifica* (London, 1665).
5 William U. S. Glanville-Richards, *Records of the Anglo-Norman House of Glanville* (London, 1882), pp. 76–7.
6 Glanvill, *Plus Ultra* (London, 1668), 'The Preface to the Reverend Clergy of the Dioces of B and W'; and *Praefatory*, pp. 1–2.

7 For a classic statement of the dual meaning of popery: Henry Neville, *Plato Redivivus*, in Caroline Robbins (ed.), *Two Republican Tracts* (Cambridge, 1969), p. 158.

8 William C. Braithwaite, *The Second Period of Quakerism*, 2nd edn (Cambridge, 1961), pp. 218, 258; Norman Penney (ed.), *Extracts from State Papers Relating to Friends 1654 to 1672* (London, 1913), pp. 121–2, 229, 244; *CSPD, 1670*, p. 220.

9 Evelyn MSS., John Beale to John Evelyn, letters written between 21 Oct. 1668 and 9 Jan. 1671.

10 Ibid., Beale to Evelyn, 20 Nov. 1669, where Beale, referring to Dissenters, speaks of 'their incredible growth.'

11 Somerset RO, DD/SFR, 8/1, fos. 23r and 61r and indices.

12 See nn. 154–5.

13 *Praefatory*, p. 2.

14 Glanvill (see n. 6), 'Preface to the Reverend Clergy.'

15 Ibid.

16 Ibid.

17 Glanville-Richards (see n. 5), p. 80; and Somerset RO, Quarter Sessions Rolls.

18 Evelyn MSS., Beale to Evelyn, letters written between 21 Oct. 1668 and 9 Jan, 1671.

19 Glanville-Richards (see n. 5), p. 80; and Evelyn MSS., Beale to Evelyn, 24 July 1669.

20 Evelyn MSS., Beale to Evelyn, 21 Oct. 1668.

21 Ibid., Beale to Evelyn, 20 Nov. 1669.

22 Glanville-Richards (see n. 5), p. 80.

23 Ibid.

24 Evelyn MSS., Beale to Evelyn, 2 Jan. 1669.

25 *AO*, iv, pp. 122–4.

26 Ibid., p. 123; and *Praefatory*, pp. 1–2.

27 Glanvill (see n. 6), 'Preface to the Reverend Clergy.'

28 *AO*, iv, pp. 123–4.

29 Evelyn MSS., Beale to Evelyn, 21 Oct. 1668.

30 Bristol RO, Records of the Diocese of Bristol, Presentments, 1637–1861, EP/V/3, Presentments, 1669–70.

31 *Conway*, p. 216; and Joseph Glanvill, *A Blow at Modern Sadducism* (London, 1668), Preface.

32 BL Add. MS. 4456, fos. 133–4, 'A true and faithful relation of a learned disputation held at the city of Bath, between two grave divines.' For another copy: Bodl. MS. Wood F22, fo. 181. *AO*, iv, p. 124. For a modern edition: Nicholas H. Steneck, '"The Ballad of Robert Crosse and Joseph Glanvill" and the Background to *Plus Ultra*,' *British Journal for the History of Science*, 14 (1981), pp. 59–74.

33 BL Add. MS. 4456, fos. 133–4.

34 Ibid.

35 Ibid.

36 *Leviathan*, p. 708.

37 BL Add. MS. 4456, fos. 133–4.

38 Ibid.

39 Ibid.
40 *Leviathan*, p. 714.
41 *CHO*, vi, p. 138.
42 *Praefatory*, p. 89; and *Reply*, p. 58.
43 *CHO*, vi, p. 456.
44 *Praefatory*, p. 3.
45 Ibid., Preface, p. 8 (unnumbered).
46 Ibid., p. 3.
47 Alan Everitt, 'The English Urban Inn, 1560–1760,' *Perspectives in English Urban History*, ed. Alan Everitt (London, 1973), pp. 91–137; and Peter Clark, 'The Alehouse as an Alternative Society,' *Puritans and Revolutionaries*, ed. Donald Pennington and Keith Thomas (Oxford, 1978), pp. 47–72, esp. 48–53.
48 [Joseph Glanvill], *The Character of a Coffee-House*, in *The Harleian Miscellany* (London, 1810), vi, pp. 465, 467.
49 Clark (see n. 47), pp. 61–7; and Everitt (see n. 47), pp. 110–14.
50 Clark (see n. 47), pp. 53–7.
51 [Glanvill] (see n. 48), p. 468; *HMCR*, 12, pt 7, p. 123; and Hill (see ch. 2, n. 13), p. 85.
52 Jackson Cope, *Joseph Glanvill, Anglican Apologist* (St Louis, Mo., 1956), p. 27.
53 *HRS*, p. 94; and Thomas Birch, *The History of the Royal Society*, 4 vols. (London, 1756–7), i, pp. 85, 507, ii, pp. 6, 47, 138, 161, 163, 175.
54 *HRS*, pp. 22, 57, 63–76, 94, 130–1, 342–77, 400, 408, 426–9; and William Coleman, 'Providence, Capitalism, and Environmental Degradation: English Apologetics in an Era of Economic Revolution,' *Journal of the History of Ideas*, 37 (1976), pp. 27–44.
55 *Legends*, Preface, p. 2 (unnumbered).
56 For Stubbe's London supporters: ibid., Preface, pp. 7–8 (unnumbered); and *PUR*, p. 135.
57 *Legends*, Preface, p. 2 (unnumbered); and *PUR*, 'Premonition to the Reader,' and p. 14.
58 *Legends*, Preface, p. 4 (unnumbered); *PUR*, pp. 14, 172–3; and *Censure*, pp. 50–3.
59 *CR*, pp. 3–4.
60 *HRS*, pp. 63–76, 130–1, 343, 400, 408, 426–9.
61 *CR*, p. 2.
62 Ibid., p. 3.
63 Ibid., pp. 12–13.
64 Baker (see Intro., n. 2), p. 365.
65 Jones (see Intro., n. 2), p. 262.
66 *Legends*, Preface, p. 3 (unnumbered).
67 Gerald M. Straka, *Anglican Reaction to the Revolution of 1688* (Madison, Wisconsin, 1962).
68 *Leviathan*, chs. 13–15; C. B. Macpherson, *The Political Theory of Possessive Individualism: Hobbes to Locke* (Oxford, 1962); and Skinner (see ch. 1, n. 48).
69 *Praefatory*, p. 6.
70 Ibid., p. 63.
71 *CR*, p. 13.

72 Corinne C. Weston, 'Concepts of Estates in Stuart Political Thought,' in *Representative Institutions in Theory and Practice*, 'Historical Papers Read at Bryn Mawr College, April, 1968, Studies Presented to the International Commission for the History of Representatives and Parliamentary Institutions,' 39 (Brussels, 1970), pp. 87–130, esp. 87–94, 121–30; and Corinne Weston and Janelle Greenberg, *Subjects and Sovereigns* (Cambridge, 1981), chs. 6–8.

73 *Legends*, p. 14.

74 *Reply*, p. 20.

75 *HRS*, p. 355.

76 *Censure*, pp. 45–7.

77 For the sixteenth-century origins of this theory: Quentin Skinner, *The Foundations of Modern Political Thought*, 2 vols. (Cambridge, 1978), ii, pp. 189–359. For the opinion that the theory disappears from print during the Restoration: Julian Franklin, *John Locke and the Theory of Sovereignty* (Cambridge, 1978), p. 88. The theory was not quite as scarce in print as Franklin thinks: Lamont (see ch. 4, n. 43), p. 98.

78 Edward Chamberlayne, *Angliae Notitia*, 3rd edn (London, 1669), pp. 60–2.

79 Royce Macgillivray, *Restoration Historians of the Civil War* (The Hague, 1974), pp. 237–42. The conservative argument is at least as old as the early sixteenth century and is answered by Sir Thomas More in terms that anticipate Stubbe: Thomas More, *Utopia*, trans. Paul Turner (Harmondsworth, UK, 1965), pp. 61–2. For the same conservative argument in seventeenth-century France: Paolo Rossi, *Philosophy, Technology and the Arts in the Early Modern Era* (New York, 1970), p. 13; and Hill, *The World Turned Upside Down* (see Intro., n. 14), pp. 40–2.

80 Chamberlayne (see n. 78), pp. 60–2.

81 Jacob, *Boyle*, pp. 134–6.

82 *CR*, 'Preface to the Reader;' and *RPM*, p. 175.

83 *PUR*, 'A Premonition to the Reader.'

84 *WRB*, i, pp. xc–xcii, Stubbe to Boyle, 17 Dec. 1669.

85 Weston (see n. 72), p. 122.

86 RS, Letter Book Supplement, A–B Copy, p. 382.

87 Ibid., p. 410.

88 Buchanan Sharp, *In Contempt of All Authority: Rural Artisans and Riot in the West of England, 1586–1660* (Berkeley and Los Angeles, 1980), pp. 243–7, 255, 259, 261–6. Among the riots for which there is evidence were those occurring in 1643 and 1655 on lands in Somerset belonging to Roger Boyle, Baron Broghill, who was Robert's older brother (ibid., pp. 244–5). Robert himself had lands in neighboring Dorset, where such riots also occurred.

89 *PUR*, p. 13.

90 *CR*, p. 13; and *Censure*, pp. 50–2.

91 *CR*, p. 12.

92 *HRS*, p. 355; and *Censure*, pp. 50–2.

93 *Censure*, p. 52.

94 Ibid., p. 53; see also *HRS*, p. 370 (Stubbe incorrectly cites p. 362).

95 *Censure*, p. 53.

96 *PUR*, pp. 15–16.

97 *RPM*, pp. 8–58.
98 Ibid., pp. 28–9.
99 Ibid., pp. 35–6.
100 *PUR*, p. 16; and *RPM*, pp. 15–24, 29–37.
101 *Leviathan*, chs. 46 and 47.
102 *RPM*, chs, 4 and 5, and pp. 145–6, 164–70, 178, 188–9.
103 Ibid., and *PUR*, pp. 15–16.
104 *RPM*, pp. 164–8.
105 Ibid., pp. 15–16, 28–9, 164–6.
106 Ibid., p. 178.
107 Ibid., pp. 43–8, 53–7; and *PUR*, pp. 15–16.
108 *PUR*, p. 16; and *CHO*, vi, p. 137.
109 *HRS*, p. 12. For Sprat's view of the pre-Constantinian church as the conventional Anglican view: Theophilus Gale, *The Court of the Gentiles*, pt 2 (Oxford, 1670), 'The Preface,' pt 3 (London, 1677), pp. 133–5, 139–40. Stubbe in his attack on Sprat in this regard may also have been answering Gale: *CHO*, viii, p. 255, and vi, p. 456.
110 *HRS*, p. 12.
111 Ibid., p. 354.
112 Ibid., pp. 13–25.
113 Wallace K. Ferguson, 'The Reinterpretation of the Renaissance,' in *Facts of the Renaissance*, ed. William H. Werkmeister (New York, Evanston and London, 1963), pp. 4–5.
114 *HRS*, p. 45. This view was echoed by Wolseley (see ch. 4, n. 53), pp. 170–1, where it is asserted, in sharp contrast to Stubbe, that Islam 'totally ruins all learning and brings men into perfect enmity with all liberal sciences.' Sir Charles was a FRS, and this, in addition to his general view of Islam and his antideistical polemic, examined in ch. 4 (see n. 53), suggests that he was in conscious dialogue with Stubbe.
115 *HRS*, p. 354.
116 Ch. 8, nn. 6, 7, 10.
117 For example: *CR*, p. 13; and *Censure*, pp. 50–3.
118 *RPM*, chs. 4 and 5, and pp. 145–6.
119 *Praefatory*. For Glanvill's collaboration with Beale: Evelyn MSS., Beale to Evelyn, 11 June 1670; for his collaboration with Oldenburg: ibid., Beale to Evelyn, 3 Aug. 1671.
120 *Legends*, Preface, p. 3 (unnumbered).
121 *Praefatory*, pp. 6–7.
122 Ibid., p. 7.
123 BL Sloane MS. 35; Virgilio Malvezzi, *Discourses upon Cornelius Tacitus*, trans, Sir Richard Baker (London, 1642); and Trajano Boccalini, *I Raggluagli di Parnasso: Or Advertisements from Parnassus*, trans. Henry, Earl of Monmouth (London, 1657). Harrington's *Oceana* also shows the influence of Boccalini's work (*PWJH*, pp. 74–6).
124 *Legends*, Preface, p. 3 (unnumbered).
125 *Praefatory*, p. 7
126 Ibid.

127 Ibid., Preface, pp. 3–4 (unnumbered).

128 Ibid., p. 8.

129 Ibid., pp. 60–1.

130 Ibid., *passim*.

131 Ibid., pp. 48–9, 62.

132 Ibid., Preface, p. 1 (unnumbered), pp. 62–3.

133 Ibid., p. 5.

134 *RPM*, pp. 29, 55–7, 146.

135 Peirce (see ch. 3, n. 80), pp. 280, 283; see also Thomas Guidott, *A Discourse of Bathe and the Hot Waters There* (London, 1676), 'A Preface to the Reader,' and *DNB*, 'Sir James Long,' whose interest in natural history and Roman antiquities would have appealed to Stubbe.

136 Glanvill was not a physician, but he was familiar with the baths and prepared a report on them: *Philosophical Transactions*, iv (1670), pp. 977–82. See also C. F. Mullett, 'Public Baths and Health in England 16th–18th Centuries,' *Supplement to the Bulletin of the History of Medicine*, no. 5 (Baltimore, 1946), pp. 75–6.

137 Joseph Glanvill, *A Further Discovery of M. Stubbe* (London, 1671), pp. 33–4.

138 Ibid., p. 34.

139 *PUR*, pp. 16, 172–3; *Leviathan*, p. 404. See *HRS*, p. 312; and *Conway*, p. 303.

140 *HRS*, pp. 342–5, 368–77, 400, 408, 426–9.

141 E. A. Burtt, *The Metaphysical Foundations of Modern Science*, rev. edn (Garden City, NY, n.d.), pp. 140–3; Marjorie Nicolson, 'The Early Stages of Cartesianism in England,' *Studies in Philology*, 26 (1929), pp. 356–74; Sterling P. Lamprecht, 'The Role of Descartes in Seventeenth-Century England,' Columbia University, *Studies in the History of Ideas*, 3 (1935), pp. 181–242; Charles Webster, 'Henry More and Descartes: Some New Sources,' *British Journal for the History of Science*, 4 (1969), pp. 359–64; and Hunter (see Intro., n. 2), pp. 181–3.

142 *PUR*, pp. 16, 172–3. More and Stubbe had discussed the matter. Here is Stubbe's account: 'When I was busy in animadverting upon *The History of the Royal Society* and Mr Glanvill, you happened to be at Ragley, and upon some incidental discourse upon the Virtuosi, I asked of you how you could adhere to them . . . That, if the mechanical and corpuscularian hypothesis deserve credit, all your late doctrines about the world, that its phenomena were vital, and not mechanical, must be grossly erroneous': *Reply*, p. 63.

143 *Conway*, p. 269; Robert A. Greene, 'Henry More and Boyle on Nature,' *Journal of the History of Ideas*, 23 (1962), pp. 451–74; and Burtt (see n. 141), p. 177.

144 *Conway*, p. 303; and *Reply*. Later in the decade More would join Glanvill in a bitter attack on another vitalist, John Webster: Thomas Jobe, 'The Devil in Restoration Science: The Glanvill–Webster Debate,' *ISIS*, 72 (1981), pp. 343–56.

145 *Conway*, p. 303.

146 *PUR*, pp. 11–12.

147 Ibid., pp. 15–16; *Censure*, p. 29; and *RPM*, *passim*.

148 *CHO*, vi, p. 456.

149 *Praefatory*, p. 3.

150 *CSPD, 1670*, p. 229.

151 Somerset RO, DD/SFR, 8/1, fo. 16v. and indices.

152 Bristol RO, 'Articles to be ministered, enquired of, and answered; concerning matters ecclesiatical: in the 3rd episcopal visitation of . . . Gilbert . . . learned bishop of Bristol in the 8th year of his consecration [1669].'

153 *Praefatory*, pp. 48–9.

154 *CHO*, vi, p. 456.

155 Bristol RO, Thomas Speed's Account Book, 1681–90, fos. 21, 94, 117; and Russell Mortimer (ed.), *Minute Book of the Men's Meeting of the Society of Friends in Bristol 1667–1686* (Bristol Record Society, 1971). For Thomas Speed as a Quaker leader: ibid., p. 216 and *passim*; Russell Mortimer (ed.), *Minute Book of the Men's Meeting of the Society of Friends in Bristol 1686–1704* (Bristol Record Society, 1977), p. xii; and *AO*, iii, p. 799, and iv, pp. 488–9.

156 George Bishop, *A Looking-Glass for the Times* (London, 1668), p. 217.

157 [Stubbe] (see ch. 2, n. 63), pp. 88–92.

158 *CSPD, 1668–9*, p. 59.

159 For Quaker attitudes in these respects: George Bishop, *A Book of Warnings* (London, 1661), pp. 28–9; and Braithwaite (see n. 8), ch. 20. Also Holt (see ch. 4, n. 3), pp. 26–8.

160 *AO*, iv, p. 124.

161 Evelyn MSS., Beale to Evelyn, 11 June 1670.

162 *Praefatory*, pp. 101–2. See also Hunter (see Intro., n. 2), pp. 166–7.

163 *WRB*, vi, p. 445; and Evelyn MSS., Beale to Evelyn, 29 April 1681.

164 *Legends*.

165 Ibid.

166 That same year he served as a go-between for Fell and his patron Viscount Conway (*CSPD, 1670*, p. 353).

167 *CHO*, vi, pp. 137, 189–90; and *WRB*, vi, p. 459.

168 *CHO*, vii, p. 225.

169 Hunter (see Intro., no. 2), p. 149.

170 Ibid., pp. 137–8, 160. For the curriculum: William T. Costello, *The Scholastic Curriculum at Early Seventeenth-Century Cambridge* (Cambridge, Mass., 1958); Patricia Reif, 'The Textbook Tradition in Natural Philosophy, 1600–1650.' *Journal of the History of Ideas*, 30 (1969), pp. 17–32; and Hugh Kearney, *Scholars and Gentlemen* (Ithaca, NY, 1970), pp. 124–8, 146–50.

171 Hunter (see Intro., n. 2), p. 143.

172 Ibid., pp. 156, 160.

173 M. R. G. Spiller, 'Conservative Opinion and the New Science, 1630–1680: With Special Reference to the Life and Works of Meric Casaubon.' Oxford University, BLitt thesis (1968), pp. 3–4, 7. See also: Michael R. G. Spiller, *'Concerning Natural Experimental Philosophie': Meric Casaubon and the Royal Society* (The Hague and Boston, 1980).

174 Spiller, 'Conservative Opinion' (see n. 173), pp. 22–4, 25. For the reading of Descartes at Cambridge: Kearney (see n. 170), pp. 150–1.

175 Spiller, 'Conservation Opinion' (see n. 173), p. 26.

176 Hunter (see Intro., n. 2), pp. 152–3.

177 Henry Stubbe, *A Further Justification of the Present War Against the United Netherlands* (London, 1673), p. 82.

178 Ibid., vi, p. 456; and Evelyn MSS., Beale to Evelyn, 11 June 1670.

179 *Praefatory*, Preface, p. 9 (unnumbered).
180 *WRB*, i, pp. xc–xcvii.
181 *CHO*, vi, p. 138.
182 Ibid.; and *WRB*, i, pp. xciii, xcv.
183 Ibid., pp, xci, xcii; and PRO, SP 29/275/151.
184 Hill, 'Milton and Marvell' (see Intro., n. 6), p. 12.
185 One of Stubbe's contemporaries, Mary Trye, was not certain what the 'aims' of his attack were. The disguise sometimes worked too well. But even she recognized that there was behind these attacks a 'disguised design': Mary Trye, *Medicatrix* (London, 1675), pp. 4, 11, 79.
186 *AO*, iii, p. 1072.
187 Ch. 8.

6. Court pen: 'ancient prudence' and royal policy

1 PRO, SP 9/202, especially (37).
2 PRO, SP 44/40, fo. 1.
3 PRO, SP 9/202 (37).
4 C. R. Boxer, 'Some Second Thoughts on the Third Anglo-Dutch War, 1672–1674,' *Transactions of the Royal Historical Society*, 5th ser., 19 (1969), pp. 67–80.
5 E.g., Jonathan Edwin, *The Dutch Usurpation* (London, 1672); Sir George Downing, *A Discourse* (London, 1672); the Earl of Castlemaine, *A Short and True Account*, 2nd edn (London, 1672); Maurice Lee, *The Cabal* (Urbana, Ill., 1965), p. 113; and K. H. D. Haley, *William of Orange and the English Opposition 1672–4* (Oxford, 1953), p. 64.
6 *CSPD, 1672*, pp. 284, 319–20, 323.
7 Peter Fraser, *The Intelligence of the Secretaries of State and their Monopoly of Licensed News, 1660–1688* (Cambridge, 1956), p. 167; Boxer (see n. 4), p. 68; and Frederick George Stephens (ed.), *Catalogue of Prints and Drawings in the British Museum, Political and Personal Satires* (London, 1870), i, pp. 586–7, 591.
8 Henry Stubbe, *A Justification of the Present War Against the United Netherlands* (London, 1672), in *The Harleian Miscellany* (London, 1746), viii, p. 164.
9 Stubbe (see ch. 5, n. 177), p. 4.
10 Ibid., p. 5.
11 Ibid., pp. 29–30.
12 Ibid., 'To the Reader.'
13 Ibid., p. 4.
14 Ibid.
15 Ibid., pp. 31–2. For indications of whom Stubbe had in mind: *CSPD, 1665–1666*, p. 342; *CSPD, 1666–1667*, pp. 537, 546; G. Lyon Turner (ed.), 'Williamson's Spy Book,' *Transactions of the Congregationalist Historical Society*, 5 (1911–12), pp. 242–58, 301–19, 345–56; J. Walker, 'The English Exiles in Holland during the Reigns of Charles II and James II,' *Transactions of the Royal Historical Society*, 4th ser., 30 (1948), pp. 111–25; K. H. D. Haley, *The First Earl of Shaftesbury* (Oxford, 1968), pp. 296–7; Maureen Duffy, *The Passionate Shepherdess* (New York, 1979), pp. 60–2, 66–71, 78–83.

16 Stubbe (see ch. 5, n. 177), pp. 30–1.
17 Ibid., p. 31.
18 Ibid.
19 Ibid., pp. 29–30.
20 Ibid., p. 30.
21 Ibid.
22 Ibid., p. 31.
23 Ibid., pp. 31–2.
24 Ibid., p. 72; and R. A. Beddard, 'The Restoration Church,' *The Restored Monarchy 1660–1688*, ed. J. R. Jones (London, 1979), pp. 163–4.
25 Stubbe (see ch. 5, n. 177), pp. 31–2.
26 Ibid., pp. 20–2.
27 Ibid., p. 22.
28 Beddard (see n. 24), pp. 156–72.
29 Frank Bate, *The Declaration of Indulgence 1672* (London, 1908), p. 85.
30 Henry Bennet, Earl of Arlington, *The Right Honourable Earl of Arlington's Letters*, 2 vols. (London, 1701), ii, p. 362.
31 Haley (see n. 15), pp. 296–8.
32 Stubbe (see ch. 5, n. 177), p. 29.
33 W. D. Christie, *A Life of Anthony Ashley Cooper, First Earl of Shaftesbury* (London, 1871), ii, Appendix I, pp. v–ix; and Roger Coke, *A Treatise Wherein Is Demonstrated that the Church and State of England Are in Equal Danger with the Trade of It* (London, 1671), 'Petitions' (unnumbered).
34 Stubbe (see ch. 5, n. 177), p. 29.
35 Ibid'. p. 28.
36 Claire Cross, *The Royal Supremacy in the Elizabethan Church* (London, 1969), p. 28; and Ferguson (see ch. 4, n. 14), pp. 178–82, 195–207.
37 Stubbe (see ch. 5, n. 177), pp. 32–61.
38 Ibid.
39 Ibid., p. 43.
40 Ibid., p. 65.
41 Ibid., p. 35.
42 Ibid., p. 72.
43 Ibid., pp. 61–7.
44 Ibid., pp. 62–7.
45 Jones (see Intro., n. 2); and Joseph M. Levine, *Dr Woodward's Shield* (Berkeley, 1977).
46 *PWJH*, pp. 43–76.
47 Ibid., pp. 128–52.
48 Ibid., pp. 131–6; and [Shaftesbury], *A Letter from a Person of Quality to His Friend in the Country* (London, 1675), p. 33.
49 Haley (see n. 15), p. 297.
50 *CSPD, October, 1672, to February, 1673*, p. 350.
51 Haley (see n. 15), pp. 297–8.
52 Ibid., p. 298.
53 [Shaftesbury] (see n. 48), p. 15.
54 Ibid., pp. 9, 15.

55 Ibid., p. 1.
56 Ibid., p. 25.
57 Ibid., pp. 1, 34.
58 Professor Pocock has recently begun to see that neo-Harringtonianism had a religious component, what he calls a civil theology: J. G. A. Pocock, 'Contexts for the Study of James Harrington,' *Il Pensiero Politico*, 2 (1978), pp. 20–35; and idem, 'England and the Enlightenment' (see Intro., n. 14), pp. 91–112.
59 Andrew Marvell, *The Rehearsal Transpros'd The Second Part*, ed. D. I. B. Smith (Oxford, 1971), pp. xxi, xvii.
60 [Henry Stubbe], *Rosemary & Bayes* (London, 1672), pp. 18–19.
61 *PWJH*, pp. 43–76, 128–52.
62 [Stubbe] (see n. 60), p. 19.
63 Ibid., p. 18.
64 Ibid., pp. 18–19.
65 Ibid., p. 18.
66 Ibid., pp. 18–22.
67 For brief notices of *Rosemary & Bayes*: Cope (see ch. 5, n. 52), p. 35; Marvell (see n. 59), p. xiv; and Annabel Patterson, *Andrew Marvell and the Civic Crown* (Princeton, 1978), p. 38.
68 Hill, 'Milton and Marvell' (see Intro., n. 6). p. 16.
69 Stubbe (see ch. 5, n. 177), p. 79.
70 Ibid., p. 80.
71 Ibid., pp. 81–2.
72 Pocock, *The Machiavellian Moment* (see Intro., n. 14), chs. 12–14.
73 Stubbe (see ch. 5, n. 177), pp. 32–3.
74 Ibid., pp. 59–60.
75 Ibid., p. 75; and idem (see n. 60), p. 22.
76 Stubbe (see ch. 5, n. 177), pp. 62–3.
77 Ibid., p. 63.
78 Ibid., pp. 47–8.
79 Ibid., p. 63.
80 Ibid., pp. 32–3.
81 *PWJH*, pp. 78–82, 91–3, 94–6.
82 Stubbe (see n. 8), pp. 9–10, 54.
83 Ibid., p. 55; and *RPM*, pp. 93–4, 112–13.
84 Marvell (see n. 59), p. xvii; see also Hill, 'Milton and Marvell' (see Intro., n. 6), pp. 14–15. For Marvell, unlike Stubbe, the Indulgence was one thing but the third Dutch War was quite another, which he thoroughly opposed: L. N. Wall, 'Marvell and the Third Dutch War,' *Notes and Queries*, ccii (1957), pp. 296–7; and Patterson (see n. 67), p. 41.
85 [Stubbe] (see n. 60), pp. 21–2.
86 Stubbe (see n. 8), p. 9.
87 Ibid.
88 *Legends*, Preface (unnumbered).
89 *Praefatory*, pp. 6–7.
90 Stubbe (see ch. 5, n. 177), p. 30.
91 *RPM*, p. 2.

7. Court to country

1 *AO*, iii, p. 1082.

2 Haley (see ch. 6, n. 15), p. 350.

3 For Seignior: George Seignior, *God, the King, and the Church* (London, 1670); idem, *Moses and Aaron* (Cambridge, 1670), pp. 6, 14–17, 59; and James Fawket, *An Account of the Late Reverend and Worthy Dr. George Seignior* (London, 1681), pp. 19–27, 29–30. For Anglesey; *HMC, 13, Appendix*, pt 6, p. 270: Arthur Annesley, Earl of Anglesey, *The King's Right of Indulgence in Spiritual Matters Asserted* (London, 1688); and *DNB*.

4 Bodl. MS., Tanner 42.12, George Seignior to William Sancroft, 1 June 1673; *HMCR*, 12, p. 518; and Marvell (see ch. 6, n. 59), p. xxii.

5 PRO, SP 44/40, fo. 124v. On Povey: Webb (see ch. 3, n. 13), p. 206; and Cundall (see ch. 3, n. 18), p. 7.

6 On the importance of the post: Webb (see ch. 3, n. 13), p. 206.

7 During the early 1670s, particularly between 1671 and 1674, the colonial legislature in Jamaica was gaining a greater voice in affairs (ibid., pp. 253–8). Did Arlington thus think this a fit place to send Stubbe? As Secretary of Jamaica he would have sat on the Governor's council (ibid, p. 206).

8 W.D. Christie (ed.), *Letters Addressed from London to Sir Joseph Williamson*, 2 vols. (London, 1874), i, p. 176. Stubbe probably knew Holmes in Bath, where he went regularly for treatment during the 1670s: Thomas Guidott. *A Collection of Treatises Relating to the City and Waters of Bath* (London, 1725), p. 352; and Peirce (see ch. 3, n. 80), pp. 241, 305–6.

9 Gilbert Burnet, *Bishop Burnet's History of His Own Time*, 2nd edn (Oxford, 1883), i, pp. 562–3; Thomas Bruce, Earl of Ailesbury, *Memoirs* (London, 1890), i, pp. 11–12; and Haley (see ch. 6, n. 15), p. 296.

10 BL Add. MS. 35838, fos. 267v–268; *HMCR, 3, Appendix*, p. 217; and *HMCR, 33*, p. 221.

11 BL Add. MS. 35838, fos. 267v–268r.

12 *HMCR, 12, Appendix*, pt 6, p. 104.

13 J. R. Jones, *Country and Court* (Cambridge, Mass., 1978), p. 182.

14 G. E. C. *The Complete Peerage*, rev. Vicary Gibbs, ed. H. A. Doubleday and Lord Howard de Walden (London, 1929), vii, pp. 176–7.

15 PRO, 30/24/5/pt 1/262.

16 Haley (see ch. 6, n. 5), p. 117.

17 Christie (ed.), (see n. 8), p. i, 164; Haley (see ch. 6, n. 5), p. 132; and *HMCR, 12, Appendix*, pt 7, p. 106.

18 Ibid.

19 Jones (see n. 13), p. 182; and John Miller, *James II* (Hove, UK, 1977), p. 74.

20 Bodl. MS. Wood 660c (14); and Bodl. MS. Tanner 42.48.

21 Haley (see ch. 6, n. 5), p. 336.

22 *AO*, iii, p. 1082.

23 Bodl. MS. Tanner 42. 48. For Tillison: Bodl. MS. Eng. lett. e. 137. 45; Bodl. MS. Tanner 42. 20, 31, 44, 48, 52, 54, 81, 86, 89, 222; and Bodl. MS. Tanner 145. 178, 183, 185.

24 The reference to 'true honour' may be an anticipation of Charles's reply to the Commons' petition in which he said: 'he could not in honour break a contract

of marriage which had been so solemnly executed.' Mary Hopkirk, *Queen over the Water* (London, 1953), p. 20.

25 Pocock, *The Machiavellian Moment* (see Intro., n. 14), pp. 406–22.

26 Bodl. MS. Tanner 42. 48.

27 *CSPD, 1673*, p. 599.

28 D. T. Witcombe, *Charles II and the Cavalier House of Commons, 1663–1674* (Manchester, 1966), p. 204.

29 *HMCR*, 5, p. 321.

30 Witcombe (see n. 28), pp. 148–9.

31 Ibid., p. 204.

32 Ibid.; and the Pepys Library, Magdalene College, Cambridge, Miscellanies VII, fos. 489–91.

33 For Malet: Somerset RO, Quarter Sessions Rolls; Caroline Robbins, *The Diary of John Milward, Esq.* (Cambridge, 1938), p. 80; BL Add. MS. 32094, fos. 357, 360, and Add. MS. 32095, fos. 109–88; Sir John Malet, *Concerning Penal Laws* (London, 1680); and William A. Shaw, *The Knights of England*, 2 vols. (London, 1906), ii, p. 242. Sir John's younger brother Michael had been a member of the Rota in 1659, was one of the most radical MPs in the Cavalier Parliament, and in November 1675 tried to introduce a bill in the Commons allowing a man to 'have as many wives as he pleases, not exceeding 12' (*HMCR*, 7, p. 493a). For Michael: Leo Miller, *John Milton among the Polygamophiles* (New York, 1974), pp. 136–7; and Witcombe (see n. 28), p. 137.

34 *AO*, iii, p. 1082.

35 Edward Arber, *The Term Catalogues*, 3 vols. (London, 1903), i, p. 149.

36 Henry Stubbe, *The History of the United Provinces of Achaia*, 'To the Reader.'

37 Ibid.

38 Ibid., p. 2.

39 Ibid., p. 3.

40 Ibid.

41 Ibid.

42 Ibid., pp. 3–4.

43 Ibid., pp. 31–2.

44 Ibid., p. 32.

45 BL Add. MS. 35838, fos. 269, 276.

46 *CSPD, 1667*, p. 338; *CSP, Ireland, 1666–1669*, p. 474; *CSP, Ireland, 1669–1670*, p. 148: *CSPD, 1670*, p. 353; *CSPD, 1671*, pp. 295, 539.

47 BL Add. MS. 35838, fos. 272r, 276.

48 Ibid., fo. 269r. There must have been deep ideological resonances between the two men. Kent's mother, the Countess Dowager, whom Stubbe also knew (ibid., fo. 272r), was in widowhood the intimate companion of John Selden towards the end of his life; and Kent for his part collected the theological manuscripts of John Wyclif: [Edward Bernard], *Catalogi Librorum Manuscriptorum Angliae et Hiberniae* (Oxford, 1697), ii, p. 392.

49 BL Add. MS. 35838, fos. 269–76.

50 Ibid., fo. 276; see also Clement Edward Pike (ed.), *Selections from the Correspondence of Arthur Capel Earl of Essex 1675–1677*, Camden Society, 3rd ser., xxiv (London, 1913), ii, p. 3. The baths were open to public view: E. S.

Turner, *Taking the Cure* (London, 1967), p. 52. There were even galleries for spectators at the Cross Bath: Celia Fiennes, *The Journeys of Celia Fiennes*, ed. Christopher Morris (London, 1949), p. 18.

51 P. Rowland James, *The Baths of Bath in the Sixteenth and Seventeenth Centuries* (Bristol, 1938), pp. 80–4.

52 BL Add. MS. 35838, fo. 274.

53 Miller (see n. 33), pp. 136–7; and *HMCR*, 7, p. 493a.

54 BL Add. MS. 35838, fos. 269v–270r, 274.

55 Ibid., fo. 274v.

56 Robert Hooke spoke with him at a coffee house in London on 12 June 1674: Hooke, *Diary*, p. 107. On 12 September 1675, Stubbe wrote to Elias Ashmole, who had supplied him with illustrations for his two books justifying the Dutch War, asking him to prepare his coat of arms: Stubbe (see ch. 6, n. 8), viii, p. 134; and C. H. Josten (ed.), *Elias Ashmole*, 5 vols. (Oxford, 1966), iv, pp. 1438–9.

57 Turner (see n. 50), p. 53. For background: James Wigmore, *Medicine and Its Practitioners during the Early Years of the History of Bath* (Bristol, 1913); Reginald Lennard, *Englishmen at Rest and Play: Some Phases of English Leisure, 1558–1714* (Oxford, 1931); and Henry Chapman, *Thermae Redivivae: The City of Bath Described* (London, 1673).

58 James (see n. 51), pp. 80–4; and Venner (see ch. 3, n. 80), 'To the Reader,' pp. 345–7, 358–9.

59 Fiennes (see n. 50), p. 19.

60 Ibid., p. 18.

61 Guidott (see n. 8), p. 75; and idem, 'An Appendix Concerning Bathe,' p. 17, in Edward Jorden, *A Discourse of Natural Bathes and Mineral Waters*, 3rd edn, rev. (London, 1669).

62 Peirce (see ch. 3, n. 80), p. 129.

63 Ibid., p. 136.

64 Ibid.

65 Ibid., p. 134.

66 Guidott (see ch. 5, n. 135), 'A Preface to the Reader.'

67 Ibid., pp. 12, 13–14; and Peirce (see ch. 3, n. 80), p. 38.

68 BL Sloane MS. 35, fo. 14v.

69 [Henry Stubbe], *Medice Cura Teipsum!* (London, 1671), p. 19.

70 Quoted in Henry Stubbe, *Directions for the Drinking the Bath-Water*, 'The Preface to the Reader,' in John Hale, *Select Observations*, trans. James Cook (London, 1679). For the medical plight of the poor in the early eighteenth century: Hill (see ch. 2, n. 13), p. 309.

71 Stubbe (see n. 70), 'The Preface to the Reader.'

72 *AO*, iii, p. 1071.

73 Ibid., p. 1082.

74 Margoliouth (ed.) (see ch. 3, n. 80), ii, p. 325.

75 *AO*, iii, p. 1082.

76 Ibid., pp. 1082–3.

77 *HMCR*, 78, *Hastings*, ii, p. 385.

78 *CSPD, 1676–1677*, p. 310.

79 Bodl. MS. Aubrey 12, fos. 325–7.

80 *HMCR*, 78, *Hastings*, ii, p. 385.
81 *CSPD, 1676–1677*, pp. 310–11.
82 For the catalogue: BL Sloane 35.
83 Hooke, *Diary*, pp. 356, 447.
84 Henry R. Plomer, *A Dictionary of the Booksellers and Printers Who Were at Work in England, Scotland and Ireland from 1641 to 1667* (London, 1907), p. 123.
85 Hooke, *Diary*, p. 389.
86 Ibid., p. 447.
87 Anon., *List of Catalogues of English Book Sales, 1676–1900, Now in the British Museum* (London, 1915), unpaginated.
88 John Lauber, *Book Auctions in England in the Seventeenth Century, 1676–1700* (London, 1898), p. 141.
89 Anon, (see n. 87), 'Introduction,' unpaginated.
90 Hooke, *Diary*, p. 389.
91 J. Williams, 'An Edition of the Correspondence of John Aubrey with Anthony à Wood and Edward Lhuyd, 1667–1696,' 2 vols. PhD thesis, University of London (1969), ii, pp. 285–6, 288: Aubrey to Wood, London, 11 September 1676.
92 Ibid., i, p. 201.
93 Bodl. MS. Aubrey 12, fo. 327; 14 November 1676. I owe this reference and the next to the courtesy of Dr Michael Hunter.
94 Ibid., fo. 325; 11 October 1676.
95 *AO*, iii, p. 1082.
96 Williams (see n. 91), i. pp. 53, 201.

8. Civil religion and radical politics: Stubbe to Toland

1 Hooke, *Diary*, pp. 344, 408.
2 Donald Wing, *Short-Title Catalogue of Books Printed in England, Scotland, Ireland, Wales, and British America, and of English Books Printed in Other Countries, 1641–1700* (New York, 1945–51), iii, p. 309.
3 J. R. Jones, *The First Whigs* (Durham, 1961); and J. P. Kenyon, *The Popish Plot* (London, 1972).
4 Henry Stubbe, *A Caveat for the Protestant Clergy*, 2nd edn (London, printed for W. Cooper at the Pelican [1678]), pp. 14–16.
5 For a record and the membership of the Green Ribbon Club: The Pepys Library, Magdalene College, Cambridge, Miscellanies VII, fos. 465–91.
6 Gilbert Burnet, *Some Passages of the Life and Death of the Right Honourable John, Earl of Rochester* (London, 1680).
7 Harth (see ch. 4, n. 53), p. 74; and Philopatris [Charles Blount], *A Just Vindication of Learning* (London, 1679), Preface.
8 [Charles Blount], *Last Sayings or Dying Legacy of Mr. Thomas Hobbes* (London, 1680).
9 Charles Blount, *Miracles No Violations of the Laws of Nature* (London, 1683); also Don Cupitt, 'The Doctrine of Analogy in the Age of Locke,' *Journal of Theological Studies*, 19 (1968), pp. 186–202.
10 Charles Blount, [Charles] Gildon et al., *The Oracles of Reason* (London, 1693), p. 156.

11 Clark (ed.), (see ch. 2, n. 43), iii, p. 481, in which a letter, dated 7 March 1695, is quoted, saying 'Certaine works of Charles Blount lately deceased were stop'd going to the press, containing atheistical and profane matters.'

12 Harth (see ch. 4, n. 53), pp. 235–44.

13 Albertus Warren, *An Apology for the Discovery of Humane Reason, Written by Mr. Clifford, Esq.* (London, 1680), p. 97.

14 Sir George Blundell, *Remarks upon a Tract Intitled A Treatise of Humane Reason. And upon Mr. Warren's Late Defence of It* (London, 1683), p. 93.

15 Pepys, *Diary*, ix, p. 361.

16 PRO, 30/24/6A, fo. 309.

17 Warren (see n. 13), 'The Epistle Dedicatory,' dated Oct. 1680.

18 Blount *et al.* (see n. 10), pp. 195, 209.

19 Ibid., p. 195; and Warren (see n. 13), *passim*.

20 Warren (see n. 13), pp. 83–6, 116–17, 142.

21 Ibid., pp. 128–9.

22 [Martin Clifford], *A Treatise of Humane Reason* (London, 1675), pp. 44–5.

23 Albertus Warren, *The Royalist Reformed* (London, 1650); and Hill (see ch. 2, n. 13), p. 175.

24 Warren (see n. 13), p. 80.

25 Pocock, *The Machiavellian Moment* (see Intro., n. 14), pp. 406–22. The most important and explicit Harringtonian political analysis to emerge during the Exclusion crisis was Henry Neville's *Plato Redivivus* (1680). Neville, however, did not do as Warren did, and apply Harringtonian analysis to the question of the *religious* settlement. Although Neville is anticlerical and shares Stubbe's and Warren's view that pure Christianity was anciently corrupted by priests for worldly ends, they depart from him in offering a Harringtonian solution to the religious crisis. Neville in fact belongs to that current in seventeenth-century English thought which sees the religious crisis as stemming entirely from the political one: See Anon., *A Paradox, That the Designe upon Religion Was Not the Cause of State Mis-Government; But an Effect of It* (London, 1644), and Neville (see ch. 5, n. 7), p. 159. Hence, Neville restricts the application of his revised Harringtonianism to politics, which he sees as the source of the trouble (ibid., p. 155). There were thus two kinds of Harringtonian analysis available during the Restoration – one offering a formula for achieving political balance and the other promoting Harringtonian civic religion.

26 *PWJH*, pp. 50–3.

27 Warren (see n. 13), p. 121.

28 Ibid., pp. 79–80.

29 Ibid., p. 123.

30 J. R. Jones, 'The Green Ribbon Club,' *Durham University Journal*, n.s., 18 (Dec. 1956), pp. 17–20.

31 Kenyon; and Jones (see n. 3).

32 *WRB*, vi, p. 450; also J. R. Jacob, 'Restoration Ideologies and the Royal Society,' *History of Science*, 18 (1980), pp. 25–38.

33 *WRB*, v, p. 159.

34 Ibid., p. 160.

35 Ibid.

36 Ibid., pp. 191–2.

37 Ibid., p. 183.

38 Ibid., pp. 222–6.

39 Ibid., pp. 250–3.

40 *HRS*, pp. 342–5, 368–77.

41 It is difficult to know who Stubbe's followers were. For indications: Evelyn MSS., Beale to Evelyn, 11 June 1670, treated in ch. 5.

42 RS, Boyle Letters, ii. fo. 65v.

43 *MC*, pp. 25, 14, 27.

44 Glanvill (see ch. 5, n. 137), p. 35.

45 *WRB*, i, p. lxxix.

46 Jacob, *Boyle*, pp. 169–70.

47 Hooke, *Diary*, pp. 13, 82, 107, 184, 344, 356, 409, 447.

48 J. A. Redwood, 'Blount, Deism and English Free Thought,' *Journal of the History of Ideas*, 35 (1974), pp. 490–8.

49 D. P. Walker, 'Edward Lord Herbert of Cherbury and Christian Apologetics,' in *The Ancient Theology* (London, 1972), ch. 5.

50 Charles Blount, *Religio Laici* (London, 1683), pp. 48–55.

51 Ibid., pp. 56–70.

52 Blount (see n. 9), 'Premonition to the Candid Reader.'

53 Ibid., p. 12.

54 *WRB*, vi, pp. 311–14.

55 John Miller, *Popery and Politics in England 1660–1688* (Cambridge, 1973), p. 247; and Evelyn, *Diary*, iv, p. 489.

56 Robin Clifton, 'The Popular Fear of Catholics during the English Revolution,' *Past and Present*, 52 (Aug., 1971), p. 36; Thomas Birch, *The Life of the Most Reverend Doctor John Tillotson* (London, 1752), p. 127; Thomas Jones (ed.), *A Catalogue of the Collection of Tracts for and against Popery (Published in or about the Reign of James II))* in the Manchester Library Founded by Humphrey Chetham, Chetham Society, vols. 48, 64 (1859–65); and Edward Cardwell (ed.), *Enchiridion Theologicum Anti-Romanism*, 3 vols. (Oxford, 1836–7).

57 For example: John Tillotson, *A Discourse against Transubstantiation* (London, 1684), pp. 36–7; and William Payne, *A Discourse Concerning the Adoration of the Host, As It Is Taught and Practised in the Church of Rome* (London, 1685), pp. 22–3.

58 Samuel Johnson, *Julian the Apostate* (London, 1682), p. 108.

59 David Abercromby, *Protestancy to Be Embrac'd: Or a New and Infallible Method to Reduce Romanists from Popery to Protestancy* (London, 1682), p. 97.

60 *WRB*, vi, p. 311.

61 Ibid., p. 313.

62 Ibid., p. 306.

63 [Robert Boyle], *Reasons Why a Protestant Should Not Turn Papist* (London, 1687), p. 19.

64 *WRB*, v, p. 190.

65 Robert Boyle, *A Free Enquiry into the Vulgarly Receiv'd Notion of Nature* (London, 1885/6), p. 414.

66 Abercromby (see n. 59); and David Abercromby, *A Moral Discourse on the Power of Interest* (London, 1690), 'The Epistle Dedicatory,' and pp. 59–60.

67 David Abercromby, *A Discourse of Wit* (London, 1685), p. 114.

68 Miller (see n. 55), pp. 206–10; and J. R. Western, *Monarchy and Revolution* (London, 1972), pp. 196–8.

69 George Villiers, 2nd Duke of Buckingham, *A Short Discourse upon the Reasonableness of Men's Having a Religion, or Worship of God*, in *The Works of George Villiers . . . Duke of Buckingham*, 2 vols. (London, 1715), ii, p. 202.

70 Ibid., p. 201.

71 Ibid., p. 200.

72 Ibid., p. 194.

73 Ibid., p. 197.

74 Cf., for example, ibid., pp. 194–200 with Blount (see n. 50), pp. 48–70.

75 Henry Maurice, *The Antithelimite* (London, 1685), pp. 5–8, 22.

76 [William Penn], *A Defence of the Duke of Buckingham, Against the Answer to His Book, and the Reply to His Letter* (London, 1685), pp. 5–6.

77 [William Penn], *Considerations Moving to a Toleration . . . Occasioned by an Excellent Discourse upon that Subject, Published by His Grace the Duke of Buckingham* (London, 1685), p. 3.

78 William Penn, *Fiction Found Out* (Worminghurst-place, 1685); this is a broadside.

79 Evelyn, *Diary*, iii, p. 521.

80 [William Penn], *A Defence of the Duke of Buckingham's Book of Religion and Worship from the Exceptions of a Nameless Author* (London, 1685), p. 10.

81 [William Walwyn], *A Manifestation from Lieutenant Col. John Lilburn, Mr. William Walwyn, Mr. Thomas Prince, and Mr. Richard Overton* (London, 1649), in G. E. Aylmer (ed.), *The Levellers and the English Revolution* (Ithaca, NY, 1975), p. 155; C. E. Whiting, *Studies in English Puritanism from the Restoration to the Revolution, 1660–1688* (London, 1931), pp. 515, 529–30; Clifton (see n. 56), pp. 33–4; and Lamont (see ch. 4, n. 43), pp. 175–88, 190–5.

82 Evelyn, *Diary*, iv, pp. 507–8; and Samuel M. Janney, *Life of William Penn* (Philadelphia, 1851), pp. 262–5.

83 Evelyn, *Diary*, iv, pp. 507–8.

84 RS, Boyle Letters, iv, fo. 39.

85 *WRB*, v, p. 198.

86 Ibid., p. 200.

87 Ibid., p. 164.

88 Jacob, *Boyle*, pp. 104–7, 141–2.

89 *WRB*, v, p. 198.

90 Gilbert Burnet, *An Exposition of the Thirty-Nine Articles of the Church of England*, ed. James R. Page (London, 1837), pp. vii–viii, 419, 424–7, 438–9, 445.

91 *WRB*, v, p. 165.

92 *Newtonians*, ch. 6.

93 Blount *et al.* (see n. 10).

94 *Newtonians*, ch. 6; *PWJH*, pp. 141–3; Pocock, *The Machiavellian Moment* (see Intro., n. 14), ch. 13; and Edmund Ludlow, *A Voyce from the Watch Tower, Part Five: 1660–1662*, ed. A. B. Worden (London, 1978), pp. 17–55.

95 John Toland, *Miscellaneous Works*, ed. Pierre Des Maizeaux, 2 vols. (London, 1747), i, p. xiv.

96 Ibid., p. xvii.

97 [John Toland], *An Apology for Mr. Toland*, in John Toland, *Christianity Not Mysterious* (London, 1702), p. 7.

98 Toland (see n. 95), i, pp. xxiv–xxv.

99 Robert South, *Twelve Sermons* (London, 1698), 'The Epistle Dedicatory.'

100 Ibid.

101 *WRB*, vi, pp. 458–9; and *CHO*, vi, pp. 129, 137, 245.

102 South (see n. 99), 'The Epistle Dedicatory.'

103 Lambeth Palace Library, MS. 673; and McLachlan (see Intro., n. 6), pp. 318–19.

104 *Newtonians*, p. 273.

105 John Toland, *The State-Anatomy of Great Britain*, 4th edn (London, n.d. [1717]), p. 27.

106 Ibid., p. 29.

107 Giancarlo Carabelli, *Tolandiana* (Florence, 1975), pp. 258–9.

108 Toland (see n. 95), ii, p. 196.

109 Ibid.

110 Toland (see n. 105), pp. 26–32; also John Toland, *Tetradymus* (London, 1720), pp. xvii–xxi.

111 Toland (see n. 105), p. 28.

112 John Milton, *Of True Religion, Heresy, Schism, Toleration* (London, 1673).

113 [John Toland], *The Life of John Milton* (London, 1699), pp. 143–7.

114 Toland (see n. 105), pp. 74–5. For the quotation from Harrington: *PWJH*, p. 400. I am grateful to Professor J. G. A. Pocock for pointing out the quotation from Harrington.

115 John Toland, *Letters to Serena* (London, 1704), 'The Preface.'

116 Margaret C. Jacob, 'John Toland and the Newtonian Ideology,' *Journal of the Warburg and Courtauld Institutes*, 32 (1969), pp. 307–31.

117 Ibid.

118 Toland, *Tetradymus* (see n. 110), pp. vii–viii; Toland (see n. 95), i, pp. lxvii, lxxiii, lxxx, lxxxiv, and ii, pp. 388, 476–7; and Toland (see n. 105), ch. 6.

119 Basil Williams, *The Whig Supremacy 1714–1760*, 2nd edn rev. by C. H. Stuart (Oxford, 1962), p. 86.

120 Ibid., pp. 69–70; and *Commonwealthman*, pp. 114–20, 227, 234–6.

121 Toland (see n. 105), ch. 6.

122 Toland (see n. 95), ii, pp. 461–95.

123 Ibid., i, p. lxxxiv, and ii, pp. 476–7.

124 John Toland, *Nazarenus*, 2nd edn rev. (London, 1718), pp. 38–40, 70–3.

125 BL Add. MS. 4465, fos. 63v–64; and Stuart Piggott, *William Stukeley* (Oxford, 1950), p. 118.

126 Toland (see n. 124), p. 76.

127 Ibid., pp. 26–9, 38–40, 70–3.

128 Ibid., p. 40.

129 Ibid., pp. 67–8.

130 Ibid., pp. 65–6. For Toland's devotion to Cicero's civic religion: Robert Sullivan, *John Toland and the Deist Controversy* (Cambridge, Mass., 1982), pp. 118–19.

131 Toland (see n. 124), pp. iii, 4, 5.

132 Ibid., pp. 72–3.

133 Ibid., p. 38.

134 Ibid., p. 77.

135 Ibid., p. 69, for example.

136 *RPM*, pp. vii, x; and Charles Hornby, *A Caveat against the Whigs* (London, 1711).

137 Thomas Mangey, *Remarks upon Nazarenus*, 2nd edn (London, 1718), p. 43. For Mangey: Humfrey Wanley, *The Diary of Humfrey Wanley*, ed. C. E. Wright and Ruth C. Wright, 2 vols. (London, the Bibliographic Society, 1966), ii, pp. 210, 348, 415, 421, 455.

138 Mangey (see n. 137), p. 43.

139 There are strong similarities in the arguments and the sources both use – for example, the heavy reliance of both on Selden (for Toland's use of Selden: Toland (see n. 124), pp. 25–6, 62, 65; for Stubbe's: ch. 4).

140 Stubbe seems to have still had a reputation. In 1718, Thomas Hearne, the Oxford highchurchman, referred to 'the famous Mr. Hen. Stubbe': *Remarks and Collections of Thomas Hearne*, 6 (1717–19), Oxford Historical Society, 43 (Oxford, 1902), p. 237. It is clear that the Stubbe referred to, is ours (ibid., and Josten (ed.), (see ch. 7, n. 56), iv, pp. 1438–9). Was Stubbe 'famous' perhaps because his manuscript was in circulation and being connected with Toland's *Nazarenus*? In this regard the date of Hearne's remark is tantalizing: 8 October 1718, some months after *Nazarenus* was published (Piggott (see n. 125), p. 118). For Hearne, like Mangey, Toland was the enemy: *Remarks and Collections of Thomas Hearne*, 7 (1719–22), Oxford Historical Society, 48 (Oxford, 1906), p. 343.

141 Jacob and Jacob (see Intro., n. 8), pp. 264–5.

142 Ibid., pp. 251–67, esp. 257, 260–2, 264–7.

143 Toland (see n. 124), p. 70.

144 For Toland's civil religion: Sullivan (see n. 130), pp. 169–72.

Epilogue: The paganizing thread

1 *RPM*, pp. vii–x.

2 *A Catalogue of the Libraries of Thomas Hollis, Esq. and Thomas Brand Hollis, Esq. Including . . . the . . . Library of . . . John Disney*, Lots 1559, 1562, 1564; and *Commonwealthman*, p. 391.

3 Caroline Robbins, 'Library of Liberty,' *Harvard Library Bulletin*, 5 (1951), p. 13.

4 *Commonwealthman*, pp. 260–8; and [F. Blackburne], *Memoirs of Thomas Hollis, Esq.*, 2 vols (London, 1780), ii, p. 576.

5 Robbins (see n. 3), pp. 17, 18.

6 *Catalogue* (see n. 2), Lots 807, 991, 1096.

7 Ibid., *passim*; Robbins (see n. 3), pp. 5–23, 181–96; and Caroline Robbins, 'The Strenuous Whig, Thomas Hollis of Lincoln's Inn,' *William & Mary Quarterly*, 3rd ser., 7 (July, 1950), p. 430.

8 Caroline Robbins, 'Thomas Brand Hollis,' *Proceedings of the American Philosophical Society*, 97, no. 3 (June, 1953), pp. 239–47; and *Commonwealthman*, p. 381.

9 Robbins (see n. 7), p. 443.

10 Ibid., p. 447.

11 *Catalogue* (see n. 2), *passim*.

12 Ibid., Lot 1521.

13 Nicholas H. Steneck, 'Greatrakes the Stroker: The Interpretations of Historians,' *ISIS*, 73 (1982), pp. 161–77.

14 Jacob, *Boyle*; and idem (see ch. 3, n. 118).

15 Jacob and Jacob (see Intro., n. 8).

16 Steneck (see n. 13), pp. 163–6.

17 See pp. 59–60 above.

18 Steneck (see n. 13), p. 166.

19 Quoted in Jacob, *Boyle*, pp. 167–8.

20 Steneck (see n. 13), p. 166.

21 Ibid., p. 167.

22 *MC*, p. 27.

23 Jacob, *Boyle*, pp. 167–8; and Steneck (see n. 13), p. 167.

24 *WRB*, i, p. lxxvii.

25 Steneck (see n. 13), p. 167.

26 Jacob, *Boyle*, p. 168.

27 *WRB*, i, pp. lxxvii–lxxix. Boyle's exact words are: 'I have long looked upon those enemies to Christianity as none of the wariest and formidablest that granting the truth of the historical part of the New Testament (which relates to miracles) have gone about to give an account of it by coelestial influences or natural (though peculiar) complexions or such conceits, which have quite lost them, in my thoughts, the title of knowing naturalists. But I must not forget that the opinion I have been opposing may possibly be disclaimed as well by you as me, though I wish some readers do you not the discourtesy to take a rise from your epistle to maintain it' (ibid., p. lxxix).

28 Steneck (see n. 13), p. 165.

29 For another instance: Jacob, *Boyle*, p. 156.

30 Ibid., *passim*.

31 Ibid., p. 169.

32 Jacob (see ch. 3, n. 118).

33 *WRB*, i, p. lxxix.

34 Jacob, *Boyle*, pp. 172–5.

35 Steneck (see n. 13), p. 168.

36 Ibid., p. 167.

37 Ibid., p. 169

38 Ibid., p. 167.

39 Ibid., p. 169.

40 *WRB*, i, p. lxxxi; and Jacob, *Boyle*, p. 175.

41 Steneck (see n. 13), p. 167.

42 *WRB*, i, p. lxxvii.

43 Ibid., p. lxxix.

44 Quoted in Jacob, *Boyle*, pp. 173–4.

45 Quoted in Steneck (see n. 13), p. 168.

46 *MC*, p. 14.

47 There were those who did 'adore him as an Apostle' (*Conway*, p. 274), which was also heretical, though not Stubbe's meaning: he was levelling Christ and the Apostles down; those who thought of Greatrakes as an Apostle were raising *him* up. Greatrakes's own account of his cures was strictly orthodox: Greatrakes (see ch. 3, n. 55), pp. 28–31.

48 Ibid., pp. 58–9, 60–1, 63; *Conway*, p. 274; and John Worthington, *The Diary and Correspondence of Dr. John Worthington*, ed. James Crossley and Richard C. Christie, Chetham Society, xxxvi (Manchester, 1855), pp. 216–17.
49 Steneck (see n. 13), pp. 170, 171–2.
50 Ibid., p. 170.
51 Jacob (see ch. 3, n. 118).
52 Quoted in Jacob, *Boyle*, pp. 167–8.
53 Steneck (see n. 13), p. 170.
54 Also: Jacob (see ch. 3, n. 118).
55 Steneck (see n. 13), p. 175.
56 Ibid., pp. 173–4.
57 Greene (see ch. 5, n. 143).
58 Steneck (see n. 13), pp. 174–5.
59 See pp. 98–101 above.
60 Steneck (see n. 13), p. 175.
61 See pp. 56–7, 60–2, 98–101 above.
62 Steneck (see n. 13), p. 176.
63 Ibid., pp. 176–7.

Bibliographical note

The documentation for the arguments advanced in this book can be found in the notes, and the historiographical questions posed have been dealt with in the Introduction. I wish now to indicate the recent works (some of which have not been cited in the notes) which have been particularly valuable to me in writing this book. The list that follows is intended to serve as an introductory guide to the study of radical ideas in England from 1650 to 1720. As such it is highly selective and even more so because it focusses on those studies which take an interdisciplinary approach or examine ideas in context. In what follows I am also interested in pointing out serious gaps in our knowledge where important work might now be done. For a fuller guide to the literature, especially the primary sources, there is an excellent bibliographical essay in: Michael Hunter, *Science and Society in Restoration England* (Cambridge, 1981).

There is no general study dealing with the social context of ideas in the last half of the seventeenth century in England; such a project would be worth undertaking. There are, however, a number of important books dealing with aspects of the problem: Christopher Hill, *The Century of Revolution 1603–1714* (Edinburgh, 1961); Ralph Davis, *The Rise of the Atlantic Economies* (Ithaca, NY, 1973); Charles Wilson, *England's Apprenticeship 1603–1763* (London, 1965); Keith Thomas, *Religion and the Decline of Magic* (London, 1971); J.G.A. Pocock, *The Machiavellian Moment* (Princeton, NJ, 1975); Hunter, *op. cit.*; C. B. Macpherson, *The Political Theory of Possessive Individualism: Hobbes to Locke* (Oxford, 1962); Joyce Appleby, *Economic Thought and Ideology in Seventeenth-Century England* (Princeton, 1978); Richard Schlatter, *The Social Ideas of Religious Leaders, 1660–1688* (Oxford, 1940); Margaret C. Jacob, *The Newtonians and the English Revolution, 1689–1720* (Ithaca, NY, 1976), with a useful chapter on the Restoration; James R. Jacob and Margaret C. Jacob, 'The Anglican Origins of Modern Science: The Metaphysical Foundations of the Whig Constitution,' *ISIS*, 71 (June 1980), pp. 251–67.

For the social and ideological context of ideas, particularly radical ideas, during the Interregnum, there are some important guideposts: B.H.G. Wormald, *Clarendon: Politics, History and Religion, 1640–1660* (Cambridge, 1951); Christopher Hill, *The World Turned Upside Down*, 2nd edn (New York, 1972); idem, *Puritanism and Revolution* (New York, 1964); P. M. Rattansi, 'Paracelsus and the Puritan Revolution,' *Ambix*, 11 (1964), pp. 24–32; idem, 'The Social Interpretation of Science in the Seventeenth Century,' *Science and Society, 1600–1900*, ed. Peter Mathias (Cambridge, 1972), pp. 1–32; Quentin Skinner, 'The Ideological Context of Hobbes's Political Thought,' *Historical Journal*, 9 (1966), pp. 286–317; Keith Thomas, 'The

Social Origins of Hobbes's Political Thought,' *Hobbes Studies*, ed. K. C. Brown (Cambridge, Mass., 1965), pp. 185–236; Charles Webster, 'New Light on the Invisible College: The Social Relations of English Science in the Mid-Seventeenth Century,' *Transactions of the Royal Historical Society*, 5th ser., 24 (1974), pp. 19–42; Buchanan Sharp, *In Contempt of All Authority: Rural Artisans and Riot in the West of England, 1586–1660* (Berkeley and Los Angeles, 1980); Geoffrey Nuttall, *The Holy Spirit in Puritan Faith and Experience* (Oxford, 1946); James Maclear, 'The Making of the Lay Tradition,' *Journal of Religion*, 33 (1953), pp. 113–36.

On the transmission of radical ideas from the Interregnum through the Restoration to the Enlightenment much more work might be done. Fundamental to any future enterprise in this field is: J. G. A. Pocock (ed.), *The Political Works of James Harrington* (Cambridge, 1977); Professor Pocock's introduction to this edition has been invaluable to this study. Also important are: George L. Mosse, 'Puritan Radicalism and the Enlightenment,' *Church History*, 29 (1960), pp. 424–39; R. L. Emerson, 'Heresy, the Social Order and English Deism,' *Church History*, 37 (1968), pp. 389–403; Herbert John McLachlan, *Socinianism in Seventeenth-Century England* (Oxford, 1951); Wilbur C. Abbott, 'English Conspiracy and Dissent, 1660–1674,' *American Historical Review*, 14 (1909), pp. 503–28, 696–722; Christopher Hill, *Milton and the English Revolution* (London, 1977); John M. Wallace, *Destiny His Choice: The Loyalism of Andrew Marvell* (Cambridge, 1968); Pierre Legouis, *Andrew Marvell*, 2nd edn (Oxford, 1968); Corinne Weston and Janelle Greenberg, *Subjects and Sovereigns* (Cambridge, 1981); J. G. A. Pocock, 'Post-Puritan England and the Problem of the Enlightenment,' *Culture and Politics from Puritanism to the Enlightenment*, ed. Perez Zagorin (Berkeley and Los Angeles, 1980), pp. 91–112. For the transmission of ideas to the Enlightenment the essential works are: Caroline Robbins, *The Eighteenth-Century Commonwealthman* (New York, 1968); Margaret C. Jacob, 'John Toland and the Newtonian Ideology,' *Journal of the Warburg and Courtauld Institutes*, 32 (1969), pp. 307–31; and idem, *The Radical Enlightenment* (London, 1981); Edmund Ludlow, *A Voyce from the Watch Tower*, pt 5: 1660–2, ed. A. B. Worden, Camden Society, 4th ser., xxi (London, 1978).

For understanding the development of scientific ideas in England during the middle decades of the seventeenth century there are two fundamental works: Charles Webster, *The Great Instauration: Science, Medicine and Reform, 1626–1660* (London, 1975); and R. G. Frank Jr, *Harvey and the Oxford Physiologists* (Berkeley, Los Angeles and London, 1980). The question of the origins of the Royal Society continues to inspire research; the latest contribution to the literature is Lotte Mulligan and Glenn Mulligan, 'Reconstructing Restoration Science: Styles of Leadership and Social Composition of the Early Royal Society,' *Social Studies of Science*, 11 (August, 1981), pp. 327–64, which cites much of the relevant literature. For understanding the ideological implications of natural philosophy during the Restoration one must begin with Thomas Sprat, *The History of the Royal Society of London* (1667), ed. J. I. Cope and H. W. Jones (London, 1959). The basic recent studies of the question are: S. I. Mintz, *The Hunting of Leviathan* (Cambridge, 1962); R. L. Colie, 'Spinoza and the Early English Deists,' *Journal of the History of Ideas*, 20 (1959), pp. 23–46; idem, 'Spinoza in England, 1665–1730,' *Proceedings of the American Philosophical Society*, 107 (1963), pp. 183–219; J. A. Redwood, 'Charles Blount (1654–93), Deism and English Free Thought,' *Journal of the History of Ideas*, 35

(1974), pp. 490–8; M. E. Prior, 'Joseph Glanvill, Witchcraft and Seventeenth-Century Science,' *Modern Philology*, 30 (1932), pp. 167–93; Barbara J. Shapiro, 'Latitudinarianism and Science in Seventeenth-Century England,' *Past and Present*, 40 (1968), pp. 16–41; J. R. Jacob, *Robert Boyle and the English Revolution* (New York, 1977); J. G. A. Pocock, 'Time, History and Eschatology in the Thought of Thomas Hobbes,' in *Politics, Language and Time* (New York, 1971); Wm Craig Diamond, 'Natural Philosophy in Harrington's Political Thought,' *Journal of the History of Philosophy*, 16 (Oct. 1978), pp. 387–98. There is also an excellent historiographical essay on the subject: Steven Shapin, 'Social Uses of Science, 1660–1800,' *The Ferment of Knowledge*, ed. R. S. Porter and G. S. Rousseau (Cambridge, 1980), pp. 93–139. Two more works throw considerable light on what might be called popular paganism in late seventeenth-century England: Henry J. Cadbury (ed.), *George Fox's 'Book of Miracles'* (Cambridge, 1948); and David Rollison, 'Property, Ideology and Popular Culture in a Gloucestershire Village,' *Past and Present*, 93 (1981), pp. 70–97.

The ideological issues posed by natural philosophy in late seventeenth-century England had deep roots in early modern European thought and culture. Essential for understanding this continuity are: Owsei Temkin, *Galenism: Rise and Decline of a Medical Philosophy* (Ithaca, NY, 1973); D. P. Walker, *Spiritual and Demonic Magic from Ficino to Campanella* (London, 1958); idem, *The Ancient Theology* (London, 1972); Frances Yates, *Giordano Bruno and the Hermetic Tradition* (London, 1964); Marc Bloch, *The Royal Touch*, trans. J. E. Anderson (London, 1973); Natalie Davis, *Society and Culture in Early Modern France* (Stanford, California, 1975); Peter Burke, *Popular Culture in Early Modern Europe* (New York, 1978); Paolo Rossi, *Philosophy, Technology and the Arts in the Early Modern Era* (New York, 1970); Carlo Ginzburg, 'High and Low: The Theme of Forbidden Knowledge in the Sixteenth and Seventeenth Centuries,' *Past and Present*, 73 (1976), pp. 28–41.

The ideological dimension of historical scholarship during the Restoration is treated in: J. G. A. Pocock, *The Ancient Constitution and the Feudal Law* (Cambridge, 1957); Royce Macgillivray, *Restoration Historians of the Civil War* (The Hague, 1974); and William M. Lamont, *Richard Baxter and the Millennium* (London, 1979). Stubbe's historicism must be seen of course against a background, the evolution of historical scholarship in early modern Europe. The relevant literature has been recently cited in: Barbara Shapiro, 'History and Natural History in 16th and 17th Century England,' in Barbara Shapiro and Robert Frank, Jr, *English Scientific Virtuosi in the 16th and 17th Centuries* (Los Angeles, 1979).

The religious and political setting in which Stubbe's polemic was conducted is best supplied by the following: R. A. Beddard, 'The Restoration Church,' *The Restored Monarchy 1660–1688*, ed. J. R. Jones (London, 1979), pp. 155–75; I. M. Green, *The Re-Establishment of the Church of England, 1660–1663* (Oxford, 1978); G. F. Nuttall and Owen Chadwick (eds.), *From Uniformity to Unity, 1662–1962* (London, 1962); John Miller, *Popery and Politics in England, 1660–88* (Cambridge, 1973); J. Bossy, *The English Catholic Community, 1560–1850* (Oxford, 1976); D. T. Witcombe, *Charles II and the Cavalier House of Commons, 1663–1674* (Manchester, 1966); K. H. D. Haley, *The First Earl of Shaftesbury* (Oxford, 1968); idem, *William of Orange and the English Opposition, 1672–4* (Oxford, 1953); J. R. Jones, *The First Whigs* (Durham, 1961); idem, 'The Green Ribbon Club,' *Durham University Journal*, n.s., 18 (Dec. 1956). For an interesting study of Jesuit missionary work among pagans that would have confirmed the worst fears of Anglicans like Boyle, there is: Jeffrey L. Klaiber, 'The

Posthumous Christianization of the Inca Empire in Colonial Peru,' *Journal of the History of Ideas*, 37 (1976), pp. 507–20, which might usefully be read with Bossy, *op. cit.*, ch. 6 and esp. pp. 391–401.

Most of the works I have listed in this bibliographical note have been written and published in the last two decades. There is a reason for this. During this period we have come to study the ideas associated with the various seventeenth-century revolutions in their social contexts in order the better to elucidate their historical meanings. This is the approach that I have quite deliberately adopted in this book. As a consequence my conclusions regarding the relationship between science and radical opinion, especially radical religious opinion, during the late seventeenth and early eighteenth centuries in England run directly contrary to the conclusions reached in the postwar historiography on the subject, perhaps best exemplified by two standard works: G. R. Cragg, *From Puritanism to the Age of Reason* (Cambridge, 1950); and Richard S. Westfall, *Science and Religion in Seventeenth-Century England* (New Haven, Conn., 1958). Both of these books take the view that religious and philosophical radicalism or deism derived from science, that it sprang from the materialistic and irreligious implications of scientific skepticism and the new mechanical conception of the universe.

I have argued in this book that the new science played its part in the growth of radical religious opinion. Stubbe, for example, read Boyle, Willis and More and interpreted what they were saying in the direction of his own paganizing naturalism. To this extent I would agree with Westfall and Cragg. But I am also arguing that Stubbe's naturalism was partially antecedent to his reading of the new philosophy, that it sprang in part from his extremely radical Protestantism which was of a kind that flourished during the mid-century crisis of the Interregnum, the period during which he reached intellectual maturity. In other words, Stubbe was a religious and political radical, and this radicalism was reinforced by what he saw to be the implications of the new science. In fact I would go further and argue that it was this antecedent radicalism that caused him to see these implications and to spin them out in works like *The Miraculous Conformist*. This gives us a picture very different from the one drawn by the older historiography. Nor does the picture apply only to Stubbe. It also fits the radical tradition that he helped to initiate, the tradition of Blount and especially Toland, and thus revises our understanding of the origins of the Enlightenment (Margaret Jacob, 'Newtonianism and the Origins of the Enlightenment: A Reassessment,' *Eighteenth Century Studies*, 11 (1977), pp. 1–25). The radical opinion associated with the early Enlightenment in England derived not only from a materialistic interpretation of the new science but also from the religious and political radicalism that can be traced back to the mid-century revolution in England.

Science was not ideologically neutral during the seventeenth and eighteenth centuries. On the one hand, it was used to support the moderately conservative views of latitudinarian churchmen. On the other, it was interpreted in a paganizing direction to provide the metaphysical foundations for civil religion. These two views, moreover, were in open conflict. Only thus can we see the full significance of the dialogue between Stubbe and the Royal Society or that between Toland and the early Newtonians. This new view of the relationship between science and the Enlightenment has been one of the principal pay-offs to come from a contextual approach to the study of ideas in the period after 1640 in England.

Index

214

n88, 213; *v.* Hobbes, 14, 48, 55; and
More, 101, 172–3; *v.* pagan naturalism,
144–53, 157, 167–9, 172–3, 208 n27;
patronage of, 43, 45, 48–9, 58, 60, 166;
and the Royal Society, 85, 152–3, 157;
social and religious views of, 48–9, 153;
Stubbe to, 51–4, 58–60, 146, 165–72; to
Stubbe, 55–7, 58–9, 146–7, 159, 164,
165–73
Boyle, Roger, Baron Broghill, 192 n88
Bristol, 79, 80, 81, 90, 102, 103, 104, 107,
137
Brooke, Lord, *see* Greville, Fulke, Baron
Brooke
Bruno, Giordano, 54
Buchanan, George, 161
Buckingham, 2nd Duke of, *see* Villiers,
George
Burnet, Gilbert, 153
Busby, Richard, 9

Calvin, John, 89
Cambridge, 105
Campanella, Tommaso, 86, 101
Casa, Joannes, 44
Casaubon, Isaac, 105
Casaubon, Meric, 105–6
Catherine of Braganza, Queen of England,
46, 135, 136
Cawdrey, Daniel, 20–1
censorship: in the Exclusion crisis, 143; at
Oxford during the Interregnum, 20–1,
23; during the Restoration, 2–3, 7, 42,
59, 63, 81, 84, 98, 129, 164; after the
Revolution of 1688–9, 154, 203 n11
Chamberlayne, Edward, 89–90
charity, *see* poor relief
Charles II, King of England, 45, 46, 50,
75–7, 98, 107, 109, 131, 148, 189 n90,
199–200 n24; and the Anglo-Dutch
wars, 111, 112, 113, 127; and the
Indulgence, 113–14, 115–16, 120–1, 122,
124, 126, 127, 128, 134; mistresses of,
130, 134, 135–6; in radical Whig theory,
142–3
Chew Magna, Somerset, 79, 81
chocolate, 45–8, 84
Christ, 52, 55, 66–7, 68, 71, 87, 92–5, 99,
101, 102, 126, 146, 157, 158, 166–7,
170–1, 208 n47
Christ Church, Oxford, 9, 10, 18, 42
Christianity: Apostolic, 11, 20, 36, 38, 44,
47, 61, 62, 70, 74, 75–6, 103, 104,
114–15, 123–6, 188 n53; Arian, 65, 67,
69–70, 92–7, 102, 123–6, 188 n53; of
Blount, 72; of Stubbe, 71, 72, 102, 104,
106–7, 188 n53; of Toland, 158, *see also*

civil religion, Arian; Galenic, 47–8;
'Mahometan', 65, 66, 72, 75–6, 77,
93–7, 99–100, 103–4, 108, 125–8, 155,
158–60; primitive, 2, 5, 18, 38, 44, 47,
61–2, 71, 93, 94–6, 103, 108, 114–15,
121, 123–6, 158; corruption of, 38, 66,
68–9, 72, 73, 94, 95, 99, 100, 115, 121,
159, 188 n53, 203 n25; government of,
67, 123, 125–6, 155–7; *v.* learning, 68,
69; seventh-century, 65
church, national, 30–1, 44, 156–7
Cicero, Marcus Tullius, 158, 206 n130
citizenship, 26–9; and armies, 29
civil religion: Arian, 102; and the 'country'
opposition, 6, 198 n58; of Harrington,
34–5, 119, 125–6, 164; and
latitudinarianism, 7; and the Royal
Society, 4, 108; of Selden, 33; of Stubbe,
2, 3, 96, 119–20, 121–7, 131, 134, 147,
156–60, 163, 164, 213; and the third
Dutch War, 5, 119–20, 121–7, 163–4; of
Toland, 155–60, 164, 206 n130, 213; of
Warren, 142–3, 203 n25. *See also*
natural religion
civil wars, English: and Harrington, 26,
142; and Hobbes, 12, 22, 40; and Stubbe,
40
clandestine manuscript, *see An Account of
the Rise and Progress of Mahometanism*
Clarendon code, 80
clergy: authority of, 11, 12–13, 14, 16–17,
34–5, 61–2, 82–3, 89–90, 95–6, 123;
Boyle on, 48; conservative Christian view
of, 2, 11, 12–13, 16–17, 36; and
Greatrakes, 50; Harrington's ideas and,
16–17, 34–5; Hoadley on, 157–8; Hobbes
on, 12–13, 16–17, 20, 24, 34, 36–7,
39–40, 73, 82–3; origin of a separate, 68,
69, 94; political function of, 118–20,
121–2, 124; Quaker view of, 38, 39, 40;
reduction of authority of, 3, 4, 11, 12,
13, 16–17, 37, 39, 61–2, 154, 156, 164;
in the universities, 78; Warren on, 141
Cleveland, Duchess of, *see* Villiers, Barbara
Clifford, Martin, 141, 142, 143
coffee houses, 80, 84, 108
Coke, Roger, 114
common people, 80, 82, 83, 84, 89–91,
102, 104, 107, 108, 119–20, 121–2
commonwealth, *see* 'good old cause'
Commonwealth, *see* Interregnum
Constantine, Emperor, 38, 69, 72, 94, 95–6;
and Charles II, 115–16, 121–8, 131;
conservative Protestant view of, 187
n43; radical Protestant view of, 187 n43
Conventicle Act (1664), 79, 80, 103, 127
Conway, Anne, Viscountess, 50, 55, 101